"CO. AYTCH"

A CONFEDERATE MEMOIR OF THE CIVIL WAR

Sam R. Watkins

A TOUCHSTONE BOOK
Published by Simon & Schuster
New York   London   Toronto   Sydney

Touchstone
Rockefeller Center
1230 Avenue of the Americas
New York, NY 10020

This Touchstone Edition 2003

TOUCHSTONE and colophon are registered trademarks
of Simon & Schuster, Inc.

For information regarding special discounts for bulk purchases,
please contact Simon & Schuster Special Sales at 1-800-456-6798
or business@simonandschuster.com

Designed by Jan Pisciotta

Manufactured in the United States of America

5   7   9   10   8   6   4

The Library of Congress has cataloged the Macmillan edition
as follows:
Watkins, Samuel R. (Samuel Rush)
"Co. Aytch"; a side show of the big show. With a new introd.
by Roy P. Basler.
p.   cm.
First published in 1882 under title: 1861 vs. 1882. "Co. Aytch,"
Maury Grays, First Tennessee Regiment
1. Tennessee Infantry. 1st Regt., 1861–1865. 2. Company H.
United States—History—Civil War, 1861–1865—Regimental
histories—Tennessee Infantry—1st—Company H.
3. United States—History—Civil War, 1861–1865—
Personal narratives—Confederate side. I. Title.
E579.5 1st .W34
973.7468   62-19123

ISBN-13: 978-0-7432-5541-7

INTRODUCTION

———•⋙◆⋘•———

"Co. Aytch" has always been my favorite among the best personal narratives of the Civil War, whether written by Confederate or Union soldiers, possibly because of a certain rapport with Private Sam Watkins' realistic, middle-country point-of-view, and a natural sympathy for the Confederate who could see the war in retrospect as Watkins did. It is this point-of-view which I believe most readers, in the North or South, a century after the events, will find compatible with their own view of the Civil War, as well perhaps as of wars of more recent vintage. As General Sherman said it bluntly, the experience of war is an experience of hell, in which the worst and the best in human nature tend to fry to the uniform crackling of survival, and yet the character of the man who emerges as a Sam Watkins testifies to the humanity that will live in hell's despite.

The parable with which Sam begins his book tells us as much about Sam by implication as do his explicit details of spilled blood, dangling guts, smell of death, and the funniest or the most pathetic episode that he records. Sam's timeless parable of how the war began conveys a wisdom of peace as well as of war. The concluding paragraph of the book confirms what we suspected at its beginning: Sam Watkins was a natural poet and a philosopher.

Styles in literature change. The abundance of certain four-letter words in autobiographical fiction about World War II, which is the modern version of what Sam was trying to say about war, would not have been natural to *"Co. Aytch,"* though it may not have been unnatural to the Civil War soldier's tongue. I think the modern reader will not find Sam's narrative the less realistic for their omission. Likewise, Sam's treatment of the theme closest to any soldier's heart is hardly that of

James Jones or James Michener, and yet no one will fail to appreciate the depth of Sam's yearning for his "Jennie" through four years of postponement. His humor will require no special taste for appreciation either. But there may be one element in his narrative which some readers of this edition will find difficult to comprehend—his absolute religious conviction. Be that as it may, I think not even the toughest skeptic will fail to recognize what Sam's religion meant to him, and even the most devout believer can relish his humorous description of the orotund prayer of an eminent Divine whose transcendental deity could have been understood only by the generals, if at all.

Not all Civil War soldiers, Confederate or Union, participated in so many major battles as Sam Watkins did, and it is safe to say that no American soldier since the Civil War fought so long and so hard: Shiloh, Corinth, Murfreesboro, Shelbyville, Chattanooga, Chickamauga, Missionary Ridge, the Hundred Days Battles, Atlanta, Jonesboro, Franklin, Nashville—this is the roll which accounts for a simple statistic. Of the 120 men enlisted in Co. H. in 1861, Sam was one of 7 alive when General William T. Sherman accepted General Joseph E. Johnston's surrender of the last major Confederate army in the field, at Greensboro, N. C., on April 26, 1865. Of the whole Army of Tennessee, in which Co. H. was a unit originally numbering 1,250 (to which were added 1,950 recruits and conscripts during the course of the war, making a total of 3,200 men), there were 65 officers and men left to be paroled on that day. Sam presents the obverse of the same coin when he records, with certainty, the scores upon scores of Union soldiers whom he shot. The incredible feats of marksmanship Sam attributes to Confederate soldiers could hardly fail to become the hard-bitten survivor's principal reason for living. Private Sam's sardonic comment would have been appreciated by General Sherman, as well as by his own commander, General John B. Hood, whose generalship he despised but would not desert: "I always shot at privates. It was they that did the shooting and killing, and if I could kill or wound a private, why, my chances were so much the better. I always looked upon officers as harmless personages." Lying exhausted on the ground the night after Chickamauga, among the dead, "scattered over the ground, and in many places piled in heaps," Sam reflected, "Dying on the field of battle and glory is about the easiest duty a soldier has to undergo."

The scenes Watkins transmits from his memory to our own are the etchings of this truth. In the dead of terrible winter in the mountains of Virginia, arriving at an outlying guard post, Sam's relief detail found them: "Some were sitting down and some were lying down; but each and every one was as cold and as hard frozen as the icicles that hung from their hands and faces and clothing—dead! . . . Two of them, a little in advance of the others, were standing with guns in their hands, as cold and as hard frozen as a monument of marble. . . ." On the 27th of June, 1864, in the "Dead Angle" at Kennesaw Mountain, "the sun rose clear and cloudless, the heavens seemed made of brass, and the earth of iron, and as the sun began to mount towards the zenith, everything became quiet, and no sound was heard save a peckerwood on a neighboring tree . . . when all at once a hundred guns from the Federal line. . . . Talk about other battles . . . in comparison with this day's fight, all other dwarf into insignificance. . . . The sun beaming down on our uncovered heads, the thermometer being one hundred and ten degrees in the shade. . . . I am satisfied that on this memorable day every man in our regiment killed from one score to four score, yea, five score men. I mean from twenty to one hundred each. All that was necessary was to load and shoot. . . . The ground was piled up with one solid mass of dead and wounded Yankees. . . . In the meantime the woods had taken fire. . . ." The imagination balks.

And yet the brutalizing ordeal could not kill the spirit that rebelled at retaliation for its own sake, as he described the hanging of two little boys as spies: "The youngest one began to beg and cry and plead most piteously. . . . The older one kicked him, and told him to stand up and show the Rebels how a Union man could die for his country. . . . The props were knocked out and the two boys were dangling in the air. I turned off sick at heart." Nor could it obliterate inhibitions. As badly and as often as Sam needed clothing and shoes, he could never bring himself to rob the well-dressed and well-shod Yankee dead: "I could not bear the thought of wearing dead men's shoes." Nor could it stifle his admiration of final courage in the most difficult of all cases to admire—deserters. The soldier Rowland, who having served out his original term of enlistment in the Conferedate Army, had decided the Confederacy was all wrong and had enlisted in the Union Army. When he was captured and sentenced to be shot, and his grave prepared the night before filled with rain, Rowland asked for a drink of it, "as he had heard water was very scarce in hell, and it would be the last he would ever drink. . . .

When the shooting detail came up, he went of his own accord and knelt down at the post. The Captain commanding the squad gave the command, 'Ready, aim, fire!' and Rowland tumbled over on his side." Who can blame Sam's resentment of the caste system which dictated that "A general could resign. That was honorable. A private could not resign, nor choose his branch of the service, and if he deserted, it was death."

Born on June 26, 1839, near Columbia, Tennessee, Sam Watkins was twenty-one when he enlisted in the spring of 1861. Prior to the war he had attended Jackson College at Columbia. After the war he married "Jennie" and at the time of writing "Co. Aytch" reported "a house full of young rebels clustering around my knees and bumping my elbows." He died on July 20, 1901, at the age of 62.

Sam's narrative was written twenty years after the war began, primarily for his own people. It appeared serially in his hometown newspaper, the Columbia, Tennessee, *Herald*, in 1881–1882. Shortly after the conclusion of this serialization, he published these reports as a book, in an edition of 2,000 copies. It has been reprinted twice in small editions, and has long been admired by Civil War buffs. Now is the time for it to reach the widest possible audience with the truth about the Civil War as Sam understood it. For, whatever his minor inaccuracies in the recording of names and the recollection of precise dates, his historical perspective was sounder than that of many more important but far less intelligent men who occupied posts of high responsibility in the years 1861–1865. The faults of the very society and system which Sam fought to defend, in spite of his recognition of those faults, were fatal: "Our cause was lost from the beginning."

Like Robert E. Lee at the top of that system, Sam Watkins, far down the line, was the prisoner of a myth whose power neither a Lee nor a Watkins could dispell or make viable by their heroism. But Sam Watkins could, twenty years after the war, in his grimly humorous parable try to lay the myth to rest. The obsolete Confederate notion that the sun rose in the east and set in the west was replaced, for Watkins at least, by a Yankee one "that the sun neither rises nor sets, the earth simply turns on its axis. . . .

"The United States has no North, no South, no East, no West. *We are one and undivided*." The italics are Sam's.

ROY P. BASLER

May 1962

Contents

"CO. AYTCH"

Chapter 1

Retrospective

"We Are One and Undivided"

A BOUT twenty years ago, I think it was—I won't be certain, though—a man whose name, if I remember correctly, was Wm. L. Yancy—I write only from memory, and this was a long time ago—took a strange and peculiar notion that the sun rose in the east and set in the west, and that the compass pointed north and south. Now, everybody knew at the time that it was but the idiosyncrasy of an unbalanced mind, and that the United States of America had no north, no south, no east, no west. Well, he began to preach the strange doctrine of there being such a thing. He began to have followers. As you know, it matters not how absurd, ridiculous and preposterous doctrines may be preached, there will be some followers. Well, one man by the name of (I think it was) Rhett, said it out loud. He was told to "s-h-e-e." Then another fellow by the name (I remember this one because it sounded like a graveyard) Toombs said so, and he was told to "sh-sh-ee-ee." Then after a while whole heaps of people began to say that they thought that there was a north and a south; and after a while hundreds and thousands and millions said that there was a south. But they were the persons who lived in the direction that the water courses run. Now, the people who lived where the water courses started from came down to see about it, and they said, "Gents, you are very much mistaken. We came over in the Mayflower, and we used to burn witches for saying that the sun rose in the east and set in the west, because the sun neither rises nor sets, the earth simply turns on its axis, and we know, cause we are Pure(i)tans." The spokesman of the party was named (I think I remember his name because it always gave me the blues when I heard it) Horrors Greeley; and another person by the name of Charles Sumner, said there ain't any north or south, east or west, and you shan't say so, either. Now, the other people who lived in the direction that the water courses run, just raised their bristles and continued saying that there is a north and there is a south. When those at the head of the water courses come out furiously mad, to coerce those in the direction that water courses run, and to make them take it back. Well, they went to gouging and biting, to pulling and scratching at a furious rate. One side elected a captain by the name of Jeff Davis, and known as one-eyed Jeff, and a first lieutenant by the name of Aleck Stephens, commonly styled Smart Aleck. The other side selected as captain a son of Nancy Hanks, of Bowling Green, and a son of old Bob Lincoln, the rail-splitter, and whose name was Abe. Well, after he was elected captain, they elected as first lieutenant an individual of doubtful blood by the name of Hannibal Hamlin, being a descendant of the generation of Ham, the bad son of old Noah, who meant to curse him blue, but overdid the thing, and cursed him black.

Well, as I said before, they went to fighting, but old Abe's side got the best of the argument. But in getting the best of the argument they called in all the people and wise men of other nations of the earth, and they, too, said that America had no cardinal points, and that the sun did not rise in the east and set in the west, and that the compass did not point either north or south.

Well, then, Captain Jeff Davis' side gave it up and quit, and they, too, went to saying that there is no north, no south, no east, no west. Well, "us boys" all took a small part in the fracas, and Shep, the prophet, remarked that the day would come when those who once believed that the American continent had cardinal points would be ashamed to own it. That day has arrived. America has no north, no south, no east, no west; the sun rises over the hills and sets over the mountains, the compass just points up and down, and we can laugh now at the absurd notion of there being a north and a south.

Well, reader, let me whisper in your ear. I was in the row, and the following pages will tell what part I took in the little unpleasant misconception of there being such a thing as a north and south.

The Bloody Chasm

In these memoirs, after the lapse of twenty years, we propose to fight our "battles o'er again."

To do this is but a pastime and pleasure, as there is nothing that so much delights the old soldier as to revisit the scenes and battle-fields with which he was once so familiar, and to recall the incidents, though trifling they may have been at the time.

The histories of the Lost Cause are all written out by "big bugs," generals and renowned historians, and like the fellow who called a turtle a "cooter," being told that no such word as cooter was in Webster's dictionary, remarked that he had as much right to make a dictionary as Mr. Webster or any other man; so have I to write a history.

But in these pages I do not pretend to write the history of the war. I only give a few sketches and incidents that came under the observation of a "high private" in the rear ranks of the rebel army. Of course, the histories are all correct. They tell of great achievements of great men, who wear the laurels of victory; have grand presents given them; high positions in civil life; presidents of corporations; governors of states; official positions, etc., and when they die, long obituaries are published, telling their many virtues, their distinguished victories, etc., and when they are buried, the whole country goes in mourning and is called upon to buy an elegant monument to erect over the remains of so distinguished and brave a general, etc. But in the following pages I propose to tell of the fellows who did the shooting and killing, the fortifying and ditching, the sweeping of the streets, the drilling, the standing guard, picket and videt, and who drew (or were to draw) eleven dollars per month and rations, and also drew the ramrod and tore the cartridge. Pardon me should I use the personal pronoun "I" too frequently, as I do not wish to be called egotistical, for I only write of what I saw as an humble private in the rear rank in an infantry regiment, commonly called "webfoot." Neither do I propose to make this a connected journal, for I write entirely from memory, and you must remember, kind reader, that these things happened twenty years ago, and twenty years is a long time in the life of any individual.

I was twenty-one years old then, and at that time I was not married. Now I have a house full of young "rebels," clustering around my knees and bumping against my elbow, while I write these reminiscences of the war of secession, rebellion, state rights, slavery, or our rights in the territories, or by whatever other name it may be called. These are all with the past now, and the North and South have long ago "shaken hands across the bloody chasm." The flag of the Southern cause has been furled never to be again unfurled; gone like a dream of yesterday, and lives only in the memory of those who lived through those bloody days and times.

Eighteen Hundred and Sixty-one

Reader mine, did you live in that stormy period? In the year of our Lord eighteen hundred and sixty-one, do you remember those stirring times? Do you recollect in that year, for the first time in your life, of hearing Dixie and the Bonnie Blue Flag? Fort Sumter was fired upon from Charleston by troops under General Beauregard, and Major Anderson, of the Federal army, surrendered. The die was cast; war was declared; Lincoln called for troops from Tennessee and all the Southern states, but Tennessee, loyal to her Southern sister states, passed the ordinance of secession, and enlisted under the Stars and Bars. From that day on, every person, almost, was eager for the war, and we were all afraid it would be over and we not be in the fight. Companies were made up, regiments organized; left, left, left, was heard from morning till night. By the right flank, file left, march, were familiar sounds. Everywhere could be seen Southern cockades made by the ladies and our sweethearts. And some who afterwards became Union men made the most fiery secession speeches. Flags made by the ladies were presented to companies, and to hear the young orators tell of how they would protect that flag, and that they would come back with the flag or come not at all, and if they fell they would fall with their backs to the field and their feet to the foe, would fairly make our hair stand on end with intense patriotism, and we wanted to march right off and whip twenty Yankees. But we soon found out that the glory of war was at home among the ladies and not upon the field of blood and carnage of death, where our comrades were mutilated and torn by shot and shell. And to see the cheek blanch and to hear the fervent prayer, aye, I might say the agony of mind were very different indeed from the patriotic times at home.

Camp Cheatham

After being drilled and disciplined at Camp Cheatham, under the administrative ability of General R. C. Foster, 3rd, for two months, we, the First, Third and Eleventh Tennessee Regiments—Maney, Brown and Rains—learned of the advance of McClelland's army into Virginia, toward Harper's Ferry and Bull Run.

The Federal army was advancing all along the line. They expected to march right into the heart of the South, set the negroes free, take our property, and whip the rebels back into the Union. But they soon found that secession was a bigger mouthful than they could swallow at one gobble. They found the people of the South in earnest.

Secession may have been wrong in the abstract, and has been tried and settled by the arbitrament of the sword and bayonet, but I am as firm in my convictions today of the right of secession as I was in 1861. The South is our country, the North is the country of those who live there. We are an agricultural people; they are a manufacturing people. They are the descendants of the good old Puritan Plymouth Rock stock, and we of the South from the proud and aristocratic stock of Cavaliers. We believe in the doctrine of State rights, they in the doctrine of centralization.

John C. Calhoun, Patrick Henry, and Randolph, of Roanoke, saw the venom under their wings, and warned the North of the consequences, but they laughed at them. We only fought for our State rights, they for Union and power. The South fell battling under the banner of State rights, but yet grand and glorious even in death. Now, reader, please pardon the digression. It is every word that we will say in behalf of the rights of secession in the following pages. The question has been long ago settled and is buried forever, never in this age or generation to be resurrected.

The vote of the regiment was taken, and we all voted to go to Virginia. The Southern Confederacy had established its capital at Richmond.

A man by the name of Jackson, who kept a hotel in Maryland, had raised the Stars and Bars, and a Federal officer by the name of Ellsworth tore it down, and Jackson had riddled his body with buckshot from a double-barreled shot-gun. First blood for the South.

Everywhere the enemy were advancing; the red clouds of war were booming up everywhere, but as this particular epoch, I refer you to the history of that period.

A private soldier is but an automaton, a machine that works by the command of a good, bad, or indifferent engineer, and is presumed to know nothing of all these great events. His business is to load and shoot, stand picket, videt, etc., while the officers sleep, or perhaps die on the field of battle and glory, and his obituary and epitaph but "one" remembered among the slain, but to what company, regiment, brigade or corps he belongs, there is no account; he is soon forgotten.

A long line of box cars was drawn up at Camp Cheatham one morning in July, the bugle sounded to strike tents and to place everything on board the cars. We old comrades have gotten together and laughed a hundred times at the plunder and property that we had accumulated, compared with our subsequent scanty wardrobe. Every soldier had enough blankets, shirts, pants and old boots to last a year, and the empty bottles and jugs would have set up a first-class drug store. In addition, every one of us had his gun, cartridge-box, knapsack and three days' rations, a pistol on each side and a long Bowie knife, that had been presented to us by William Wood, of Columbia, Tenn. We got in and on top of the box cars, the whistle sounded, and amid the waving of hats, handkerchiefs and flags, we bid a long farewell and forever to old Camp Cheatham.

Arriving at Nashville, the citizens turned out *en masse* to receive us, and here again we were reminded of the good old times and the "gal we left behind us." Ah, it is worth soldiering to receive such welcomes as this.

The Rev. Mr. Elliott invited us to his college grove, where had been prepared enough of the good things of earth to gratify the tastes of the most fastidious epicure. And what was most novel, we were waited on by the most beautiful young ladies (pupils of his school). It was charming, I tell you. Rev. C. D. Elliott was our Brigade Chaplain all through the war, and Dr. C. T. Quintard the Chaplain of the First Tennessee Regiment—two of the best men who ever lived. (Quintard is the present Bishop of Tennessee).

On the Road

Leaving Nashville, we went bowling along twenty or thirty miles an hour, as fast as steam could carry us. At every town and station citizens and ladies were waving their handkerchiefs and hurrahing for Jeff Davis and the Southern Confederacy. Magnificent banquets were prepared for us all along the entire

route. It was one magnificent festival from one end of the line
to the other. At Chattanooga, Knoxville, Bristol, Farmville,
Lynchburg, everywhere, the same demonstrations of joy and
welcome greeted us. Ah, those were glorious times; and you,
reader, see why the old soldier loves to live over again that
happy period.

But the Yankees are advancing on Manassas. July 21st finds
us a hundred miles from that fierce day's battle. That night, after
the battle is fought and won, our train draws up at Manassas
Junction.

Well, what news? Everyone was wild, nay, frenzied with the
excitement of victory, and we felt very much like the "boy the
calf had run over." We felt that the war was over, and we would
have to return home without even seeing a Yankee soldier. Ah,
how we envied those that were wounded. We thought at that
time that we would have given a thousand dollars to have been
in the battle, and to have had our arm shot off, so we could have
returned home with an empty sleeve. But the battle was over,
and we left out.

Staunton

From Manassas our train moved on to Staunton, Virginia.
Here we again went into camp, overhauled kettles, pots, buckets, jugs and tents, and found everything so tangled up and
mixed that we could not tell tuther from which.

We stretched our tents, and the soldiers once again felt that
restraint and discipline which we had almost forgotten en route
to this place. But, as the war was over now, our captains,
colonels and generals were not "hard on the boys;" in fact, had
begun to electioneer a little for the Legislature and for Congress.
In fact, some wanted, and were looking forward to the time, to
run for Governor of Tennessee.

Staunton was a big place; whisky was cheap, and good Virginia
tobacco was plentiful, and the currency of the country was gold
and silver.

The State Asylums for the blind and insane were here, and we visited all the places of interest.

Here is where we first saw the game called "chuck-a-luck," afterwards so popular in the army. But, I always noticed that chuck won, and luck always lost.

Faro and roulette were in full blast; in fact, the skum had begun to come to the surface, and shoddy was the gentleman. By this, I mean that civil law had been suspended; the ermine of the judges had been overridden by the sword and bayonet. In other words, the military had absorbed the civil. Hence the gambler was in his glory.

Warm Springs, Virginia

One day while we were idling around camp, June Tucker sounded the assembly, and we were ordered aboard the cars. We pulled out for Millboro; from there we had to foot it to Bath Alum and Warm Springs. We went over the Allegheny Mountains.

I was on every march that was ever made by the First Tennessee Regiment during the whole war, and at this time I cannot remember of ever experiencing a harder or more fatiguing march. It seemed that mountain was piled upon mountain. No sooner would we arrive at a place that seemed to be the top than another view of a higher, and yet higher mountain would rise before us. From the foot to the top of the mountain the soldiers lined the road, broken down and exhausted. First one blanket was thrown away, and then another; now and then a good pair of pants, old boots and shoes, Sunday hats, pistols and Bowie knives strewed the road. Old bottles and jugs and various and sundry articles were lying pell-mell everywhere. Up and up, and onward and upward we pulled and toiled, until we reached the very top, when there burst upon our view one of the grandest and most beautiful landscapes we ever beheld.

Nestled in the valley right before us is Bath Alum and Warm Springs. It seemed to me at that time, and since, a glimpse of a better and brighter world beyond, to the weary Christian pilgrim who may have been toiling on his journey for years. A glad shout arose from those who had gained the top, which cheered and encouraged the others to persevere. At last we got to Warm Springs. Here they had a nice warm dinner waiting for us. They had a large bath-house at Warm Springs. A large pool of water arranged so that a person could go in any depth he might desire. It was a free thing, and we pitched in. We had no idea of the enervating effect it would have upon our physical systems, and as the water was but little past tepid, we stayed in a good long time. But when we came out we were as limp as dishrags. About this time the assembly sounded and we were ordered to march. But we couldn't march worth a cent. There we had to stay until our systems had had sufficient recuperation. And we would wonder what all this marching was for, as the war was over anyhow.

The second day after leaving Warm Springs we came to Big Springs. It was in the month of August, and the biggest white frost fell that I ever saw in winter.

The Yankees were reported to be in close proximity to us, and Captain Field[1] with a detail of ten men was sent forward on the scout. I was on the detail, and when we left camp that evening, it was dark and dreary and drizzling rain. After a while the rain began to come down harder and harder, and every one of us was wet and drenched to the skin—guns, cartridges and powder. The next morning about daylight, while standing videt, I saw a body of twenty-five or thirty Yankees approaching, and I raised my gun for the purpose of shooting, and pulled down, but the cap popped. They discovered me and popped three or four caps at me; their powder was wet also. Before I could get on a fresh cap, Captain Field came running up with his seven-shooting rifle, and the first fire he killed a Yankee. They broke and run. Captain Field did all the firing, but every time he pulled down he brought a Yankee. I have forgotten the number that he did kill, but if I am not mistaken it was either twenty or twenty-one, for I re-

---

[1]Captain Hume R. Feild, commanding officer of Company H and later Colonel of the First Tennessee Regiment. Watkins consistently misspelled the name.

member the incident was in almost every Southern paper at that time, and the general comments were that one Southern man was equal to twenty Yankees. While we were in hot pursuit, one truly brave and magnanimous Yankee, who had been badly wounded, said, "Gentlemen, you have killed me, but not a hundred yards from here is the main line." We did not go any further, but halted right there, and after getting all the information that we could out of the wounded Yankee, we returned to camp.

One evening, General Robert E. Lee came to our camp. He was a fine-looking gentleman, and wore a moustache. He was dressed in blue cottonade and looked like some good boy's grandpa. I felt like going up to him and saying, good evening, Uncle Bob! I am not certain at this late day that I did not do so. I remember going up mighty close and sitting there and listening to his conversation with the officers of our regiment. He had a calm and collected air about him, his voice was kind and tender, and his eye was as gentle as a dove's. His whole make-up of form and person, looks and manner had a kind of gentle and soothing magnetism about it that drew every one to him and made them love, respect, and honor him. I fell in love with the old gentleman and felt like going home with him. I know I have never seen a finer looking man, nor one with more kind and gentle features and manners. His horse was standing nipping the grass, and when I saw that he was getting ready to start I ran and caught his horse and led him up to him. He took the reins of the bridle in his hand and said, "thank you, my son," rode off, and my heart went with him. There was none of his staff with him; he had on no sword or pistol, or anything to show his rank. The only thing that I remember he had was an opera-glass hung over his shoulder by a strap.

Leaving Big Springs, we marched on day by day, across Greenbrier and Gauley rivers to Huntersville, a little but sprightly town hid in the very fastnesses of the mountains. The people live exceedingly well in these mountains. They had plenty of honey and buckwheat cakes, and they called buttermilk "sour-milk," and sour-milk weren't fit for pigs; they couldn't see how folks drank sour-milk. But sourkraut was good. Every-thing seemed to grow in the mountains—potatoes, Irish and sweet; onions, snap beans, peas—though the country was very thinly populated. Deer, bear, and foxes, as well as wild turkeys, and rabbits and squirrels abounded everywhere. Apples and peaches were abundant, and everywhere the people had apple-butter for every meal; and occasionally we would come across a small-sized distillery, which we would at once start to doing duty. We drank the singlings while they were hot, but like the old woman who could not eat corn bread until she heard that they made whisky out of corn, then she could manage to "worry a lit-tle of it down;" so it was with us and the singlings.

From this time forward, we were ever on the march—tramp, tramp, tramp—always on the march. Lee's corps, Stonewall Jackson's division—I refer you to the histories for the marches and tramps made by these commanders the first year of the war. Well, we followed them.

Cheat Mountain

One evening about 4 o'clock, the drummers of the regiment began to beat their drums as hard as they could stave, and I saw men running in every direction, and the camp soon became one scene of hurry and excitement. I asked some one what all this hubbub meant. He looked at me with utter astonishment. I saw soldiers running to their tents and grabbing their guns and car-tridge-boxes and hurry out again, the drums still rolling and rat-tling. I asked several other fellows what in the dickens did all this mean? Finally one fellow, who seemed scared almost out of his wits, answered between a wail and a shriek, "Why, sir, they are beating the long roll." Says I, "What is the long roll for?" "The long roll, man, the long roll! Get your gun; they are beat-ing the long roll!" This was all the information that I could get. It was the first, last, and only long roll that I ever heard. But, then everything was new, and Colonel Maney, ever prompt, or-dered the assembly. Without any command or bugle sound, or anything, every soldier was in his place. Tents, knapsacks and everything was left indiscriminately.

We were soon on the march, and we marched on and on and on. About night it began to rain. All our blankets were back in camp, but we were expected every minute to be ordered into action. That night we came to Mingo Flats. The rain still poured. We had no rations to eat and nowhere to sleep. Some of us got some fence rails and piled them together and worried through the night as best we could. The next morning we were ordered to march again, but we soon began to get hungry, and we had about half halted and about not halted at all. Some of the boys were picking blackberries. The main body of the regiment was marching leisurely along the road, when bang, debang, debang, bang, and a volley of buck and ball came hurling right through the two advance companies of the regiment—companies H and K. We had marched into a Yankee ambuscade.

All at once everything was a scene of consternation and confusion; no one seemed equal to the emergency. We did not know whether to run or stand, when Captain Field gave the command to fire and charge the bushes. We charged the bushes and saw the Yankees running through them, and we fired on them as they retreated. I do not know how many Yankees were killed, if any. Our company (H) had one man killed, Pat Hanley, an Irishman, who had joined our company at Chattanooga. Hugh Padgett and Dr. Hooper, and perhaps one or two others, were wounded.

After the fighting was over, where, O where, was all the fine rigging heretofore on our officers? They could not be seen. Corporals, sergeants, lieutenants, captains, all had torn all the fine lace off their clothing. I noticed that at the time and was surprised and hurt. I asked several of them why they had torn off the insignia of their rank, and they always answered, "Humph, you think that I was going to be a target for the Yankees to shoot at?" You see, this was our first battle, and the officers had not found out that minnie as well as cannon balls were blind; that they had no eyes and could not see. They thought that the balls would hunt for them and not hurt the privates. I always shot at privates. It was they that did the shooting and killing, and if I could kill or wound a private, why, my chances were so much the better. I always looked upon officers as harmless personages. Colonel Field, I suppose, was about the only Colonel of the war that did as much shooting as the private soldier. If I shot at an officer, it was at long range, but when we got down to close quarters I always tried to kill those that were trying to kill me.

Sewell Mountain

From Cheat Mountain we went by forced marches day and night, over hill and everlasting mountains, and through lovely and smiling valleys, sometimes the country rich and productive, sometimes rough and broken, through towns and villages, the names of which I have forgotten, crossing streams and rivers, but continuing our never ceasing, unending march, passing through the Kanawha Valley and by the salt-works, and nearly back to the Ohio river, when we at last reached Sewell Mountain. Here we found General John B. Floyd strongly entrenched and fortified and facing the advance of the Federal army. Two days before our arrival he had charged and captured one line of the enemy's works. I know nothing of the battle. See the histories for that. I only write from memory, and that was twenty years ago, but I remember reading in the newspapers at that time of some distinguished man, whether he was captain, colonel or general, I have forgotten, but I know the papers said "he sought the bauble, reputation, at the cannon's mouth, and went to glory from the death-bed of fame." I remember it sounded gloriously in print. Now, reader, this is all I know of this grand battle. I only recollect what the newspapers said about it, and you know that a newspaper always tells the truth. I also know that beef livers sold for one dollar apiece in gold; and here is where we were first paid off in Confederate money. Remaining here a few days, we commenced our march again.

Sewell Mountain, Harrisonburg, Lewisburg, Kanawha Salt-works, first four, forward and back, seemed to be the programme of that day. Rosecrans, that wiley old fox, kept Lee and Jackson both busy trying to catch him, but Rosey would not be caught. March, march, march; tramp, tramp, tramp, back through the valley to Huntersville and Warm Springs, and up through the most beautiful valley—the Shenandoah—in the world, passing towns and elegant farms and beautiful residences, rich pastures and abundant harvests, which a Federal General (Fighting Joe Hooker), later in the war, ordered to be so sacked and destroyed that a "crow passing over this valley would have to carry his rations."[2] Passing on, we arrived at Winchester. The first night we arrived at this place, the wind blew a perfect hurricane, and every tent and marquee in Lee's and Jackson's army was blown down. This is the first sight we had of Stonewall Jackson, riding upon his old sorrel horse, his feet drawn up as if his stirrups were much too short for him, and his old dingy military cap hanging well forward over his head, and his nose erected in the air, his old rusty sabre rattling by his side. This is the way the grand old hero of a hundred battles looked. His spirit is yonder with the blessed ones that have gone before, but his history is one that the country will ever be proud of, and his memory will be cherished and loved by the old soldiers who followed him through the war.

Romney

Our march to and from Romney was in midwinter in the month of January, 1862. It was the coldest winter known to the oldest inhabitant of these regions. Situated in the most mountainous country in Virginia, and away up near the Maryland and Pennsylvania line, the storm king seemed to rule in all of his majesty and power. Snow and rain and sleet and tempest

---

[2] The reference is obviously to Sheridan's systematic devastation of the Valley in 1864. Hooker did not command in that area.

seemed to ride and laugh and shriek and howl and moan and groan in all their fury and wrath. The soldiers on this march got very much discouraged and disheartened. As they marched along icicles hung from their clothing, guns, and knapsacks; many were badly frost bitten, and I heard of many freezing to death along the road side. My feet peeled off like a peeled onion on that march, and I have not recovered from its effects to this day. The snow and ice on the ground being packed by the soldiers tramping, the horses hitched to the artillery wagons were continually slipping and sliding and falling and wounding themselves and sometimes killing their riders. The wind whistling with a keen and piercing shriek, seemed as if they would freeze the marrow in our bones. The soldiers in the whole army got rebellious—almost mutinous—and would curse and abuse Stonewall Jackson; in fact, they called him "Fool Tom Jackson." They blamed him for the cold weather; they blamed him for everything, and when he would ride by a regiment they would take occasion, *sotto voce*, to abuse him, and call him "Fool Tom Jackson," and loud enough for him to hear. Soldiers from all commands would fall out of ranks and stop by the road side and swear that they would not follow such a leader any longer.

When Jackson got to Romney, and was ready to strike Banks and Meade in a vital point, and which would have changed, perhaps, the destiny of the war and the South, his troops refused to march any further, and he turned, marched back to Winchester and tendered his resignation to the authorities at Richmond. But the great leader's resignation was not accepted. It was in store for him to do some of the hardest fighting and greatest generalship that was done during the war.

One night at this place (Romney), I was sent forward with two other soldiers across the wire bridge as picket. One of them was named Schwartz and the other Pfifer—he called it Fifer, but spelled it with a P—both full-blooded Dutchmen, and belonging to Company E, or the German Yagers, Captain Harsh, or, as he was more generally called, "God-for-dam."

When we had crossed the bridge and taken our station for the night, I saw another snow storm was coming. The zig-zag lightnings began to flare and flash, and sheet after sheet of wild flames seemed to burst right over our heads and were hissing around us. The very elements seemed to be one aurora borealis with continued lightning. Streak after streak of lightning seemed to be piercing each the other, the one from the north and the other from the south. The white clouds would roll up, looking like huge snow balls, encircled with living fires. The earth and hills and trees were covered with snow, and the lightnings seemed to be playing "King, King Canico" along its crusted surface. If it thundered at all, it seemed to be between a groaning and a rumbling sound. The trees and hills seemed white with livid fire. I can remember that storm now as the grandest picture that has ever made any impression on my memory. As soon as it quit lightning, the most blinding snow storm fell that I ever saw. It fell so thick and fast that I got hot. I felt like pulling off my coat. I was freezing. The winds sounded like sweet music. I felt grand, glorious, peculiar; beautiful things began to play and dance around my head, and I supposed I must have dropped to sleep or something, when I felt Schwartz grab me, and give me a shake, and at the same time raised his gun and fired, and yelled out at the top of his voice, "Here is your mule." The next instant a volley of minnie balls was scattering the snow all around us. I tried to walk, but my pants and boots were stiff and frozen, and the blood had ceased to circulate in my lower limbs. But Schwartz kept on firing, and at every fire he would yell out, "Yer is yer mool!" Pfifer could not speak English, and I reckon he said "Here is your mule" in Dutch. About the same time we were hailed from three Confederate officers, at full gallop right toward us, not to shoot. And as they galloped up to us and thundered right across the bridge, we discovered it was Stonewall Jackson and two of his staff. At the same time the Yankee cavalry charged us, and we, too, ran back across the bridge.

Standing Picket on the Potomac

Leaving Winchester, we continued up the valley.

The night before the attack on Bath or Berkly Springs, there fell the largest snow I ever saw.

Stonewall Jackson had seventeen thousand soldiers at his command. The Yankees were fortified at Bath. An attack was ordered, our regiment marched upon top of a mountain overlooking the movements of both armies in the valley below. About 4 o'clock one grand charge and rush was made, and the Yankees were routed and skedaddled.

By some circumstance or other, Lieutenant J. Lee Bullock came in command of the First Tennessee Regiment. But Lee was not a graduate of West Point, you see.

The Federals had left some spiked batteries on the hill side, as we were informed by an old citizen, and Lee, anxious to capture a battery, gave the new and peculiar command of, "Soldiers, you are ordered to go forward and capture a battery; just piroute up that hill; piroute, march. Forward, men; piroute carefully." The boys "pirouted" as best they could. It may have been a new command, and not laid down in Hardee's or Scott's tactics; but Lee was speaking plain English, and we understood his meaning perfectly, and even at this late day I have no doubt that every soldier who heard the command thought it a legal and technical term used by military graduates to go forward and capture a battery.

At this place (Bath), a beautiful young lady ran across the street. I have seen many beautiful and pretty women in my life, but she was the prettiest one I ever saw. Were you to ask any member of the First Tennessee Regiment who was the prettiest woman he ever saw, he would unhesitatingly answer that he saw her at Berkly Springs during the war, and he would continue the tale, and tell you of Lee Bullock's piroute and Stonewall Jackson's charge.

We rushed down to the big spring bursting out of the mountain side, and it was hot enough to cook an egg. Never did I see soldiers more surprised. The water was so hot we could not drink it.

The snow covered the ground and was still falling.

That night I stood picket on the Potomac with a detail of the Third Arkansas Regiment. I remember how sorry I felt for the poor fellows, because they had enlisted for the war, and we for only twelve months. Before nightfall I took in every object and commenced my weary vigils. I had to stand all night. I could hear the rumblings of the Federal artillery and wagons, and hear the low shuffling sound made by troops on the march. The snow came pelting down as large as goose eggs. About midnight the snow ceased to fall, and became quiet. Now and then the snow would fall off the bushes and make a terrible noise. While I was peering through the darkness, my eyes suddenly fell upon the outlines of a man. The more I looked the more I was convinced that it was a Yankee picket. I could see his hat and coat— yes, see his gun. I was sure that it was a Yankee picket. What was I to do? The relief was several hundred yards in the rear. The more I looked the more sure I was. At last a cold sweat broke out all over my body. Turkey bumps rose. I summoned all the nerves and bravery that I could command, and said: "Halt! who goes there?" There being no response, I became resolute. I did not wish to fire and arouse the camp, but I marched right up to it and stuck my bayonet through and through it. It was a stump. I tell the above, because it illustrates a part of many a private's recollections of the war; in fact, a part of the hardships and suffering that they go through.

One secret of Stonewall Jackson's success was that he was such a strict disciplinarian. He did his duty himself and was ever at his post, and he expected and demanded of everybody to do the same thing. He would have a man shot at the drop of a hat, and drop it himself. The first army order that was ever read to us after being attached to his corps, was the shooting to death by musketry of two men who had stopped on the battlefield to carry off a wounded comrade. It was read to us in line of battle at Winchester.

Schwartz and Pfifer

At Valley Mountain the finest and fattest beef I ever saw was issued to the soldiers, and it was the custom to use tallow for lard. Tallow made good shortening if the biscuits were eaten hot, but if allowed to get cold they had a strong taste of tallow in their flavor that did not taste like the flavor of vanilla or lemon in ice cream and strawberries; and biscuits fried in tallow were something upon the principle of 'possum and sweet potatoes. Well, Pfifer had got the fat from the kidneys of two hindquarters and made a cake of tallow weighing about twenty-five pounds. He wrapped it up and put it carefully away in his knapsack. When the assembly sounded for the march, Pfifer strapped on his knapsack. It was pretty heavy, but Pfifer was "well heeled." He knew the good frying he would get out of that twenty-five pounds of nice fat tallow, and he was willing to tug and toil all day over a muddy and sloppy road for his anticipated hot tallow gravy for supper. We made a long and hard march that day, and about dark went into camp. Fires were made up and water brought, and the soldiers began to get supper. Pfifer was in a good humor. He went to get that twenty-five pounds of good, nice, fat tallow out of his knapsack, and on opening it, lo and behold! it was a rock that weighed about thirty pounds. Pfifer was struck dumb with amazement. He looked bewildered, yea, even silly. I do not think he cursed, because he could not do the subject justice. He looked at that rock with the death stare of a doomed man. But he suspected Schwartz. He went to Schwartz's knapsack, and there he found his cake of tallow. He went to Schwartz and would have killed him had not soldiers interfered and pulled him off by main force. His eyes blazed and looked like those of a tiger when he has just torn his victim limb from limb. I would not have been in Schwartz's shoes for all the tallow in every beef in Virginia. Captain Harsh made Schwartz carry that rock for two days to pacify Pfifer.

The Court-Martial

One incident came under my observation while in Virginia that made a deep impression on my mind. One morning, about daybreak, the new guard was relieving the old guard. It was a bitter cold morning, and on coming to our extreme outpost, I saw a soldier—he was but a mere boy—either dead or asleep at his post. The sergeant commanding the relief went up to him and shook him. He immediately woke up and seemed very much frightened. He was fast asleep at his post. The sergeant had him arrested and carried to the guard-house.

Two days afterwards I received notice to appear before a court-martial at nine. I was summoned to appear as a witness against him for being asleep at his post in the enemy's country. An example had to be made of some one. He had to be tried for his life. The court-martial was made up of seven or eight officers of a different regiment. The witnesses all testified against him, charges and specifications were read, and by the rules of war he had to be shot to death by musketry. The Advocate-General for the prosecution made the opening speech. He read the law in a plain, straightforward manner, and said that for a soldier to go to sleep at his post of duty, while so much depended upon him, was the most culpable of all crimes, and the most inexcusable. I trembled in my boots, for on several occasions I knew I had taken a short nap, even on the very outpost. The Advocate-General went on further to say, that the picket was the sentinel that held the lives of his countrymen and the liberty of his country in his hands, and it mattered not what may have been his record in the past. At one moment he had forfeited his life to his country. For discipline's sake, if for nothing else, you gentlemen that make up this court-martial find the prisoner guilty. It is necessary for you to be firm, gentlemen, for upon your decision depends the safety of our country. When he had finished, thinks I to myself, "Gone up the spout, sure; we will have a first-class funeral here before night."

Well, as to the lawyer who defended him, I cannot now remember his speeches; but he represented a fair-haired boy leaving his home and family, telling his father and aged mother and darling little sister farewell, and spoke of his proud step, though a mere boy, going to defend his country and his loved ones; but at one weak moment, when nature, tasked and taxed beyond the bounds of human endurance, could stand no longer, and upon the still and silent picket post, when the whole army was hushed in slumber, what wonder is it that he, too, may have fallen asleep while at his post of duty.

Some of you gentlemen of this court-martial may have sons, may have brothers; yes, even fathers, in the army. Where are they tonight? You love your children, or your brother or father. This mere youth has a father and mother and sister away back in Tennessee. They are willing to give him to his country. But oh! gentlemen, let the word go back to Tennessee that he died upon the battlefield, and not by the hands of his own comrades for being asleep at his post of duty. I cannot now remember the speeches, but one thing I do know, that he was acquitted, and I was glad of it.

"The Death Watch"

One more scene I can remember. Kind friends—you that know nothing of a soldier's life—I ask you in all candor not to doubt the following lines in this sketch. You have no doubt read of the old Roman soldier found amid the ruins of Pompeii, who had stood there for sixteen hundred years, and when he was excavated was found at his post with his gun clasped in his skeleton hands. You believe this because it is written in history. I have heard politicians tell it. I have heard it told from the sacred desk. It is true; no one doubts it.

Now, were I to tell something that happened in this nineteenth century exactly similar, you would hardly believe it. But whether you believe it or not, it is for you to say. At a little village called Hampshire Crossing, our regiment was ordered to go to a little stream called St. John's Run, to relieve the 14th Georgia Regiment and the 3rd Arkansas. I cannot tell the facts as I desire to. In fact, my hand trembles so, and my feelings are so overcome, that it is hard for me to write at all. But we went to the place that we were ordered to go to, and when we arrived there we found the guard sure enough. If I remember correctly, there were just eleven of them. Some were sitting down and some were laying down; but each and every one was as cold and as hard frozen as the icicles that hung from their hands and faces and clothing—dead! They had died at their post of duty. Two of them, a little in advance of the others, were standing with their guns in their hands, as cold and as hard frozen as a monument of marble—standing sentinel with loaded guns in their frozen hands! The tale is told. Were they true men? Does He who noteth the sparrow's fall, and numbers the hairs of our heads, have any interest in one like ourselves? Yes; He doeth all things well. Not a sparrow falls to the ground without His consent.

Virginia, Farewell

After having served through all the valley campaign, and marched through all the wonders of Northwest Virginia, and being associated with the army of Virginia, it was with sorrow and regret that we bade farewell to "Old Virginia's shore," to go to other fields of blood and carnage and death. We had learned to love Virginia; we love her now. The people were kind and good to us. They divided their last crust of bread and rasher of bacon with us. We loved Lee, we loved Jackson; we loved the name, association and people of Virginia. Hatton, Forbes, Anderson, Gilliam, Govan, Loring, Ashby and Schumaker were names with which we had been long associated. We hated to leave all our old comrades behind us. We felt that we were proving recreant to the instincts of our own manhood, and that we were leaving those who had stood by us on the march and battlefield when they most needed our help. We knew the 7th and

14th Tennessee regiments; we knew the 3rd Arkansas, the 14th Georgia, and 42nd Virginia regiments. Their names were as familiar as household words. We were about to leave the bones of Joe Bynum and Gus Allen and Patrick Hanly. We were about to bid farewell to every tender association that we had formed with the good people of Virginia, and to our old associates among the soldiers of the Grand Army of Virginia. *Virginia, farewell!* Away back yonder, in good old Tennessee, our homes and loved ones are being robbed and insulted, our fields laid waste, our cities sacked, and our people slain. Duty as well as patriotism calls us back to our native home, to try and defend it, as best we can, against an invading army of our then enemies; and, Virginia, once more we bid you a long farewell!

Chapter 2

Shiloh

THIS was the first big battle in which our regiment had ever been engaged. I do not pretend to tell of what command distinguished itself; of heroes; of blood and wounds; of shrieks and groans; of brilliant charges; of cannon captured, etc. I was but a private soldier, and if I happened to look to see if I could find out anything, "Eyes right, guide center," was the order. "Close up, guide right, halt, forward, right oblique, left oblique, halt, forward, guide center, eyes right, dress up promptly in the rear, steady, double quick, charge bayonets, fire at will," is about all that a private soldier ever knows of a battle. He can see the smoke rise and the flash of the enemy's guns, and he can hear the whistle of the minnie and cannon balls, but he has got to load and shoot as hard as he can tear and ram cartridge, or he will soon find out, like the Irishman who had been shooting blank cartridges, when a ball happened to strike him, and he halloed out, "Faith, Pat, and be jabbers, them fellows are shooting bullets." But I nevertheless remember many things that came under my observation in this battle. I remember a man by the name of Smith stepping deliberately out of the ranks and shooting his finger off to keep out of the fight; of another poor fellow who was accidentally shot and killed by the discharge of another person's gun, and of others suddenly taken sick with colic. Our regiment was the advance guard on Saturday evening, and did a little skirmishing; but General Gladden's brigade passed us and assumed a position in our immediate front. About daylight on Sunday morning, Chalmers' brigade relieved Gladden's, As Gladden rode by us, a courier rode up and told him something. I do not know what it was, but I heard Gladden say, "Tell General Bragg that I have as keen a scent for Yankees as General Chalmers has."

On Sunday morning, a clear, beautiful, and still day, the order was given for the whole army to advance, and to attack immediately. We were supporting an Alabama brigade. The fire opened—bang, bang, bang, a rattle de bang, bang, bang, a boom, de bang, bang, bang, boom, bang, boom, bang, boom, bang, boom, bang, boom, whirr-siz-siz-siz—a ripping, roaring boom, bang! The air was full of balls and deadly missiles. The litter corps was carrying off the dying and wounded. We could hear the shout of the charge and the incessant roar of the guns, the rattle of the musketry, and knew that the contending forces were engaged in a breast to breast struggle. But cheering news continued to come back. Every one who passed would be hailed with, "Well, what news from the front?" "Well, boys, we are driving 'em. We have captured all their encampments, everything that they had, and all their provisions and army stores, and everything."

As we were advancing to the attack and to support the Alabama brigade in our front, and which had given way and were stricken with fear, some of the boys of our regiment would laugh at them, and ask what they were running for, and would commence to say "Flicker! flicker! flicker!" like the bird called the yellowhammer, "Flicker! flicker! flicker!" As we advanced, on the edge of the battlefield, we saw a big fat colonel of the 23rd Tennessee regiment badly wounded, whose name, if I remember correctly, was Matt. Martin. He said to us, "Give 'em goss, boys. That's right, my brave First Tennessee. Give 'em Hail Columbia!" We halted but a moment, and said I, "Colonel, where are you wounded?" He answered in a deep bass voice, "My son, I am wounded in the arm, in the leg, in the head, in the body, and in another place which I have a delicacy in mentioning." That is what the gallant old Colonel said. Advancing a little further on, we saw General Albert Sidney Johnson[1] surrounded by his staff and Governor Harris, of Tennessee. We saw some little commotion among those who surrounded him, but we did not know at the time that he was dead. The fact was kept from the troops.

About noon a courier dashed up and ordered us to go forward and support General Bragg's center. We had to pass over the ground where troops had been fighting all day.

I had heard and read of battlefields, seen pictures of battlefields, of horses and men, of cannon and wagons, all jumbled together, while the ground was strewn with dead and dying and wounded, but I must confess that I never realized the "pomp and circumstance" of the thing called glorious war until I saw this. Men were lying in every conceivable position; the dead lying with their eyes wide open, the wounded begging piteously for help, and some waving their hats and shouting to us to go forward. It all seemed to me a dream; I seemed to be in a sort of haze, when siz, siz, siz, the minnie balls from the Yankee line began to whistle around our ears, and I thought of the Irishman when he said, "Sure enough, those fellows are shooting bullets!"

Down would drop first one fellow and then another, either killed or wounded, when we were ordered to charge bayonets. I had been feeling mean all the morning as if I had stolen a sheep, but when the order to charge was given, I got happy. I felt happier than a fellow does when he professes religion at a big Methodist camp-meeting. I shouted. It was fun then. Everybody looked happy. We were crowding them. One more charge, then their lines waver and break. They retreat in wild confusion. We were jubilant; we were triumphant. Officers could not curb the men to keep in line. Discharge after discharge was poured into the retreating line. The Federal dead and wounded covered the ground.

---

[1] General Albert Sidney Johnston, commander of Confederate forces in the West, killed later in the day. Watkins habitually omitted the "t" in spelling the last name.

When in the very midst of our victory, here comes an order to halt. What! halt after today's victory? Sidney Johnson killed, General Gladden killed, and a host of generals and other brave men killed, and the whole Yankee army in full retreat.

These four letters, h-a-l-t, O, how harsh they did break upon our ears. The victory was complete, but the word "halt" turned victory into defeat.

The soldiers had passed through the Yankee camps and saw all the good things that they had to eat in their sutlers' stores and officers' marquees, and it was but a short time before every soldier was rummaging to see what he could find.

The harvest was great and the laborers were not few.

The negro boys, who were with their young masters as servants, got rich. Greenbacks were plentiful, good clothes were plentiful, rations were not in demand. The boys were in clover.

This was Sunday.

On Monday the tide was reversed.

Now, those Yankees were whipped, fairly whipped, and according to all the rules of war they ought to have retreated. But they didn't. Flushed with their victories at Fort Henry and Fort Donelson and the capture of Nashville, and the whole State of Tennessee having fallen into their hands, victory was again to perch upon their banners, for Buell's army, by forced marches, had come to Grant's assistance at the eleventh hour.

Gunboats and transports were busily crossing Buell's army all of Sunday night. We could hear their boats ringing their bells, and hear the puff of smoke and steam from their boilers. Our regiment was the advance outpost, and we saw the skirmish line of the Federals advancing and then their main line and then their artillery. We made a good fight on Monday morning, and I was taken by surprise when the order came for us to retreat instead of advance. But as I said before, reader, a private soldier is but an automaton, and knows nothing of what is going on among the generals, and I am only giving the chronicles of little things and events that came under my own observation as I saw them then and remember them now. Should you desire to find out more about the battle, I refer you to history.

One incident I recollect very well. A Yankee colonel, riding a fine gray mare, was sitting on his horse looking at our advance as if we were on review. W. H. rushed forward and grabbed his horse by the bridle, telling him at the same time to surrender. The Yankee seized the reins, set himself back in the saddle, put the muzzle of his pistol in W. H.'s face and fired. About the time he pulled trigger, a stray ball from some direction struck him in the side and he fell off dead, and his horse becoming frightened, galloped off, dragging him through the Confederate lines. His pistol had missed its aim.

I have heard hundreds of old soldiers tell of the amount of greenback money they saw and picked up on the battlefield of Shiloh, but they thought it valueless and did not trouble themselves with bringing it off with them.

One fellow, a courier, who had had his horse killed, got on a mule he had captured, and in the last charge, before the final and fatal halt was made, just charged right ahead by his lone self, and the soldiers said, "Just look at that brave man, charging right in the jaws of death." He began to seesaw the mule and grit his teeth, and finally yelled out, "It arn't me, boys, it's the blarsted old mule. Whoa! Whoa!"

On Monday morning I too captured me a mule. He was not a fast mule, and I soon found out that he thought he knew as much as I did. He was wise in his own conceit. He had a propensity to take every hog path he came to. All the bombasting that I could give him would not make him accelerate his speed. If blood makes speed, I do not suppose he had a drop of any kind in him. If I wanted him to go on one side of the road he was sure to be possessed of an equal desire to go on the other side. Finally I and my mule fell out. I got a big hickory and would frail him over the head, and he would only shake his head and flop his ears, and seem to say, "Well, now, you think you are smart, don't you?" He was a resolute mule, slow to anger, and would have made an excellent merchant to refuse bad pay, or I will pay your credit, for his whole composition seemed to be made up the one word—no. I frequently thought it would be pleasant to split the difference with that mule, and I would gladly have done so if I could have gotten one-half of his no. Me and mule worried along until we came to a creek. Mule did not desire to cross, while I was trying to persuade him with a big stick, a rock in his ear, and a twister on his nose. The caisson of a battery was about to cross. The driver said, "I'll take your mule over for you." So he got a large two-inch rope, tied one end around the mule's neck and the other to the caisson, and ordered the driver to whip up. The mule was loath to take to the water. He was no Baptist, and did not believe in immersion, and had his views about crossing streams, but the rope began to tighten, the mule to squeal out his protestations against such villainous proceedings. The rope, however, was stronger than the mule's "no," and he was finally prevailed upon by the strength of the rope to cross the creek. On my taking the rope off he shook himself and seemed to say, "You think that you are mighty smart folks, but you are a leetle too smart." I gave it up that that mule's "no" was a little stronger than my determination. He seemed to be in deep meditation. I got on him again, when all of a sudden he lifted his head, pricked up his ears, began to champ his bit, gave a little squeal, got a little faster, and finally into a gallop and then a run. He seemed all at once to have remembered or to have forgotten something, and was now making up for lost time. With all my pulling and seesawing and strength I could not stop him until he brought up with me at Corinth, Mississippi.

Chapter 3

Corinth

WELL, here we were, again "reorganizing," and after our lax discipline on the road to and from Virginia, and after a big battle, which always disorganizes an army, what wonder is it that some men had to be shot, merely for discipline's sake? And what wonder that General Bragg's name became a terror to deserters and evil doers? Men were shot by scores, and no wonder the army had to be reorganized. Soldiers had enlisted for twelve months only, and had faithfully complied with their volunteer obligations; the terms for which they had enlisted had expired, and they naturally looked upon it that they had a right to go home. They had done their duty faithfully and well. They wanted to see their families; in fact, wanted to go home anyhow. War had become a reality; they were tired of it. A law had been passed by the Confederate States Congress called the conscript act. A soldier had no right to volunteer and to choose the branch of service he preferred.[1] He was conscripted.

From this time on till the end of the war, a soldier was simply a machine, a conscript. It was mighty rough on rebels. We cursed the war, we cursed Bragg, we cursed the Southern Confederacy. All our pride and valor had gone, and we were sick of war and the Southern Confederacy.

---

[1] Watkins was in error on this point. The conscription act allowed soldiers held to service by its terms thirty days to enter units of their own choice.

A law was made by the Confederate States Congress about this time allowing every person who owned twenty negroes to go home. It gave us the blues; we wanted twenty negroes. Negro property suddenly became very valuable, and there was raised the howl of "rich man's war, poor man's fight." The glory of the war, the glory of the South, the glory and the pride of our volunteers had no charms for the conscript.

We were directed to re-elect our officers, and the country was surprised to see the sample of a conscript's choice. The conscript had no choice. He was callous, and indifferent whether he had a captain or not. Those who were at first officers had resigned and gone home, because they were officers. The poor private, a contemptible conscript, was left to howl and gnash his teeth. The war might as well have ended then and there. The boys were "hacked," nay, whipped. They were shorn of the locks of their glory. They had but one ambition now, and that was to get out of the army in some way or other. They wanted to join the cavalry or artillery or home guards or pioneer corps or to be "yaller dogs," or anything.

[The average staff officer and courier were always called "yaller dogs," and were regarded as non-combatants and a nuisance, and the average private never let one pass without whistling and calling dogs. In fact, the general had to issue an army order threatening punishment for the ridicule hurled at staff officers and couriers. They were looked upon as simply "hangers on," or in other words, as yellow sheep-killing dogs, that if you would say "booh" at, would yelp and get under their master's heels. Mike Snyder was General George Maney's "yaller dog," and I believe here is where Joe Jefferson, in Rip Van Winkle, got the name of Rip's dog Snyder. At all times of day or night you could hear, "wheer, hyat, hyat, haer, haer, hugh, Snyder, whoopee, hyat, whoopee, Snyder, here, here," when a staff officer or courier happened to pass. The reason of this was that the private knew and felt that there was just that much more loading, shooting and fighting for him; and there are the fewest number of instances on record where a staff officer or courier ever fired a gun in their country's cause; and even at this late day, when I hear an old soldier telling of being on some general's staff, I always think of the letter "E." In fact, later in the war I was detailed as special courier and staff officer for General Hood, which office I held three days. But while I held the office in passing a guard I always told them I was on Hood's staff, and ever afterwards I made those three days' staff business last me the balance of the war. I could pass any guard in the army by using the magic words, "staff officer." It beat all the countersigns ever invented. It was the "open sesame" of war and discipline.]

Their last hope had set. They hated war. To their minds the South was a great tyrant, and the Confederacy a fraud. They were deserting by thousands. They had no love or respect for General Bragg. When men were to be shot or whipped, the whole army was marched to the horrid scene to see a poor trembling wretch tied to a post and a platoon of twelve men drawn up in line to put him to death, and the hushed command of "Ready, aim, fire!" would make the soldier, or conscript, I should say, loathe the very name of Southern Confederacy. And when some miserable wretch was to be whipped and branded for being absent ten days without leave, we had to see him kneel down and have his head shaved smooth and slick as a peeled onion, and then stripped to the naked skin. Then a strapping fellow with a big rawhide would make the blood flow and spurt at every lick, the wretch begging and howling like a hound, and then he was branded with a red hot iron with the letter D on both hips, when he was marched through the army to the music of the "Rogue's March." It was enough. None of General Bragg's soldiers ever loved him. They had no faith in his ability as a general. He was looked upon as a merciless tyrant. The soldiers were very scantily fed. Bragg never was a good feeder or commissary-general. Rations with us were always scarce. No extra rations were ever allowed to the negroes who were with us as servants. No coffee or whisky or tobacco were ever allowed to be issued to the troops. If they obtained these luxuries, they were not from the government. These luxuries were withheld in order to crush the very heart and spirit of his troops. We were crushed. Bragg was the great autocrat. In the mind of the soldier, his word was law. He loved to crush the spirit of his men. The more of a hang-dog look they had about them the better was General Bragg pleased. Not a single soldier in the whole army ever loved or respected him. But he is dead now.

Peace to his ashes!

We became starved skeletons; naked and ragged rebels. The chronic diarrhœa became the scourge of the army. Corinth became one vast hospital. Almost the whole army attended the sick call every morning. All the water courses went dry, and we used water out of filthy pools.

Halleck was advancing; we had to fortify Corinth. A vast army, Grant, Buell, Halleck, Sherman, all were advancing on Corinth. Our troops were in no condition to fight. In fact, they had seen enough of this miserable yet tragic farce. They were ready to ring down the curtain, put out the footlights and go home. They loved the Union anyhow, and were always opposed to this war. But breathe softly the name of Bragg. It had more terror than the advancing hosts of Halleck's army. The shot and shell would come tearing through our ranks. Every now and then a soldier was killed or wounded, and we thought what "magnificent" folly. Death was welcome. Halleck's whole army of blue coats had no terror now. When we were drawn up in line of battle, a detail of one-tenth of the army was placed in our rear to shoot us down if we ran. No pack of hounds under the master's lash, or body of penitentiary convicts were ever under greater surveillance. We were tenfold worse than slaves; our morale was a thing of the past; the glory of war and the pride of manhood had been sacrificed upon Bragg's tyrannical holocaust. But enough of this.

Rowland Shot to Death

One morning I went over to the 23rd Tennessee Regiment on a visit to Captain Gray Armstrong and Colonel Jim Niel, both of whom were glad to see me, as we were old ante-bellum friends.

While at Colonel Niel's marquee I saw a detail of soldiers bring out a man by the name of Rowland, whom they were going to shoot to death with musketry, by order of a court-martial, for desertion. I learned that he had served out the term for which he had originally volunteered, had quit our army and joined that of the Yankees, and was captured with Prentiss' Yankee brigade at Shiloh. He was being hauled to the place of execution in a wagon, sitting on an old gun box, which was to be his coffin. When they got to the grave, which had been dug the day before, the water had risen in it, and a soldier was baling it out. Rowland spoke up and said, "Please hand me a drink of that water, as I want to drink out of my own grave so the boys will talk about it when I am dead, and remember Rowland." They handed him the water and he drank all there was in the bucket, and handing it back asked them to please hand him a little more, as he had heard that water was very scarce in hell, and it would be the last he would ever drink. He was then carried to the death post, and there he began to cut up jack generally. He began to curse Bragg, Jeff. Davis, and the Southern Confederacy, and all the rebels at a terrible rate. He was simply arrogant and very insulting. I felt that he deserved to die. He said he would show the rebels how a Union man could die. I do not know what all he did say. When the shooting detail came up, he went of his own accord and knelt down at the post. The Captain commanding the squad gave the command, "Ready, aim, fire!" and Rowland tumbled over on his side. It was the last of Rowland.

Killing a Yankee Sharpshooter

In our immediate front, at Corinth, Mississippi, our men were being picked off by sharpshooters, and a great many were killed, but no one could tell where the shots came from. At one particular post it was sure death. Every detail that had been sent to this post for a week had been killed. In distributing the detail this post fell to Tom Webb and myself. They were bringing off a dead boy just as we went on duty. Colonel George C. Porter, of the 6th Tennessee, warned us to keep a good lookout. We took our stands. A minnie ball whistled right by my head. I don't think it missed me an eighth of an inch. Tom had sat down on an old chunk of wood, and just as he took his seat, zip! a ball took the chunk of wood. Tom picked it up and began laughing at our tight place. Happening to glance up towards the tree tops, I saw a smoke rising above a tree, and about the same time I saw a Yankee peep from behind the tree, up among the bushes. I quickly called Tom's attention to it, and pointed out the place. We could see his ramrod as he handled it while loading his gun; saw him raise his gun, as we thought, to put a cap on it. Tom in the meantime had lain flat on his belly and placed his gun across the chunk he had been sitting on. I had taken a rest for my gun by the side of a sapling, and both of us had dead aim at the place where the Yankee was. Finally we saw him sort o' peep round the tree, and we moved about a little so that he might see us, and as we did so, the Yankee stepped out in full view, and bang, bang! Tom and I had both shot. We saw that Yankee tumble out like a squirrel. It sounded like distant thunder when that Yankee struck the ground. We heard the Yankees carry him off. One thing I am certain of, and that is, not another Yankee went up that tree that day, and Colonel George C. Porter complimented Tom and I very highly on our success. This is where I first saw a jack o'lantern (*ignis fatui*). That night, while Tom and I were on our posts, we saw a number of very dim lights, which seemed to be in motion. At first we took them to be Yankees moving about with lights. Whenever we could get a shot we would blaze away. At last one got up very close, and passed right between Tom and I. I don't think I was ever more scared in my life. My hair stood on end like the quills of the fretful porcupine; I could not imagine what on earth it was. I took it to be some hellish machination of a Yankee trick. I did not know whether to run or stand, until I heard Tom laugh and say, "Well, well, that's a jack o'lantern."

Colonel Field

Before proceeding further with these memoirs, I desire to give short sketches of two personages with whom we were identified and closely associated until the winding up of the ball. The first is Colonel Hume R. Field. Colonel Field was born a soldier. I have read many descriptions of Stonewall Jackson. Colonel Field was his exact counterpart. They looked somewhat alike, spoke alike, and alike were trained military soldiers. The War Department at Richmond made a grand mistake in not making him a "commander of armies." He was not a brilliant man; could not talk at all. He was a soldier. His conversation was yea and nay. But when you could get "yes, sir," and "no, sir," out of him his voice was as soft and gentle as a maid's when she says "yes" to her lover. Fancy, if you please, a man about thirty years old, a dark skin, made swarthy by exposure to sun and rain, very black eyes that seemed to blaze with a gentle luster. I never saw him the least excited in my life. His face was a face of bronze. His form was somewhat slender, but when you looked at him you saw at the first glance that this would be a dangerous man in a ground skuffle, a foot race, or a fight. There was nothing repulsive or forbidding or even domineering in his looks. A child or a dog would make up with him on first sight. He knew not what fear was, or the meaning of the word fear. He had no nerves, or rather, has a rock or tree any nerves? You might as well try to shake the nerves of a rock or tree as those of Colonel Field. He was the bravest man, I think, I ever knew. Later in the war he was known by every soldier in the army; and the First Tennessee Regiment, by his manipulations, became the regiment to occupy "tight places." He knew his men. When he struck the Yankee line they felt the blow. He had, himself, set the example, and so trained his regiment that all the armies in the world could not whip it. They might kill every man in it, is true, but they would die game to the last man. His men all loved him. He was no disciplinarian, but made his regiment what it was by his own example. And every day on the march you would see some poor old ragged rebel riding his fine gray mare, and he was walking.

Captain Joe P. Lee

The other person I wish to speak of is Captain Joe P. Lee. Captain Henry J. Webster was our regular captain, but was captured while on furlough, sent to a northern prison and died there, and Joe went up by promotion. He was quite a young man, about twenty-one years old, but as brave as any old Roman soldier that ever lived. Joe's face was ever wreathed in smiles, and from the beginning to the end he was ever at the head of his company. I do not think that any member of the company ever did call him by his title. He was called simply "Joe Lee," or more frequently "Black Perch." While on duty he was strict and firm, but off duty he was "one of us boys." We all loved and respected him, but everybody knows Joe, and further comment is unnecessary.

I merely mention these two persons because in this rapid sketch I may have cause occasionally to mention them, and only wish to introduce them to the reader, so he may understand more fully my ideas. But, reader, please remember that I am not writing a history at all, and do not propose in these memoirs to be anybody's biographer. I am only giving my own impressions. If other persons think differently from me it is all right, and I forgive them.

Corinth Forsaken

One morning a detail was sent to burn up and destroy all the provisions and army stores, and to blow up the arsenal. The town was in a blaze of fire and the arsenal was roaring and popping and bellowing like pandemonium turned loose as we marched through Corinth on the morning of the evacuation. We bade farewell to Corinth. Its history was black and dark and damning. No little speck of green oasis ever enlivened the dark recesses of our memory while at this place. It's a desert that lives only in bitter memories. It was but one vast graveyard that entombed the life and spirit of once brave and chivalrous men. We left it to the tender mercies of the Yankees without one tear of sorrow or regret, and bade it farewell forever.

Chapter 4

Tupelo

WE WENT into summer quarters at Tupelo. Our principal occupation at this place was playing poker, chuck-a-luck and cracking graybacks (lice). Every soldier had a brigade of lice on him, and I have seen fellows so busily engaged in cracking them that it reminded me of an old woman knitting. At first the boys would go off in the woods and hide to louse themselves, but that was unnecessary, the ground fairly crawled with lice. Pharaoh's people, when they were resisting old Moses, never enjoyed the curse of lice more than we did. The boys would frequently have a louse race. There was one fellow who was winning all the money; his lice would run quicker and crawl faster than anybody's lice. We could not understand it. If some fellow happened to catch a fierce-looking louse, he would call on Dornin for a race. Dornin would come and always win the stake. The lice were placed in plates—this was the race course—and the first that crawled off was the winner. At last we found out D.'s trick; he always heated his plate.

Billy P. said he had no lice on him.

"Did you ever look?"

"No."

"How do you know then?"

"If ignorance is bliss 'tis folly to be wise," said Billy.

"Why, there is one crawling on your bosom now."

Billy took him and put him back in his bosom and said to the louse, "You stay there now; this makes the fourth time I have put you back, and if I catch you out again today I'll martyr you."

Billy was philosophic—the death of one louse did not stop the breed.

The Court-Martial at Tupelo

At this place was held the grand court-martial. Almost every day we would hear a discharge of musketry, and knew that some poor, trembling wretch had bid farewell to mortal things here below. It seemed to be but a question of time with all of us as to when we too would be shot. We were afraid to chirp. So far now as patriotism was concerned, we had forgotten all about that, and did not now so much love our country as we feared Bragg. Men were being led to the death stake every day. I heard of many being shot, but did not see but two men shot myself. I do not know to what regiment they belonged, but I remember that they were mere beardless boys. I did not learn for what crime or the magnitude of their offenses. They might have deserved death for all I know.

I saw an old man, about sixty years old, whose name was Dave Brewer, and another man, about forty-five, by the name of Rube Franklin, whipped. There was many a man whipped and branded that I never saw or heard tell of. But the reason I remembered these two was that they belonged to Company A of the 23rd Tennessee Regiment, and I knew many men in the regiment.

These two men were hung up by the hands, after having their heads shaved, to a tree, put there for the purpose, with the prongs left on them, and one hand was stretched toward one prong and the other hand to another prong, their feet, perhaps just touching the ground. The man who did the whipping had a thick piece of sole-leather, the end of which was cut in three strips, and this tacked on to the end of a paddle. After the charges and specifications had been read (both men being stark naked), the whipper "lit in" on Rube, who was the youngest. I do not think he intended to hit as hard as he did, but, being excited himself, he blistered Rube from head to foot. Thirty-nine lashes was always the number. Now, three times thirty-nine makes one hundred and seventeen. When he struck at all, one lick would make three whelps. When he had finished Rube, the Captain commanding the whipping squad told him to lay it on old man Brewer as light as the law would allow, that old man Brewer was so old that he would die—that he could not stand it. He struck old man Dave Brewer thirty-nine lashes, but they were laid on light. Old Dave didn't beg and squall like Rube did. He j-e-s-t did whip old man Dave. Like the old preacher who caught the bear on Sunday. They had him up before the church, agreed to let him off if he did not again set his trap. "Well," he said, "brethren, I j-e-s-t did set it."

Raiding on Roastingears

At this place General Bragg issued an order authorizing citizens to defend themselves against the depredations of soldiers—to shoot them down if caught depredating.

Well, one day Byron Richardson and myself made a raid on an old citizen's roastingear patch. We had pulled about all the corn that we could carry. I had my arms full and was about starting for camp when an old citizen raised up and said, "Stop there! drop that corn." He had a double-barreled shotgun cocked and leveled at my breast.

"Come and go with me to General Bragg's headquarters. I intend to take you there, by the living God!"

I was in for it. Directed to go in front, I was being marched to Bragg's headquarters. I could see the devil in the old fellow's eye. I tried to beg off with good promises, but the old fellow was deaf to all entreaty. I represented to him all of our hardships and suffering. But the old fellow was inexorable. I was being steadily carried toward Bragg's headquarters. I was determined not to see General Bragg, even if the old citizen shot me in the back.

When all at once a happy thought struck me. Says I, "Mister, Byron Richardson is in your field, and if you will go back we can catch him and you can take both of us to General Bragg." The old fellow's spunk was up. He had captured me so easy, he no doubt thought he could whip a dozen. We went back a short distance, and there was Byron, who had just climbed over the fence and had his arms full, when the old citizen, diverted from me, leveled his double-barrel at Byron, when I made a grab for his gun, which was accidentally discharged in the air, and with the assistance of Byron, we had the old fellow and his gun both. The table was turned. We made the old fellow gather as much as he could carry, and made him carry it nearly to camp, when we dismissed him, a wiser if not a better and richer man. We took his gun and bent it around a black jack tree. He was at the soldiers' mercy.

Chapter 5

Kentucky

We Go into Kentucky

A<small>FTER</small> being thoroughly reorganized at Tupelo, and the troops had recovered their health and spirits, we made an advance into Kentucky. We took the cars at Tupelo and went to Mobile, from thence across Mobile Bay to Montgomery, Alabama, then to Atlanta, from there to Chattanooga, and then over the mountains afoot to the blue-grass regions of Kentucky— the dark and bloody ground. Please remember, patient reader, that I write entirely from memory. I have no data or diary or anything to go by, and memory is a peculiar faculty. I find that I cannot remember towns and battles, and remember only the little things. I remember how gladly the citizens of Kentucky received us. I thought they had the prettiest girls that God ever made. They could not do too much for us. They had heaps and stacks of cooked rations along our route, with wine and cider everywhere, and the glad shouts of "Hurrah for our Southern boys!" greeted and welcomed us at every house. Ah, the boys felt like soldiers again. The bands played merrier and livelier tunes. It was the patient convalescing; the fever had left him, he was getting fat and strong; the old fire was seen to illuminate his eyes; his step was buoyant and proud; he felt ashamed that he had ever been "hacked"; he could fight now. It was the same old proud soldier of yore. The bands played "Dixie" and the "Bonnie Blue Flag," the citizens cheered, and the ladies waved their handkerchiefs and threw us bouquets. Ah, those were halcyon days, and your old soldier, kind reader, loves to recall that happy period. Mumfordsville[1] had been captured with five thousand prisoners. New recruits were continually joining our ranks.

Camp Dick Robinson, that immense pile of army stores, had fallen into our hands. We rode upon the summit of the wave of success. The boys had got clean clothes, and had their faces washed. I saw then what I had long since forgotten—a "cockade." The Kentucky girls made cockades for us, and almost every soldier had one pinned on his hat. But stirring events were hastening on, the black cloud of battle and war had begun then to appear much larger than a man's hand, in fact we could see the lightning flash and hear the thunder roar.

We were at Harrodsburg; the Yankees were approaching Perryville under General Buell. The Yankees had been dogging our rear, picking up our stragglers and capturing some of our wagon trains.

This good time that we were having was too good to last. We were in an ecstasy akin to heaven. We were happy; the troops were jubilant; our manhood blood pulsated more warmly; our patriotism was awakened; our pride was renewed and stood ready for any emergency; we felt that one Southern man could whip twenty Yankees. All was lovely and the goose hung high. We went to dances and parties every night.

When General Chalmers marched to Perryville, in flanking and surrounding Mumfordsville, we marched the whole night long. We, the private soldiers, did not know what was going on among the generals. All that we had to do was march, march, march. It mattered not how tired, hungry, or thirsty we were. All that we had to do was to march that whole night long, and every staff officer who would pass, some fellow would say, "Hey, mis-

---

[1]Munfordville, Kentucky, captured by Bragg's troops on September 16, 1862.

ter, how far is it to Mumfordsville?" He would answer, "five miles." It seemed to me we traveled a hundred miles and were always within five miles of Mumfordsville. That night we heard a volley of musketry in our immediate front, and did not know what it meant, but soon we came to where a few soldiers had lighted some candles and were holding them over the body of a dead soldier. It was Captain Allison, if I remember rightly, of General Cheatham's staff. He was very bloody, and had his clothes riddled with balls. I heard that he rode on in front of the advance guard of our army, and had no doubt discovered the Yankee picket, and came galloping back at full speed in the dark, when our advance guard fired on and killed him.

We laid down in a graveyard that night and slept, and when we awoke the sun was high in the heavens, shining in our faces. Mumfordsville had surrendered. The next day Dr. C. T. Quintard let me ride his horse nearly all day, while he walked with the webfeet.

The Battle of Perryville

In giving a description of this most memorable battle, I do not pretend to give you figures, and describe how this general looked and how that one spoke, and the other one charged with drawn sabre, etc. I know nothing of these things—see the history for that. I was simply a soldier of the line, and I only write of the things I saw. I was in every battle, skirmish and march that was made by the First Tennessee Regiment during the war, and I do not remember of a harder contest and more evenly fought battle than that of Perryville. If it had been two men wrestling, it would have been called a "dog fall." Both sides claim the victory—both whipped.

I stood picket in Perryville the night before the battle—a Yankee on one side of the street, and I on the other. We got very friendly during the night, and made a raid upon a citizen's pantry, where we captured a bucket of honey, a pitcher of sweet milk, and three or four biscuit. The old citizen was not at home—he and his whole household had gone visiting, I believe. In fact, I think all of the citizens of Perryville were taken with a sudden notion of promiscuous visiting about this time; at least they were not at home to all callers.

At length the morning dawned. Our line was drawn up on one side of Perryville, the Yankee army on the other. The two enemies that were soon to meet in deadly embrace seemed to be eyeing each other. The blue coats lined the hillside in plain view. You could count the number of their regiments by the number of their flags. We could see the huge war dogs frowning at us, ready at any moment to belch forth their fire and smoke, and hurl their thunderbolts of iron and death in our very midst.

I wondered why the fighting did not begin. Never on earth were our troops more eager for the engagement to open. The Yankees commenced to march toward their left, and we marched almost parallel to our right—both sides watching each other's maneuvers and movements. It was but the lull that precedes the storm. Colonel Field was commanding our brigade, and Lieutenant-Colonel Patterson our regiment. About 12 o'clock, while we were marching through a corn field, in which the corn had been shocked, they opened their war dogs upon us. The beginning of the end had come. Here is where Captain John F. Wheless was wounded, and three others, whose names I have forgotten. The battle now opened in earnest, and from one end of the line to the other seemed to be a solid sheet of blazing smoke and fire. Our regiment crossed a stream, being preceded by Wharton's Texas Rangers, and we were ordered to attack at once with vigor. Here General Maney's horse was shot. From this moment the battle was a mortal struggle. Two lines of battle confronted us. We killed almost every one in the first line, and were soon charging over the second, when right in our immediate front was their third and main line of battle from which four Napoleon guns poured their deadly fire.

We did not recoil, but our line was fairly hurled back by the leaden hail that was poured into our very faces. Eight color-bearers were killed at one discharge of their cannon. We were right up among the very wheels of their Napoleon guns. It was death to retreat now to either side. Our Lieutenant-Colonel Patterson halloed to charge and take their guns, and we were soon in a hand-to-hand fight—every man for himself—using the butts of our guns and bayonets. One side would waver and fall back a few yards, and would rally, when the other side would fall back, leaving the four Napoleon guns; and yet the battle raged. Such obstinate fighting I never had seen before or since. The guns were discharged so rapidly that it seemed the earth itself was in a volcanic uproar. The iron storm passed through our ranks, mangling and tearing men to pieces. The very air seemed full of stifling smoke and fire which seemed the very pit of hell, peopled by contending demons.

Our men were dead and dying right in the very midst of this grand havoc of battle. It was a life to life and death to death grapple. The sun was poised above us, a great red ball sinking slowly in the west, yet the scene of battle and carnage continued. I cannot describe it. The mantle of night fell upon the scene. I do not know which side whipped, but I know that I helped bring off those four Napoleon guns that night though we were mighty easy about it.

They were given to Turner's Battery of our brigade and had the name of our Lieutenant-Colonel Patterson and our color-bearer, Mitchell, both of whom were killed, inscribed on two of the pieces. I have forgotten the names inscribed on the other two pieces. I saw these very four guns surrendered at Missionary Ridge. But of this another time.

The battle of Perryville presented a strange scene. The dead, dying, and wounded of both armies, Confederate and Federal, were blended in inextricable confusion. Now and then a cluster of dead Yankees and close by a cluster of dead Rebels. It was like the Englishman's grog—'alf and 'alf. Now, if you wish, kind reader, to find out how many were killed and wounded, I refer you to the histories.

I remember one little incident that I laughed at while in the very midst of battle. We were charging through an old citizen's

yard, when a big yellow cur dog ran out and commenced snap-
ping at the soldiers' legs—they kicking at him to keep him off.
The next morning he was lying near the same place, but he was
a dead dog.

I helped bring off our wounded that night. We worked the
whole night. The next morning about daylight a wounded comrade, Sam Campbell, complained of being cold, and asked me to
lie down beside him. I did so, and was soon asleep; when I
awoke the poor fellow was stiff and cold in death. His spirit had
flown to its home beyond the skies.

After the battle was over, John T. Tucker, Scott Stephens,
A. S. Horsley and I were detailed to bring off our wounded that
night, and we helped to bring off many a poor dying comrade—
Joe Thompson, Billy Bond, Byron Richardson, the two Allen
boys—brothers, killed side by side—and Colonel Patterson, who
was killed standing right by my side. He was first shot through
the hand, and was wrapping his handkerchief around it, when
another ball struck and killed him. I saw W. J. Whitthorne, then
a strippling boy of fifteen years of age, fall, shot through the
neck and collar-bone. He fell apparently dead, when I saw him
all at once jump up, grab his gun and commence loading and firing, and I heard him say, "D—n 'em, I'll fight 'em as long as I
live." Whit thought he was killed, but he is living yet. We helped
bring off a man by the name of Hodge, with his under jaw shot
off, and his tongue lolling out. We brought off Captain Lute B.
Irvine. Lute was shot through the lungs and was vomiting blood
all the while, and begging us to lay him down and let him die.
But Lute is living yet. Also, Lieutenant Woldridge, with both
eyes shot out. I found him rambling in a briar-patch. About fifty
members of the Rock City Guards were killed and nearly one
hundred wounded. They were led by Captains W. D. Kelley,
Wheless, and Steele. Lieutenant Thomas H. Maney was badly
wounded. I saw dead on the battlefield a Federal General by the
name of Jackson. It was his brigade that fought us so obstinately
at this place, and I did hear that they were made up in Kentucky.
Colonel Field, then commanding our brigade, and on his fine

gray mare, rode up almost face to face with General Jackson, before he was killed, and Colonel Field was shooting all the time with his seven-shooting rifle. I cannot tell the one-half, or even remember at this late date, the scenes of blood and suffering that I witnessed on the battlefield of Perryville. But its history, like all the balance, has gone into the history of the war, and it has been twenty years ago, and I write entirely from memory. I remember Lieutenant Joe P. Lee and Captain W. C. Flournoy standing right at the muzzle of the Napoleon guns, and the next moment seemed to be enveloped in smoke and fire from the discharge of the cannon. When the regiment recoiled under the heavy firing and at the first charge, Billy Webster and I stopped behind a large oak tree and continued to fire at the Yankees until the regiment was again charging upon the four Napoleon guns, heavily supported by infantry. We were not more than twenty paces from them; and here I was shot through the hat and cartridge-box. I remember this, because at that time Billy and I were in advance of our line, and whenever we saw a Yankee rise to shoot, we shot him; and I desire to mention here that a braver or more noble boy was never created on earth than was Billy Webster. Everybody liked him. He was the flower and chivalry of our regiment. His record as a brave and noble boy will ever live in the hearts of his old comrades that served with him in Company H. He is up yonder now, and we shall meet again. In these memoirs I only tell what I saw myself, and in this way the world will know the truth. Now, citizen, let me tell you what you never heard before, and this is this—there were many men with the rank and pay of general, who were not generals; there were many men with the rank and pay of privates who would have honored and adorned the name of general. Now, I will state further that a private soldier was a private.

It mattered not how ignorant a corporal might be, he was always right; it mattered not how intelligent the private might be (and so on up); the sergeant was right over the corporal, the sergeant-major over the sergeant, the lieutenant over him, and the captain over him, and the major over him, and the colonel over

him, and the general over him, and so on up to Jeff Davis. You
see, a private had no right to know anything, and that is why
generals did all the fighting, and that is today why generals and
colonels and captains are great men. They fought the battles of
our country. The privates did not. The generals risked their reputation, the private soldier his life. No one ever saw a private in
battle. His history would never be written. It was the generals
that everybody saw charge such and such, with drawn sabre, his
eyes flashing fire, his nostrils dilated, and his clarion voice ringing above the din of battle—"in a horn," over the left.

Bill Johns and Marsh Pinkard would have made Generals
that would have distinguished themselves and been an honor to
the country.

I know today many a private who would have made a good
General. I know of many a General who was better fitted to be
excused from detail and fights, to hang around a camp and draw
rations for the company. A private had no way to distinguish
himself. He had to keep in ranks, either in a charge or a retreat.
But now, as the Generals and Colonels fill all the positions of
honor and emoluments, the least I say, the better.

The Retreat Out of Kentucky

From Perryville we went to Camp Dick Robinson and drew
three days' rations, and then set fire to and destroyed all those
great deposits of army stores which would have supplied the
South for a year. We ate those rations and commenced our retreat out of Kentucky with empty haversacks and still emptier
stomachs.

We supposed our general and commissaries knew what they
were doing, and at night we would again draw rations, but we
didn't.

The Yankee cavalry are worrying our rear guards. There is
danger of an attack at any moment. No soldier is allowed to
break ranks.

We thought, well surely we will draw rations tonight. But we didn't. We are marching for Cumberland Gap; the country has long ago been made desolate by the alternate occupation of both armies. There are no provisions in the country. It has long since been laid waste. We wanted rations, but we did not get them.

Fourth day out—Cumberland Gap in the distance—a great indenture in the ranges of Cumberland mountains. The scene was grand. But grand scenery had but little attraction for a hungry soldier. Surely we will get rations at Cumberland Gap. Toil on up the hill, and when half way up the hill, "Halt!"—march back down to the foot of the hill to defend the cavalry. I was hungry. A cavalryman was passing our regiment with a pile of scorched dough on the pummel of his saddle. Says I, "'Halt!' I am going to have a pattock of that bread." "Don't give it to him! don't give it to him!" was yelled out from all sides. I cocked my gun and was about to raise it to my shoulder, when he handed me over a pattock of scorched dough, and every fellow in Company H made a grab for it, and I only got about two or three mouthfuls. About dark a wild heifer ran by our regiment, and I pulled down on her. We killed and skinned her, and I cut off about five pounds of hindquarter. In three minutes there was no sign of that beef left to tell the tale. We ate that beef raw and without salt.

Only eight miles now to Cumberland Gap, and we will get rations now. But we didn't. We descended the mountain on the southern side. No rations yet.

Well, says I, this won't do me. I am going to hunt something to eat, Bragg or no Bragg. I turned off the road and struck out through the country, but had gone but a short distance before I came across a group of soldiers clambering over something. It was Tom Tuck with a barrel of sorghum that he had captured from a good Union man. He was selling it out at five dollars a quart. I paid my five dollars, and by pushing and scrouging I finally got my quart. I sat down and drank it; it was bully; it was not so good; it was not worth a cent; I was sick, and have never loved sorghum since.

Along the route it was nothing but tramp, tramp, tramp, and

no sound or noise but the same inevitable, monotonous tramp, tramp, tramp, up hill and down hill, through long and dusty lanes, weary, wornout and hungry. No cheerful warble of a merry songster would ever greet our ears. It was always tramp, tramp, tramp. You might, every now and then, hear the occasional words, "close up;" but outside of that, it was but the same tramp, tramp, tramp. I have seen soldiers fast asleep, and no doubt dreaming of home and loved ones there, as they staggered along in their places in the ranks. I know that on many a weary night's march I have slept, and slept soundly, while marching along in my proper place in the ranks of the company, stepping to the same step as the soldier in front of me did. Sometimes, when weary, broken down and worn out, some member of the regiment would start a tune, and every man would join in. John Branch was usually the leader of the choir. He would commence a beautiful tune. The words, as I remembered them now, were "Dear Paul, Just Twenty Years Ago." After singing this piece he would commence on a lively, spirit-stirring air to the tune of "Old Uncle Ned." Now, reader, it has been twenty years ago since I heard it, but I can remember a part of it now. Here is is:

> "There was an ancient individual whose cognomen was
>   Uncle Edward.
> He departed this life long since, long since.
> He had no capillary substance on the top of his cranium,
> The place where the capillary substance ought to vegetate.
>
> His digits were as long as the bamboo piscatorial imple-
>   ment of the Southern Mississippi.
> He had no oculars to observe the beauties of nature.
> He had no ossified formation to masticate his daily ra-
>   tions,
> So he had to let his daily rations pass by with impunity."

Walker Coleman raises the tune of "I'se a gwine to jine the rebel band, a fightin' for my home."

Now, reader, the above is all I can now remember of that very beautiful and soul-stirring air. But the boys would wake up and step quicker and livelier for some time, and Arthur Fulghum would holloa out, "All right; go ahead!" and then would toot! toot! as if the cars were starting—puff! puff! puff and then he would say, "Tickets, gentlemen; tickets, gentlemen" like he was conductor on a train of cars. This little episode would be over, and then would commence the same tramp, tramp, tramp, all night long. Step by step, step by step, we continued to plod and nod and stagger and march, tramp, tramp, tramp. After a while we would see the morning star rise in the east, and then after a while the dim gray twilight, and finally we could discover the outlines of our file leader, and after a while could make out the outlines of trees and other objects. And as it would get lighter and lighter, and day would be about to break, cuckoo, cuckoo, cuckoo, would come from Tom Tuck's rooster. [Tom carried a game rooster, that he called "Fed" for Confederacy, all through the war in a haversack.] And then the sun would begin to shoot his slender rays athwart the eastern sky, and the boys would wake up and begin laughing and talking as if they had just risen from a good feather bed, and were perfectly refreshed and happy. We would usually stop at some branch or other about breakfast time, and all wash our hands and faces and eat breakfast, if we had any, and then commence our weary march again. If we were halted for one minute, every soldier would drop down, and resting on his knapsack, would go to sleep. Sometimes the sleeping soldiers were made to get up to let some general and his staff pass by. But whenever that was the case, the general always got a worse cursing than when Noah cursed his son Ham black and blue. I heard Jessee Ely do this once.

We march on. The scene of a few days ago comes unbidden to my mind. Tramp, tramp, tramp, the soldiers are marching. Where are many of my old friends and comrades, whose names were so familiar at every roll call, and whose familiar "Here" is no more? They lie yonder at Perryville, unburied, on the field of battle. They lie where they fell. More than three hundred and fifty members of my regiment, the First Tennessee, numbered among the killed and wounded—one hundred and eighty-five slain on the field of battle. Who are they? Even then I had to try to think up the names of all the slain of Company H alone. Their spirits seemed to be with us on the march, but we know that their souls are with their God. Their bones, today, no doubt, bleach upon the battlefield. They left their homes, families, and loved ones a little more than one short twelve months ago, dressed in their gray uniforms, amid the applause and cheering farewells of those same friends. They lie yonder; no friendly hands ever closed their eyes in death; no kind, gentle, and loving mother was there to shed a tear over and say farewell to her darling boy; no sister's gentle touch ever wiped the death damp from off their dying brows. Noble boys; brave boys! They willingly gave their lives to their country's cause. Their bodies and bones are mangled and torn by the rude missiles of war. They sleep the sleep of the brave. They have given their all to their country. We miss them from our ranks. There are no more hard marches and scant rations for them. They have accomplished all that could be required of them. They are no more; their names are soon forgotten. They are put down in the roll-book as killed. They are forgotten. We will see them no more until the last reveille on the last morning of the final resurrection. Soldiers, comrades, friends, noble boys, farewell! we will meet no more on earth, but up yonder some day we will have a grand reunion.

Knoxville

The first night after crossing Cumberland Gap—I have forgotten the date, but I know it was very early in the fall of the year; we had had no frost or cold weather, and our marches all through Kentucky had been characterized by very dry weather, it not having rained a drop on us during the whole time—about four o'clock in the morning it began to snow, and the next morning the ground was covered with a deep snow; the trees and grass and everything of the vegetable kingdom still green.

When we got back to Knoxville we were the lousiest, dirtiest, raggedest looking Rebels you ever saw. I had been shot through the hat and cartridge-box at Perryville, and had both on, and the clothing I then had on was all that I had in the world. William A. Hughes and I were walking up the street looking at the stores, etc., when we met two of the prettiest girls I ever saw. They ran forward with smiling faces, and seemed very glad to see us. I thought they were old acquaintances of Hughes, and Hughes thought they were old acquaintances of mine. We were soon laughing and talking as if we had been old friends, when one of the young ladies spoke up and said, "Gentlemen, there is a supper for the soldiers at the Ladies' Association rooms, and we are sent out to bring in all the soldiers we can find." We spoke up quickly and said, "Thank you, thank you, young ladies," and I picked out the prettiest one and said, "Please take my arm," which she did, and Hughes did the same with the other one, and we went in that style down the street. I imagine we were a funny looking sight. I know one thing, I felt good all over, and as proud as a boy with his first pants, and when we got to that supper room those young ladies waited on us, and we felt as grand as kings. To you, ladies, I say, God bless you!

Ah, "Sneak"

Almost every soldier in the army—generals, colonels, captains, as well as privates—had a nick-name; and I almost believe that had the war continued ten years, we would have forgotten our proper names. John T. Tucker was called "Sneak," A. S. Horsley was called "Don Von One Horsley," W. A. Hughes was called "Apple Jack," Green Rieves was called "Devil Horse," the surgeon of our regiment was called "Old Snake," Bob Brank was called "Count," the colonel of the Fourth was called "Guide Post," E. L. Lansdown was called "Left Tenant," some were called by the name of "Greasy," some "Buzzard," others "Hog," and "Brutus," and "Cassius," and "Cæsar," "Left Center," and "Bolderdust," and "Old Hannah;" in fact, the nick-names were singular and peculiar, and when a man got a nick-name it stuck to him like the Old Man of the Sea did to the shoulders of Sinbad, the sailor.

On our retreat the soldiers got very thirsty for tobacco (they always used the word thirsty), and they would sometimes come across an old field off which the tobacco had been cut and the suckers had re-sprouted from the old stalk, and would cut off these suckers and dry them by the fire and chew them. "Sneak" had somehow or other got hold of a plug or two, and knowing that he would be begged for a chew, had cut it up in little bits of pieces about one-fourth of a chew. Some fellow would say, "Sneak, please give me a chew of tobacco." Sneak would say, "I don't believe I have a piece left," and then he would begin to feel in his pockets. He would pull that hand out and feel in another pocket, and then in his coat pockets, and hid away down in an odd corner of his vest pocket he would accidentally find a little chew, just big enough to make "spit come." Sneak had his pockets full all the time. The boys soon found out his inuendoes and subterfuges, but John would all the time appear as innocent of having tobacco as a pet lamb that has just torn down a nice vine that you were so careful in training to run over the front porch. Ah, John, don't deny it now!

I Jine the Cavalry

When we got to Charleston, on the Hiwassee river, there we found the First Tennessee Cavalry and Ninth Battalion, both of which had been made up principally in Maury county, and we knew all the boys. We had a good old-fashioned handshaking all around. Then I wanted to "jine the cavalry." Captain Asa G. Freeman had an extra horse, and I got on him and joined the cavalry for several days, but all the time some passing cavalryman would make some jocose remark about "Here is a webfoot who wants to jine the cavalry, and has got a bayonet on his gun and a knapsack on his back." I felt like I had got into the wrong pen, but anyhow I got to ride all of three days. I remember that Mr. Willis B. Embry gave me a five-pound package of Kallickanick smoking tobacco, for which I was very grateful. I think he was quartermaster of the First Tennessee Cavalry, and as good a man and as clever a person as I ever knew. None knew him but to love him. I was told that he was killed by a lot of Yankee soldiers after he had surrendered to them, all the time begging for his life, asking them please not kill him. But He that noteth the sparrow's fall doeth all things well. Not one ever falls to the ground without His consent.

Chapter 6

Murfreesboro

WE CAME from Knoxville to Chattanooga, and seemed destined to make a permanent stay here. We remained several months, but soon we were on the tramp again.

From Chattanooga, Bragg's army went to Murfreesboro.

The Federal army was concentrating at Nashville. There was no rest for the weary. Marches and battles were the order of the day.

Our army stopped at Murfreesboro. Our advanced outpost was established at Lavergne. From time to time different regiments were sent forward to do picket duty. I was on picket at the time the advance was made by Rosecrans. At the time mentioned, I was standing about two hundred yards off the road, the main body of the pickets being on the Nashville and Murfreesboro turnpike, and commanded by Lieutenant Hardy Murfree, of the Rutherford Rifles.

I had orders to allow no one to pass. In fact, no one was expected to pass at this point, but while standing at my post, a horseman rode up behind me. I halted him, and told him to go down to the main picket on the road and pass, but he seemed so smiling that I thought he knew me, or had a good joke to tell me. He advanced up, and pulling a piece of paper out of his pocket, handed it to me to read. It was an order from General Leonidas Polk to allow the bearer to pass. I read it, and looked up to hand it back to him, when I discovered that he had a pistol cocked and leveled in my face, and says he, "Drop that gun; you are my prisoner." I saw there was no use in fooling about it. I knew if I resisted he would shoot me, and I thought then that he was about to perform that detestable operation. I dropped the gun.

I did not wish to spend my winter in a Northern prison, and what was worse, I would be called a deserter from my post of duty.

The Yankee picket lines were not a half mile off. I was perfectly willing to let the spy go on his way rejoicing—for such he was—but he wanted to capture a Rebel.

And I had made up my mind to think likewise. There I was, a prisoner sure, and no mistake about it.

His pistol was leveled, and I was ordered to march. I was afraid to halloo to the relief, and you may be sure I was in a bad fix.

Finally says I, "Let's play quits. I think you are a soldier; you look like a gentleman. I am a videt; you know the responsibility resting on me. You go your way, and leave me here. Is it a bargain?"

Says he, "I would not trust a Secesh on his word, oath, or bond. March, I say."

I soon found out that he had caught sight of the relief on the road, and was afraid to shoot. I quickly made up my mind. My gun was at my feet, and one step would get it. I made a quick glance over my shoulder, and grabbed at my gun. He divined my motive, and fired. The ball missed its aim. He puts spurs to his horse, but I pulled down on him, and almost tore the fore shoulder of his horse entirely off, but I did not capture the spy, though I captured the horse, bridle and saddle. Major Allen, of the Twenty-seventh Tennessee Regiment, took the saddle and bridle, and gave me the blanket. I remembered the blanket had the picture of a "big lion" on it, and it was almost new. When we fell back, as the Yankee sharpshooters advanced, we left the poor old horse nipping the short, dry grass. I saw a Yankee skirmisher run up and grab the horse and give a whoop as if he had captured a Rebel horse. But they continued to advance upon us, we firing and retreating slowly. We had several pretty sharp brushes with them that day. I remember that they had to cross an open field in our front, and we were lying behind a fence, and as they advanced, we kept up firing, and would run them back every time, until they brought up a regiment that whooped, and yelled, and charged our skirmish line, and then we fell back again. I think we must have killed a good many in the old field, because we were firing all the time at the solid line as they advanced upon us.

Battle of Murfreesboro

The next day, the Yankees were found out to be advancing. Soon they came in sight of our picket. We kept falling back and firing all day, and were relieved by another regiment about dark. We rejoined our regiment. Line of battle was formed on the north bank of Stone's River—on the Yankee side. Bad generalship, I thought.

It was Christmas. John Barleycorn was general-in-chief. Our generals, and colonels, and captains, had kissed John a little too often. They couldn't see straight. It was said to be buckeye whisky. They couldn't tell our own men from Yankees. The private could, but he was no general, you see. But here they were— the Yankees—a battle had to be fought. We were ordered forward. I was on the skirmish line. We marched plumb into the Yankee lines, with their flags flying.

I called Lieutenant Colonel Frierson's attention to the Yankees, and he remarked, "Well, I don't know whether they are Yankees or not, but if they are, they will come out of there mighty quick."

The Yankees marched over the hill out of sight.

We were ordered forward to the attack. We were right upon the Yankee line on the Wilkerson turnpike. The Yankees were shooting our men down by scores. A universal cry was raised, "You are firing on your own men." "Cease firing, cease firing," I hallooed; in fact, the whole skirmish line hallooed, and kept on telling them that they were Yankees, and to shoot; but the order was to cease firing, you are firing on your own men.

Captain James, of Cheatham's staff, was sent forward and killed in his own yard. We were not twenty yards off from the Yankees, and they were pouring the hot shot and shells right into our ranks; and every man was yelling at the top of his voice, "Cease firing, you are firing on your own men; cease firing, you are firing on your own men."

Oakley, color-bearer of the Fourth Tennessee Regiment, ran right up in the midst of the Yankee line with his colors, begging his men to follow. I hallooed till I was hoarse, "They are Yankees, they are Yankees; shoot, they are Yankees."

The crest occupied by the Yankees was belching loud with fire and smoke, and the Rebels were falling like leaves of autumn in a hurricane. The leaden hail storm swept them off the field. They fell back and re-formed. General Cheatham came up and advanced. I did not fall back, but continued to load and shoot, until a fragment of a shell struck me on the arm, and then a minnie ball passed through the same paralyzing my arm, and wounded and disabled me. General Cheatham, all the time, was calling on the men to go forward, saying, "Come on, boys, and follow me."

The impression that General Frank Cheatham made upon my mind, leading the charge on the Wilkerson turnpike, I will never forget. I saw either victory or death written on his face. When I saw him leading our brigade, although I was wounded at the time, I felt sorry for him, he seemed so earnest and concerned, and as he was passing me I said, "Well, General, if you are determined to die, I'll die with you." We were at that time at least a hundred yards in advance of the brigade, Cheatham all the time calling upon the men to come on. He was leading the charge in person. Then it was that I saw the power of one man, born to command, over a multitude of men then almost routed and demoralized. I saw and felt that he was not fighting for glory, but that he was fighting for his country because he loved that country, and he was willing to give his life for his country and the success of our cause. He deserves a wreath of immortality, and a warm place in every Southron's heart, for his brave and glorious example on that bloody battlefield of Murfreesboro. Yes, his history will ever shine in beauty and grandeur as a name among the brightest in all the galaxy of leaders in the history of our cause.

Now, another fact I will state, and that is, when the private soldier was ordered to charge and capture the twelve pieces of artillery, heavily supported by infantry, Maney's brigade raised a whoop and yell, and swooped down on those Yankees like a whirl-a-gust of woodpeckers in a hail storm, paying the blue coated rascals back with compound interest; for when they did come, every man's gun was loaded, and they marched upon the blazing crest in solid file, and when they did fire, there was a sudden lull in the storm of battle, because the Yankees were nearly all killed. I cannot remember now of ever seeing more dead men and horses and captured cannon, all jumbled together, than that scene of blood and carnage and battle on the Wilkerson turnpike. The ground was literally covered with blue coats dead; and, if I remember correctly, there were eighty dead horses.

By this time our command had re-formed, and charged the blazing crest.

The spectacle was grand. With cheers and shouts they charged up the hill, shooting down and bayoneting the flying cannoneers, General Cheatham, Colonel Field and Joe Lee cutting and slashing with their swords. The victory was complete. The whole left wing of the Federal army was driven back five miles from their original position. Their dead and wounded were in our lines, and we had captured many pieces of artillery, small arms, and prisoners.

When I was wounded, the shell and shot that struck me, knocked me winding. I said, "O, O, I'm wounded," and at the same time I grabbed my arm. I thought it had been torn from my shoulder. The brigade had fallen back about two hundred yards, when General Cheatham's presence reassured them, and they soon were in line and ready to follow so brave and gallant a leader, and had that order of "cease firing, you are firing on our own men," not been given, Maney's brigade would have had the honor of capturing eighteen pieces of artillery, and ten thousand prisoners. This I do know to be a fact.

As I went back to the field hospital, I overtook another man walking along. I do not know to what regiment he belonged, but I remember of first noticing that his left arm was entirely gone. His face was as white as a sheet. The breast and sleeve of his coat had been torn away, and I could see the frazzled end of his shirt sleeve, which appeared to be sucked into the wound. I looked at it pretty close, and I said "Great God!" for I could see his heart throb, and the respiration of his lungs. I was filled with wonder and horror at the sight. He was walking along, when all at once he dropped down and died without a struggle or a groan. I could tell of hundreds of such incidents of the battlefield, but tell only this one, because I remember it so distinctly.

Robbing a Dead Yankee

In passing over the battlefield, I came across a dead Yankee colonel. He had on the finest clothes I ever saw, a red sash and fine sword. I particularly noticed his boots. I needed them, and had made up my mind to wear them out for him. But I could not bear the thought of wearing dead men's shoes. I took hold of the foot and raised it up and made one trial at the boot to get it off. I happened to look up, and the colonel had his eyes wide open, and seemed to be looking at me. He was stone dead, but I dropped that foot quick. It was my first and last attempt to rob a dead Yankee.

After the battle was over at Murfreesboro, that night, John Tucker and myself thought that we would investigate the contents of a fine brick mansion in our immediate front, but between our lines and the Yankees', and even in advance of our videts. Before we arrived at the house we saw a body of Yankees approaching, and as we started to run back they fired upon us.

Our pickets had run in and reported a night attack. We ran forward, expecting that our men would recognize us, but they opened fire upon us. I never was as bad scared in all my whole life, and if any poor devil ever prayed with fervency and true piety, I did it on that occasion. I thought, "I am between two fires." I do not think that a flounder or pancake was half as flat as I was that night; yea, it might be called in music, low flat.

Chapter 7

Shelbyville

IT is a bad thing for an army to remain too long at one place. The men soon become discontented and unhappy, and we had no diversion or pastime except playing poker and chuck-a-luck. All the money of the regiment had long ago been spent, but grains of corn represented dollars, and with these we would play as earnestly and as zealously as if they were so much money, sure enough.

A Foot Race

One of those amusing episodes that frequently occur in the army, happened at this place. A big strapping fellow by the name of Tennessee Thompson, always carried bigger burdens than any other five men in the army. For example, he carried two quilts, three blankets, one gum oil cloth, one overcoat, one axe, one hatchet, one camp-kettle, one oven and lid, one coffee pot, besides his knapsack, haversack, canteen, gun, cartridge-box, and three days' rations. He was a rare bird, anyhow. Tennessee usually had his hair cut short on one side and left long on the other, so that he could give his head a bow and a toss and throw the long hairs over on the other side, and it would naturally part itself without a comb. Tennessee was the wit and good nature of the company; always in a good humor, and ever ready to do any duty when called upon. In fact, I would sometimes get out of heart and low spirited, and would hunt up Tennessee to have a little fun. His bye-word was "Bully for Bragg; he's hell on retreat, and will whip the Yankees yet." He was a good and brave soldier, and followed the fortunes of Company H from the beginning to the end.

Well, one day he and Billy Webster bet twenty-five dollars, put up in Bill Martin's hands, as to which could run the faster. John Tucker, Joe Lee, Alf. Horsley and myself were appointed judges. The distance was two hundred yards. The ground was measured off, and the judges stationed. Tennessee undressed himself, even down to his stocking feet, tied a red handkerchief around his head, and another one around his waist, and walked deliberately down the track, eyeing every little rock and stick and removing them off the track. Comes back to the starting point and then goes down the track in half canter; returns again, his eyes flashing, his nostrils dilated, looking the impersonation of the champion courser of the world; makes two or three apparently false starts; turns a somersault by placing his head on the ground and flopping over on his back; gets up and whickers like a horse; goes half-hammered, hop, step, and jump—he says, to loosen up his joints—scratches up the ground with his hands and feet, flops his arms and crows like a rooster, and says, "Bully for Bragg; he's hell on a retreat," and announces his readiness. The drum is tapped, and off they start. Well, Billy Webster beat him one hundred yards in the two hundred, and Tennessee came back and said, "Well, boys, I'm beat; Billy Martin, hand over the stakes to Billy Webster. I'm beat, but hang me if I didn't outrun the whole Yankee army coming out of Kentucky; got away from Lieutenant Lansdown and the whole detail at Chattanooga with half a hog, a fifty pound sack of flour, a jug of Meneesee commissary whisky, and a camp-kettle full of brown sugar. I'm beat. Billy Martin, hand over the stakes. Bully for Bragg; he's hell on a retreat." Tennessee was trying bluff. He couldn't run worth a cent; but there was no braver or truer man ever drew a ramrod or tore a cartridge than Tennessee.

Eating Mussels

Reader, did you ever eat a mussel? Well, we did, at Shelbyville. We were camped right upon the bank of Duck river, and one day Fred Dornin, Ed Voss, Andy Wilson and I went in the river mussel hunting. Every one of us had a meal sack. We would feel down with our feet until we felt a mussel and then dive for it. We soon filled our sacks with mussels in their shells. When we got to camp we cracked the shells and took out the mussels. We tried frying them, but the longer they fried the tougher they got. They were a little too large to swallow whole. Then we stewed them, and after a while we boiled them, and then we baked them, but every flank movement we would make on those mussels the more invulnerable they would get. We tried cutting them up with a hatchet, but they were so slick and tough the hatchet would not cut them. Well, we cooked them, and buttered them, and salted them, and peppered them, and battered them. They looked good, and smelt good, and tasted good; at least the fixings we put on them did, and we ate the mussels. I went to sleep that night. I dreamed that my stomach was four grindstones, and that they turned in four directions, according to the four corners of the earth. I awoke to hear four men yell out, "O, save, O, save me from eating any more mussels!"

"Poor" Berry Morgan

One of those sad, unexpected affairs, that remind the living that even in life we are in the midst of death, happened at Shelbyville. Our regiment had been out to the front, on duty, and was returning to camp. It was nearly dark, and we saw a black wind cloud rising. The lightning's flash and the deep muttering thunders warned us to seek shelter as speedily as possible. Some of us ran in under the old depot shed, and soon the storm struck us. It was a tornado that made a track through the woods beyond Shelbyville, and right through the town, and we could follow its course for miles where it had blown down the timber, twisting and piling it in every shape. Berry Morgan and I had ever been close friends, and we threw down our blankets and were lying side by side, when I saw roofs of houses, sign boards, and brickbats flying in every direction. Nearly half of the town was blown away in the storm. While looking at the storm without, I felt the old shed suddenly jar and tremble, and suddenly become unroofed, and it seemed to me that ten thousand brickbats had fallen in around us. I could hear nothing for the roaring of the storm, and could see nothing for the blinding rain and flying dirt and bricks and other rubbish. The storm lasted but a few minutes, but those minutes seemed ages. When it had passed, I turned to look at "poor Berry." Poor fellow! his head was crushed in by a brickbat, his breast crushed in by another, and I think his arm was broken, and he was otherwise mutilated. It was a sad sight. Many others of our regiment were wounded.

Berry was a very handsome boy. He was what everybody would call a "pretty man." He had fair skin, blue eyes, and fine curly hair, which made him look like an innocent child. I loved Berry. He was my friend—as true as the needle to the pole. But God, who doeth all things well, took his spirit in the midst of the storm to that beautiful home beyond the skies. I thank God I am no infidel. We will meet again.

Wright Shot to Death with Musketry

I saw a young boy about seventeen or eighteen years old, by the name of Wright, and belonging to General Marcus J. Wright's brigade, shot to death with musketry at this place. The whole of Cheatham's division had to march out and witness the horrid scene. Now, I have no doubt that many, if not all, would have gone without being forced to do so, but then you know that was Bragg's style. He wanted always to display his tyranny, and to intimidate his privates as much as possible. The young man was hauled in a wagon, sitting on his coffin, to the place where the grave was to be dug, and a post was planted in the ground. He had to sit there for more than two hours, looking on at the preparations for his death. I went up to the wagon, like many others, to have a look at the doomed man. He had his hat pulled down over his eyes, and was busily picking at the ends of his fingers. The guard who then had him in charge told me that one of the culprit's own brothers was one of the detail to shoot him. I went up to the wagon and called him, "Wright!" He made no reply, and did not even look up. Then I said, "Wright, why don't you jump out of that wagon and run?" He was callous to everything. I was sorry for him. When the division was all assembled, and the grave dug, and the post set, he was taken out of the wagon, and tied to the post. He was first tied facing the post, and consequently would have been shot in the back, but was afterwards tied with his back to the post. The chaplain of the regiment read a chapter in the Bible, sang a hymn, and then all knelt down and prayed. General Wright went up to the pinioned man, shook hands with him, and told him good-bye, as did many others, and then the shooting detail came up, and the officer in charge gave the command, "Ready, aim, fire!" The crash of musketry broke upon the morning air. I was looking at Wright. I heard him almost shriek, "O, O, God!" His head dropped forward, the rope with which he was pinioned keeping him from falling. I turned away and thought how long, how long will I have to witness these things?

Dave Sublett Promoted

While at Shelbyville, a vacancy occurring in Captain Ledbetter's company, the Rutherford Rifles, for fourth corporal, Dave Sublett became a candidate for the position. Now, Dave was a genius. He was a noble and brave fellow, and at one time had been a railroad director. He had a distinguished air always about him, but Dave had one fault, and that was, he was ever prone to get tight. He had been a Union man, and even now he always had a good word for the Union. He was sincere, but ec-

centric. The election for fourth corporal was drawing nigh. Dave
sent off and got two jugs of *spiritus vini frumenti*, and treated
the boys. Of course, his vote would be solid. Every man in that
company was going to cast his vote for him. Dave got happy and
wanted to make a speech. He went to the butcher's block which
was used to cut up meat on—he called it Butchers' Hall—got
upon it amid loud cheering and hurrahs of the boys. He spoke
substantially as follows:

"Fellow Citizens—I confess that it is with feelings of diffi-
dence and great embarrassment on my part that I appear before
you on this occasion. But, gentlemen and fellow-citizens, I desire to serve you in an humble capacity, as fourth corporal of
Company I. Should you see cause to elect me, no heart will beat
with more gratitude than my own. Gentlemen, you well know
that I was ever a Union man:

> "'A union of lakes, and a union of lands,
> A union that no one can sever;
> A union of hearts, and a union of hands,
> A glorious union forever.'

[Cheers and applause.]

"Fellow citizens, I can look through the dim telescope of the
past and see Kansas, bleeding Kansas, coming like a fair young
bride, dressed in her bridal drapery, her cheek wet and mois-
tened with the tears of love. I can see her come and knock gently at the doors of the Union, asking for admittance. [Wild
cheering.] Looking further back, I can see our forefathers of the
revolution baring their bosoms to the famine of a seven years'
war, making their own bosoms a breastwork against the whole
hosts of King George III. But, gentlemen, as I before remarked,
I desire to ask at your hands the high, distinguished and lucra-
tive office, my fellow-citizens, and for which I will ever feel
grateful—the office of fourth corporal in your company."
[Cheers.]

Now, Dave had a competitor who was a states' rights democrat. If I mistake not, his name was Frank Haliburton. Now, Frank was an original secessionist. He felt that each state was a separate, sovereign government of itself, and that the South had the same rights in the territories as they of the North. He was fighting for secession and state rights upon principle. When Sublett had finished his speech, Frank took the stand and said:

"Gentlemen and Fellow-Citizens—I am a candidate for fourth corporal, and if you will elect me I will be grateful, and will serve you to the best of my ability. My competitor seems to harp considerably upon his Union record, and Union love. If I mistake not, my fellow-citizens, it was old George McDuffie that stood up in the senate chamber of the United States and said, 'When I hear the shout of "glorious Union," methinks I hear the shout of a robber gang.' McDuffie saw through his prophetic vision the evils that would result, and has foretold them as if by inspiration from above.

"Fellow-citizens, under the name of Union our country is invaded today.

"These cursed Yankees are invading our country, robbing our people, and desolating our land, and all under the detestable and damning name of Union. Our representatives in congress have been fighting them for fifty years. Compromise after compromise has been granted by the South. We have used every effort to conciliate those at the North. They have turned a deaf ear to every plea. They saw our country rich and prosperous, and have come indeed, like a gang of robbers, to steal our property and murder our people. But, fellow-citizens, I for one am ready to meet them, and desire that you elect me fourth corporal of Company I, so that I can serve you in a more efficient manner, while we meet as a band of brothers, the cursed horde of Northern Hessians and hirelings. I thank you for your attention, gentlemen, and would thank you for your votes."

Well, the election came off, and Dave was elected by an overwhelming majority. But the high eminence of military distinction enthralled him. He seemed to live in an atmosphere of greatness and glory, and was looking eagerly forward to the time when he would command armies. He had begun to climb the ladder of glory under most favorable and auspicious circumstances. He felt his consequence and keeping. He was detailed once, and only once, to take command of the third relief of camp guard. Ah, this thing of office was a big thing. He desired to hold a council of war with Generals Bragg, Polk, Hardee, and Kirby Smith. He first visited General Polk. His war metal was up. He wanted a fight just then and there, and a fight he must have, at all hazards, and to the last extremity. He became obstreperous, when General Polk called a guard and had him marched off to the guard-house. It was then ordered that he should do extra fatigue duty for a week. The guard would take him to the woods with an ax, and he would make two or three chops on a tree and look up at it and say:

"Woodman, spare that tree; touch not a single bough;
In youth it sheltered me, and I'll protect it now."

He would then go to another tree; but at no tree would he make more than two or three licks before he would go to another. He would hit a limb and then a log; would climb a tree and cut at a limb or two, and keep on this way until he came to a hard old stump, which on striking his ax would bound and spring back. He had found his desire; the top of that stump became fun and pleasure. Well, his time of misdemeanor expired and he was relieved. He went back and reported to Colonel Field, who informed him that he had been reduced to the ranks. He drew himself up to his full height and said: "Colonel, I regret exceedingly to be so soon deprived of my new fledged honors that I have won on so many a hard fought and bloody battlefield, but if I am reduced to the ranks as a private soldier, I can but exclaim, like Moses of old, when he crossed the Red sea in defiance of Pharaoh's hosts, 'O, how the mighty have fallen!'" He then marched off with the air of the born soldier.

Down Duck River in a Canoe

"Ora pro nobis"

At this place, Duck river wended its way to Columbia. On one occasion it was up—had on its Sunday clothes—a-booming. Andy Wilson and I thought that we would slip off and go down the river in a canoe. We got the canoe and started. It was a leaky craft. We had not gone far before the thing capsized, and we swam ashore. But we were outside of the lines now, and without passes. (We would have been arrested anyhow.) So we put our sand paddles to work and landed in Columbia that night. I loved a maid, and so did Andy, and some poet has said that love laughs at grates, bars, locksmiths, etc. I do not know how true this is, but I do know that when I went to see my sweetheart that night I asked her to pray for me, because I thought the prayers of a pretty woman would go a great deal further "up yonder" than mine would. I also met Cousin Alice, another beautiful woman, at my father's front gate, and told her that she must pray for me, because I knew I would be court-martialed as soon as I got back; that I had no idea of deserting the army and only wanted to see the maid I loved. It took me one day to go to Columbia and one day to return, and I stayed at home only one day, and went back of my own accord. When I got back to Shelbyville, I was arrested and carried to the guard-house, and when court-martialed was sentenced to thirty days' fatigue duty and to forfeit four months' pay at eleven dollars per month, making forty-four dollars. Now, you see how dearly I paid for that trip. But, fortunately for me, General Leonidas Polk has issued an order that very day promising pardon to all soldiers absent without leave if they would return. I got the guard to march me up to his headquarters and told him of my predicament, and he ordered my release, but said nothing of remitting the fine. So when we were paid off at Chattanooga I was left out. The Confederate States of America were richer by forty-four dollars.

"Sheneral Owleydousky"

General Owleydousky,[1] lately imported from Poland, was
Bragg's inspector general. I remember of reading in the newspapers of where he tricked Bragg at last. The papers said he
stole all of Bragg's clothes one day and left for parts unknown.
It is supposed he went back to Poland to act as "Ugh! Big Indian;
fight heap mit Bragg." But I suppose it must have left Bragg in
a bad fix—somewhat like Mr. Jones, who went to ask the old
folks for Miss Willis. On being told that she was a very poor girl,
and had no property for a start in life, he simply said, "All right;
all I want is the naked girl."

On one occasion, while inspecting the arms and accou-
trements of our regiments, when he came to inspect Company
H he said, "Shentlemens, vatfor you make de pothook out of de
sword and de bayonet, and trow de cartridge-box in de mud? I
dust report you to Sheneral Bragg. Mine gracious!" Approaching Orderly Sergeant John T. Tucker, and lifting the flap of his
cartridge-box, which was empty, he said, "Bah, bah, mon Dieu;
I dust know dot you ish been hunting de squirrel and de rabbit.
Mon Dieu! you sharge yourself mit fifteen tollars for wasting
sixty cartridges at twenty-five cents apiece. Bah, bah, mon Dieu;
I dust report you to Sheneral Bragg." Approaching Sergeant
A. S. Horsley, he said, "Vy ish you got nodings mit your knapsack? Sir, you must have somedings mit your knapsack." Alf ran
into his tent and came back with his knapsack in the right
shape. Well, old Owleydousky thought he would be smart and
make an example of Alf, and said, "I wish to inspect your clod-
ings." He took Alf's knapsack and on opening it, what do you
suppose was in it? Well, if you are not a Yankee and good at
guessing, I will tell you, if you won't say anything about it, for

---

[1]In his references to this officer Watkins was indulging in a bit of burlesque. Hy-
polite Oladowski, a highly proficient technician of Polish background, was
Bragg's ordnance officer, not inspector general. He was a colonel and not a general.

Alf might get mad if he were to hear it. He found Webster's Unabridged Dictionary, Cruden's Concordance, Macauley's History of England, Jean Valjean, Fantine, Cosset, Les Miserables, The Heart of Midlothian, Ivanhoe, Guy Mannering, Rob Roy, Shakespeare, the History of Ancient Rome, and many others which I have now forgotten. He carried literature for the regiment. He is in the same old business yet, only now he furnishes literature by the car load.

Chapter 8

Chattanooga

Back to Chattanooga

ROSECRANS' army was in motion. The Federals were advancing, but as yet they were afar off. Chattanooga must be fortified. Well do we remember the hard licks and picks that we spent on these same forts, to be occupied afterwards by Grant and his whole army, and we on Lookout Mountain and Missionary Ridge looking at them.

Am Visited by My Father

About this time my father paid me a visit. Rations were mighty scarce. I was mighty glad to see him, but ashamed to let him know how poorly off for something to eat we were. We were living on parched corn. I thought of a happy plan to get him a good dinner, so I asked him to let us go up to the colonel's tent. Says I, "Colonel Field, I desire to introduce you to my father, and as rations are a little short in my mess, I thought you might have a little better, and could give him a good dinner." "Yes," says Colonel Field, "I am glad to make the acquaintance of your father, and will be glad to divide my rations with him. Also, I would like you to stay and take dinner with me," which I assure you, O kind reader, I gladly accepted. About this time a young

African, Whit, came in with a frying-pan of parched corn and dumped it on an old oil cloth, and said, "Master, dinner is ready." That was all he had. He was living like ourselves—on parched corn.

We continued to fortify and build breastworks at Chattanooga. It was the same drudge, drudge day by day. Occasionally a Sunday would come; but when it did come, there came inspection of arms, knapsacks and cartridge-boxes. Every soldier had to have his gun rubbed up as bright as a new silver dollar. W. A. Hughes had the brightest gun in the army, and always called it "Florence Fleming." The private soldier had to have on clean clothes, and if he had lost any cartridges he was charged twenty-five cents each, and had to stand extra duty for every cartridge lost. We always dreaded Sunday. The roll was called more frequently on this than any other day. Sometimes we would have preaching. I remember one text that I thought the bottom had been knocked out long before: "And Peter's wife's mother lay sick of fever." That text always did make a deep impression on me. I always thought of a young divine who preached it when first entering the ministry, and in about twenty years came back, and happening to preach from the same text again, an old fellow in the congregation said, "Mr. Preacher, ain't that old woman dead yet?" Well, that was the text that was preached to us soldiers one Sunday at Chattanooga. I could not help thinking all the time, "Ain't that old woman dead yet?" But he announced that he would preach again at 3 o'clock. We went to hear him preach at 3 o'clock, as his sermon was so interesting about "Peter's wife's mother lay sick of a fever." We thought, maybe it was a sort of sickly subject, and he would liven us up a little in the afternoon service.

Well, he took his text, drawled out through his nose like "small sweetness long drawn out:" "M-a-r-t-h-a, thou art w-e-a-r-i-e-d and troubled about many things, but M-a-r-y hath chosen that good part that shall never be taken from her." Well, you see, O gentle and fair reader, that I remember the text these long gone twenty years. I do not remember what he preached about, but I remember thinking that he was a great ladies' man, at any rate, and whenever I see a man who loves and respects the ladies, I think him a good man.

The next sermon was on the same sort of a text: "And the Lord God caused a deep sleep to fall on Adam and took out of"—he stopped here and said *e* meant out of, that *e*, being translated from the Latin and Greek, meant out of, and took *e*, or rather out of a rib and formed woman. I never did know why he expaciated so largely on *e;* don't understand it yet, but you see, reader mine, that I remember but the little things that happened in that stormy epoch. I remember the *e* part of the sermon more distinctly than all of his profound eruditions of theology, dogmas, creeds and evidences of Christianity, and I only write at this time from memory of things that happened twenty years ago.

"Out A Larking"

At this place, we took Walter Hood out "a larking." The way to go "a larking" is this: Get an empty meal bag and about a dozen men and go to some dark forest or open field on some cold, dark, frosty or rainy night, about five miles from camp. Get someone who does not understand the game to hold the bag in as stooping and cramped a position as is possible, to keep perfectly still and quiet, and when he has got in the right fix, the others to go off to drive in the larks. As soon as they get out of sight, they break in a run and go back to camp, and go to sleep, leaving the poor fellow all the time holding the bag.

Well, Walter was as good and as clever a fellow as you ever saw, was popular with everybody, and as brave and noble a fellow as ever tore a cartridge, or drew a ramrod, or pulled a trigger, but was the kind of a boy that was easily "roped in" to fun or fight or anything that would come up. We all loved him. Poor fellow, he is up yonder—died on the field of glory and honor. He gave his life, 'twas all he had, for his country. Peace to his memory. That night we went "a larking," and Walter held the bag. I did not see him till next morning. While I was gulping down my coffee, as well as laughter, Walter came around, looking sort of sheepish and shy like, and I was trying to look as solemn as a judge. Finally he came up to the fire and kept on eyeing me out of one corner of his eye, and I was afraid to look at him for fear of breaking out in a laugh. When I could hold in no longer, I laughed out, and said, "Well, Walter, what luck last night?" He was very much disgusted, and said, "Humph! you all think that you are smart. I can't see anything to laugh at in such foolishness as that." He said, "Here; I have brought your bag back." That conquered me. After that kind of magnanimous act in forgiving me and bringing my bag back so pleasantly and kindly, I was his friend, and would have fought for him. I felt sorry that we had taken him out "a larking."

Hanging Two Spies

I can now recall to memory but one circumstance that made a deep impression on my mind at the time. I heard that two spies were going to be hung on a certain day, and I went to the hanging. The scaffold was erected, two coffins were placed on the platform, the ropes were dangling from the cross beam above. I had seen men shot, and whipped, and shaved, and branded at Corinth and Tupelo, and one poor fellow named Wright shot at Shelbyville. They had all been horrid scenes to me, but they were Rebels, and like begets like. I did not know when it would be my time to be placed in the same position, you see, and "a fellow feeling makes us wondrous kind." I did not know what was in store in the future for me. Ah, there was the rub, don't you see. This shooting business wasn't a pleasant thing to think about. But Yankees—that was different. I wanted to see a Yankee spy hung. I wouldn't mind that. I would like to see him agonize. A spy; O, yes, they had hung one of our regiment at Pulaski—Sam Davis. Yes, I would see the hanging. After a while I saw a guard approach, and saw two little boys in their midst, but did not see the Yankees that I had been looking for.

The two little boys were rushed upon the platform. I saw that they were handcuffed. "Are they spies?" I was appalled; I was horrified; nay, more, I was sick at heart. One was about fourteen and the other about sixteen years old, I should judge. The ropes were promptly adjusted around their necks by the provost marshal. The youngest one began to beg and cry and plead most piteously. It was horrid. The older one kicked him, and told him to stand up and show the Rebels how a Union man could die for his country. Be a man! The charges and specifications were then read. The props were knocked out and the two boys were dangling in the air. I turned off sick at heart.

Eating Rats

While stationed at this place, Chattanooga, rations were very scarce and hard to get, and it was, perhaps, economy on the part of our generals and commissaries to issue rather scant rations.

About this time we learned that Pemberton's army, stationed at Vicksburg, were subsisting entirely on rats. Instead of the idea being horrid, we were glad to know that "necessity is the mother of invention," and that the idea had originated in the mind of genius. We at once acted upon the information, and started out rat hunting; but we couldn't find any rats. Presently we came to an old out-house that seemed to be a natural harbor for this kind of vermin. The house was quickly torn down and out jumped an old residenter, who was old and gray. I suppose that he had been chased before. But we had jumped him and were determined to catch him, or "burst a boiler." After chasing him backwards and forwards, the rat finally got tired of this foolishness and started for his hole. But a rat's tail is the last that goes in the hole, and as he went in we made a grab for his tail. Well, tail hold broke, and we held the skin of his tail in our hands. But we were determined to have that rat. After hard work we caught him. We skinned him, washed and salted him, buttered and peppered him, and fried him. He actually looked nice. The delicate aroma of the frying rat came to our hungry nostrils. We were keen to eat a piece of rat; our teeth were on edge; yea, even our mouth watered to eat a piece of rat. Well, after a while, he was said to be done. I got a piece of cold corn dodger, laid my piece of the rat on it, eat a little piece of bread, and raised the piece of rat to my mouth, when I happened to think of how that rat's tail did slip. I had lost my appetite for dead rat. I did not eat any rat. It was my first and last effort to eat dead rats.

Swimming the Tennessee with Roastingears

The Tennessee river is about a quarter of a mile wide at Chattanooga. Right across the river was an immense corn-field. The green corn was waving with every little breeze that passed; the tassels were bowing and nodding their heads; the pollen was flying across the river like little snowdrops, and everything seemed to say, "Come hither, Johnny Reb; come hither, Johnny; come hither." The river was wide, but we were hungry. The roastingears looked tempting. We pulled off our clothes and launched into the turbid stream, and were soon on the other bank. Here was the field, and here were the roastingears; but where was the raft or canoe?

We thought of old Abraham and Isaac and the sacrifice: "My son, gather the roastingears, there will be a way provided."

We gathered the roastingears; we went back and gathered more roastingears, time and again. The bank was lined with green roastingears. Well, what was to be done? We began to shuck the corn. We would pull up a few shucks on one ear, and tie it to the shucks of another—first one and then another—until we had at least a hundred tied together. We put the train of corn into the river, and as it began to float off we jumped in, and taking the foremost ear in our mouth, struck out for the other bank. Well, we made the landing all correct.

I merely mention the above incident to show to what extremity soldiers would resort. Thousands of such occurrences were performed by the private soldiers of the Rebel army.

Am Detailed to Go Foraging

One day I was detailed to go with a wagon train way down in Georgia on a foraging expedition. It was the first time since I had enlisted as a private that I had struck a good thing. No roll call, no drilling, no fatigue duties, building fortifications, standing picket, dress parade, reviews, or retreats, had to be answered to—the same old monotonous roll call that had been answered five thousand times in these three years. I felt like a free man. The shackles of discipline had for a time been unfettered. This was bliss, this was freedom, this was liberty. The sky looked brighter, the birds sang more beautiful and sweeter than I remember to have ever heard them. Even the little streamlets and branches danced and jumped along the pebbly beds, while the minnows sported and frollicked under the shining ripples. The very flocks and herds in the pasture looked happy and gay. Even the screech of the wagons, that needed greasing, seemed to send forth a happy sound. It was fine, I tell you.

The blackberries were ripe, and the roadsides were lined with this delicious fruit. The Lord said that he would curse the ground for the disobedience of man, and henceforth it should bring forth thorns and briars; but the very briars that had been cursed were loaded with the abundance of God's goodness. I felt, then, like David in one of his psalms—"The Lord is good, the Lord is good, for his mercy endureth forever."

Please Pass the Butter

For several days the wagon train continued on until we had arrived at the part of country to which we had been directed. Whether they bought or pressed the corn, I know not, but the old gentleman invited us all to take supper with him. If I had ever eaten a better supper than that I have forgotten it. They had biscuit for supper. What! flour bread? Did my eyes deceive me? Well, there were biscuit—sure enough flour bread—and sugar and coffee—genuine Rio—none of your rye or potato coffee, and butter—regular butter—and ham and eggs, and turnip greens, and potatoes, and fried chicken, and nice clean plates—none of your tin affairs—and a snow-white table-cloth and napkins, and white-handled knives and silver forks. At the head of the table was the madam, having on a pair of golden spectacles, and at the foot the old gentleman. He said grace. And, to cap the climax, two handsome daughters. I know that I had never seen two more beautiful ladies. They had on little white aprons, trimmed with jaconet edging, and collars as clean and white as snow. They looked good enough to eat, and I think at that time I would have given ten years of my life to have kissed one of them. We were invited to help ourselves. Our plates were soon filled with the tempting food and our tumblers with California beer. We would have liked it better had it been twice as strong, but what it lacked in strength we made up in quantity. The old lady said, "Daughter, hand the gentleman the butter." It was the first thing that I had refused, and the reason that I did so was because my plate was full already. Now, there is nothing that will offend a lady so quick as to refuse to take butter when handed to you. If you should say, "No, madam, I never eat butter," it is a direct insult to the lady of the house. Better, far better, for you to have remained at home that day. If you don't eat butter, it is an insult; if you eat too much, she will make your ears burn after you have left. It is a regulator of society; it is a civilizer; it is a luxury and a delicacy that must be touched and handled with care and courtesy on all occasions. Should you desire to get on the good side of a lady, just give a broad, sweeping, slathering compliment to her butter. It beats kissing the dirty-faced baby; it beats anything. Too much praise cannot be bestowed upon the butter, be it good, bad, or indifferent to your notions of things, but to her, her butter is always good, superior, excellent. I did not know this characteristic of the human female at the time, or I would have taken a delicate slice of the butter. Here is a sample of the colloquy that followed:

"Mister, have some butter?"

"Not any at present, thank you, madam."

"Well, I insist upon it; our butter is nice."

"O, I know it's nice, but my plate is full, thank you."

"Well, take some anyhow."

One of the girls spoke up and said:

"Mother, the gentleman don't wish butter."

"Well, I want him to know that our butter is clean, anyhow."

"Well, madam, if you insist upon it, there is nothing that I love so well as warm biscuit and butter. I'll thank you for the butter."

I dive in. I go in a little too heavy. The old lady hints in a delicate way that they sold butter. I dive in heavier. That cake of butter was melting like snow in a red hot furnace. The old lady says, "We sell butter to the soldiers at a mighty good price."

I dive in afresh. She says, "I get a dollar a pound for that butter," and I remark with a good deal of nonchalance, "Well, madam, it is worth it," and dive in again. I did not marry one of the girls.

We Evacuate Chattanooga

One morning while sitting around our camp fires we heard a boom, and a bomb shell passed over our heads. The Yankee army was right on the other bank of the Tennessee river. Bragg did not know of their approach until the cannon fired.

Rosecrans' army is crossing the Tennessee river. A part are already on Lookout Mountain. Some of their cavalry scouts had captured some of our foraging parties in Wills valley. The air was full of flying rumors. Wagons are being packed, camps are broken up, and there is a general hubbub everywhere. But your old soldier is always ready at a moment's notice. The assembly is sounded; form companies, and we are ready for a march, or a fight, or a detail, or anything. If we are marched a thousand miles or twenty yards, it is all the same. The private soldier is a machine that has no right to know anything. He is a machine that moves without any volition of his own. If Edison could invent a wooden man that could walk and load and shoot, then you would have a good sample of the private soldier, and it would have this advantage—the private soldier eats and the wooden man would not.

We left Chattanooga, but whither bound we knew not, and cared not; but we marched toward Chickamauga and crossed at Lee & Gordon's mill.

The Bull of the Woods

On our way to Lafayette from Lee & Gordon's mill, I remember a ludicrous scene, almost bordering on sacrilege. Rosecrans' army was very near us, and we expected before three days elapsed to be engaged in battle. In fact, we knew there must be a fight or a foot race, one or the other. We could smell, as it were, "the battle afar off."

One Sabbath morning it was announced that an eloquent and able LL. D., from Nashville, was going to preach, and as the occasion was an exceedingly solemn one, we were anxious to hear this divine preach from God's Holy Word; and as he was one of the "big ones," the whole army was formed in close column and stacked their arms. The cannon were parked, all pointing back toward Chattanooga. The scene looked weird and picturesque. It was in a dark wilderness of woods and vines and overhanging limbs. In fact, it seemed but the home of the owl and the bat, and other varmints that turn night into day. Everything looked solemn. The trees looked solemn, the scene looked solemn, the men looked solemn, even the horses looked solemn. You may be sure, reader, that we felt solemn.

The reverend LL. D. had prepared a regular war sermon before he left home, and of course had to preach it, appropriate or not appropriate; it was in him and had to come out. He opened the service with a song. I did remember the piece that was sung, but right now I cannot recall it to memory; but as near as I can now recollect here is his prayer, *verbatim et literatim:*

"Oh, Thou immaculate, invisible, eternal and holy Being, the exudations of whose effulgence illuminates this terrestrial sphere, we approach Thy presence, being covered all over with wounds and bruises and putrifying sores, from the crowns of our heads to the soles of our feet. And Thou, O Lord, art our dernier resort. The whole world is one great machine, managed by Thy puissance. The beautific splendors of Thy face irradiate the celestial region and felicitate the saints. There are the most exuberant profusions of Thy grace, and the sempiternal efflux of Thy glory. God is an abyss of light, a circle whose center is everywhere and His circumference nowhere. Hell is the dark world made up of spiritual sulphur and other ignited ingredients, disunited and unharmonized, and without that pure balsamic oil that flows from the heart of God."

When the old fellow got this far, I lost the further run of his prayer, but regret very much that I did so, because it was so grand and fine that I would have liked very much to have kept such an appropriate prayer for posterity. In fact, it lays it on heavy over any prayer I ever heard, and I think the new translators ought to get it and have it put in their book as a sample prayer. But they will have to get the balance of it from the eminent LL. D. In fact, he was so "high larnt" that I don't think anyone understood him but the generals. The colonels might every now and then have understood a word, and maybe a few of the captains and lieutenants, because Lieutenant Lansdown told me he understood every word the preacher said, and further informed me that it was none of your one-horse, old-fashioned country prayers that privates knew anything about, but was bang-up, first-rate, orthodox.

Well, after singing and praying, he took his text. I quote entirely from memory. "Blessed be the Lord God, who teaches my hands to war and my fingers to fight." Now, reader, that was the very subject we boys did not want to hear preached on—on that occasion at least. We felt like some other subject would have suited us better. I forget how he commenced his sermon, but I remember that after he got warmed up a little, he began to pitch in on the Yankee nation, and gave them particular fits as to their

geneology. He said that we of the South had descended from the
royal and aristocratic blood of the Huguenots of France, and of
the cavaliers of England, etc.; but that the Yankees were the descendants of the crop-eared Puritans and witch burners, who
came over in the Mayflower, and settled at Plymouth Rock. He
was warm on this subject, and waked up the echoes of the forest. He said that he and his brethren would fight the Yankees in
this world, and if God permit, chase their frightened ghosts in
the next, through fire and brimstone.

About this time we heard the awfullest racket, produced by
some wild animal tearing through the woods toward us, and
the cry, "Look out! look out! hooie! hooie! hooie! look out!" and
there came running right through our midst a wild bull, mad
with terror and fright, running right over and knocking down
the divine, and scattering Bibles and hymn books in every direction. The services were brought to a close without the dox-
ology.

This same brave chaplain rode along with our brigade, on an
old string-haltered horse, as we advanced to the attack at
Chickamauga, exhorting the boys to be brave, to aim low, and to
kill the Yankees as if they were wild beasts. He was eloquent and
patriotic. He stated that if he only had a gun he too would go
along as a private soldier. You could hear his voice echo and re-
echo over the hills. He had worked up his patriotism to a pitch
of genuine bravery and daring that I had never seen exhibited,
when fliff, fluff, fluff, *fluff*, FLUFF, *FLUFF*—a whir, a BOOM! and a
shell screams through the air. The reverend LL. D. stops to listen, like an old sow when she hears the wind, and says, "Remember, boys, that he who is killed will sup tonight in
Paradise." Some soldier hallooed at the top of his voice, "Well,
parson, you come along and take supper with us." Boom! whir!
a bomb burst, and the parson at that moment put spurs to his
horse and was seen to limber to the rear, and almost every soldier yelled out, "The parson isn't hungry, and never eats supper."
I remember this incident, and so does every member of the First
Tennessee Regiment.

Presentment, or the Wing of the Angel of Death

Presentment is always a mystery. The soldier may at one moment be in good spirits, laughing and talking. The wing of the death angel touches him. He knows that his time has come. It is but a question of time with him then. He knows that his days are numbered. I cannot explain it. God has numbered the hairs of our heads, and not a sparrow falls without His knowledge. How much more valuable are we than many sparrows?

We had stopped at Lee & Gordon's mill, and gone into camp for the night. Three days' rations were being issued. When Bob Stout was given his rations he refused to take them. His face wore a serious, woe-begone expression. He was asked if he was sick, and said "No," but added, "Boys, my days are numbered, my time has come. In three days from today, I will be lying right yonder on that hillside a corpse. Ah, you may laugh; my time has come. I've got a twenty dollar gold piece in my pocket that I've carried through the war, and a silver watch that my father sent me through the lines. Please take them off when I am dead, and give them to Captain Irvine, to give to my father when he gets back home. Here are my clothing and blanket that any one who wishes them may have. My rations I do not wish at all. My gun and cartridge-box I expect to die with."

The next morning the assembly sounded about two o'clock. We commenced our march in the darkness, and marched twenty-five miles to a little town by the name of Lafayette, to the relief of General Pillow, whose command had been attacked at that place. After accomplishing this, we marched back by another road to Chickamauga. We camped on the banks of Chickamauga on Friday night, and Saturday morning we commenced to cross over. About twelve o'clock we had crossed. No sooner had we crossed than an order came to double quick. General Forrest's cavalry had opened the battle. Even then the spent balls were falling amongst us with that peculiar thud so familiar to your old soldier.

Double quick! There seemed to be no rest for us. Forrest is

needing reinforcements. Double quick, close up in the rear! siz, siz, double quick, boom, hurry up, bang, bang, a rattle de bang, bang, siz, boom, boom, boom, hurry up, double quick, boom, bang, halt, front, right dress, boom, boom, and three soldiers are killed and twenty wounded. Billy Webster's arm was torn out by the roots and he killed, and a fragment of shell buried itself in Jim McEwin's side, also killing Mr. Fain King, a conscript from Mount Pleasant. Forward, guide center, march, charge bayonets, fire at will, commence firing. (This is where the LL. D. ran.) We debouched through the woods, firing as we marched, the Yankee line about two hundred yards off. Bang, bang, siz, siz. It was a sort of running fire. We kept up a constant fire as we advanced. In ten minutes we were face to face with the foe. It was but a question as to who could load and shoot the fastest. The army was not up. Bragg was not ready for a general battle. The big battle was fought the next day, Sunday. We held our position for two hours and ten minutes in the midst of a deadly and galling fire, being enfiladed and almost surrounded, when General Forrest galloped up and said, "Colonel Field, look out, you are almost surrounded; you had better fall back." The order was given to retreat. I ran through a solid line of blue coats. As I fell back, they were upon the right of us, they were upon the left of us, they were in front of us, they were in the rear of us. It was a perfect hornets' nest. The balls whistled around our ears like the escape valves of ten thousand engines. The woods seemed to be blazing; everywhere, at every jump, would rise a lurking foe. But to get up and dust was all we could do. I was running along by the side of Bob Stout. General Preston Smith stopped me and asked if our brigade was falling back. I told him it was. He asked me the second time if it was Maney's brigade that was falling back. I told him it was. I heard him call out, "Attention, forward!" One solid sheet of leaden hail was falling around me. I heard General Preston Smith's brigade open. It seemed to be platoons of artillery. The earth jarred and trembled like an earthquake. Deadly missiles were flying in every direction. It was the very incarnation of death itself. I could almost hear the shriek of the death angel passing over the scene. General Smith was killed in ten minutes after I saw him. Bob Stout and myself stopped. Said I, "Bob, you weren't killed, as you expected." He did not reply, for at that very moment a solid shot from the Federal guns struck him between the waist and the hip, tearing off one leg and scattering his bowels all over the ground. I heard him shriek out, "O, O, God!" His spirit had flown before his body struck the ground. Farewell, friend; we will meet over yonder.

When the cannon ball struck Billy Webster, tearing his arm out of the socket, he did not die immediately, but as we were advancing to the attack, we left him and the others lying where they fell upon the battlefield; but when we fell back to the place where we had left our knapsacks, Billy's arm had been dressed by Dr. Buist, and he seemed to be quite easy. He asked Jim Fogey to please write a letter to his parents at home. He wished to dictate the letter. He asked me to please look in his knapsack and get him a clean shirt, and said that he thought he would feel better if he could get rid of the blood that was upon him. I went to hunt for his knapsack and found it, but when I got back to where he was, poor, good Billy Webster was dead. He had given his life to his country. His spirit is with the good and brave. No better or braver man than Billy Webster ever drew the breath of life. His bones lie yonder today, upon the battlefield of Chickamauga. I loved him; he was my friend. Many and many a dark night have Billy and I stood together upon the silent picket post. Ah, reader, my heart grows sick and I feel sad while I try to write my recollections of that unholy and uncalled for war. But He that ruleth the heavens doeth all things well.

Chapter 9

Chickamauga

Battle of Chickamauga

SUNDAY morning of that September day, the sun rose over the eastern hills clear and beautiful. The day itself seemed to have a Sabbath-day look about it. The battlefield was in a rough and broken country, with trees and undergrowth, that ever since the creation had never been disturbed by the ax of civilized man. It looked wild, weird, uncivilized.

Our corps (Polk's), being in the engagement the day before, were held in reserve. Reader, were you ever held in reserve of an attacking army? To see couriers dashing backward and forward; to hear the orders given to the brigades, regiments and companies; to see them forward in line of battle, the battle-flags waving; to hear their charge, and then to hear the shock of battle, the shot and shell all the while sizzing, and zipping, and thudding, and screaming, and roaring, and bursting, and passing right over your heads; to see the litter corps bringing back the wounded continually, and hear them tell how their command was being cut to pieces, and that every man in a certain regiment was killed, and to see a cowardly colonel (as we saw on this occasion—he belonged to Longstreet's corps) come dashing back looking the very picture of terror and fear, exclaiming, "O, men, men, for God's sake go forward and help my men! they are being cut all to pieces! we can't hold our position. O, for God's sake, please go and help my command!" To hear some of our boys ask, "What regiment is that? What regiment is that?" He replies, such and such regiment. And then to hear some fellow ask, "Why ain't you with them, then, you cowardly puppy? Take off that coat and those chicken guts; coo, sheep; baa, baa, black sheep; flicker, flicker; ain't you ashamed of yourself? flicker, flicker; I've got a notion to take my gun and kill him," etc. Every word of this is true; it actually happened. But all that could demoralize, and I may say intimidate a soldier, was being enacted, and he not allowed to participate. How we were moved from one position to another, but always under fire; our nerves strung to their utmost tension, listening to the roar of battle in our immediate front, to hear it rage and then get dimmer until it seems to die out entirely; then all at once it breaks out again, and you think now in a very few minutes you will be ordered into action, and then all at once we go double-quicking to another portion of the field, the battle raging back from the position we had left. General Leonidas Polk rides up and happening to stop in our front, some of the boys halloo out, "Say, General, what command is that which is engaged now?" The general kindly answers, "That is Longstreet's corps. He is driving them this way, and we will drive them that way, and crush them between the 'upper and nether millstone.'" Turning to General Cheatham, he said, "General, move your division and attack at once." Everything is at once set in motion, and General Cheatham, to give the boys a good sendoff, says, "Forward, boys, and give 'em h—l." General Polk also says a good word, and that word was, "Do as General Cheatham says, boys." (You know he was a preacher and couldn't curse.) After marching in solid line, see-sawing, right obliqueing, left obliqueing, guide center and close up; commence firing—fire at will; charge and take their breastworks; our pent-up nervousness and demoralization of all day is suddenly gone. We raise one long, loud, cheering shout and charge right upon their breastworks. They are pouring their deadly missiles into our advancing ranks from under their head-logs. We do not stop to look around to see who is killed and wounded, but press right up their breastworks, and plant our battle-flag upon it. They waver and break and run in every direction, when General John C. Breckinridge's division, which had been supporting us, march up and pass us in full pursuit of the routed and flying Federal army.

After the Battle

We remained upon the battlefield of Chickamauga all night. Everything had fallen into our hands. We had captured a great many prisoners and small arms, and many pieces of artillery and wagons and provisions. The Confederate and Federal dead, wounded, and dying were everywhere scattered over the battle-field. Men were lying where they fell, shot in every conceivable part of the body. Some with their entrails torn out and still hanging to them and piled up on the ground beside them, and they still alive. Some with their under jaw torn off, and hanging by a fragment of skin to their cheeks, with their tongues lolling from their mouth, and they trying to talk. Some with both eyes shot out, with one eye hanging down on their cheek. In fact, you might walk over the battlefield and find men shot from the crown of the head to the tip end of the toe. And then to see all those dead, wounded and dying horses, their heads and tails drooping, and they seeming to be so intelligent as if they comprehended everything. I felt like shedding a tear for those innocent dumb brutes.

Reader, a battlefield, after the battle, is a sad and sorrowful sight to look at. The glory of war is but the glory of battle, the shouts, and cheers, and victory.

A soldier's life is not a pleasant one. It is always, at best, one of privations and hardships. The emotions of patriotism and pleasure hardly counterbalance the toil and suffering that he has to undergo in order to enjoy his patriotism and pleasure. Dying on the field of battle and glory is about the easiest duty a soldier has to undergo. It is the living, marching, fighting, shooting soldier that has the hardships of war to carry. When a brave soldier is killed he is at rest. The living soldier knows not at what moment he, too, may be called on to lay down his life on the altar of his country. The dead are heroes, the living are but men compelled to do the drudgery and suffer the privations incident to the thing called "glorious war."

A Night Among the Dead

We rested on our arms where the battle ceased. All around us everywhere were the dead and wounded, lying scattered over the ground, and in many places piled in heaps. Many a sad and heart-rending scene did I witness upon this battlefield of Chickamauga. Our men died the death of heroes. I sometimes think that surely our brave men have not died in vain. It is true, our cause is lost, but a people who loved those brave and noble heroes should ever cherish their memory as men who died for them. I shed a tear over their memory. They gave their all to their country. Abler pens than mine must write their epitaphs, and tell of their glories and heroism. I am but a poor writer, at best, and only try to tell of the events that I saw.

One scene I now remember, that I can imperfectly relate. While a detail of us were passing over the field of death and blood, with a dim lantern, looking for our wounded soldiers to carry to the hospital, we came across a group of ladies, looking among the killed and wounded for their relatives, when I heard one of the ladies say, "There they come with their lanterns." I approached the ladies and asked them for whom they were looking. They told me the name, but I have forgotten it. We passed on, and coming to a pile of our slain, we had turned over several of our dead, when one of the ladies screamed out, "O, there he is! Poor fellow! Dead, dead, dead!" She ran to the pile of slain and raised the dead man's head and placed it on her lap and began kissing him and saying, "O, O, they have killed my darling, my darling, my darling! O, mother, mother, what must I do! My poor, poor darling! O, they have killed him, they have killed him!" I could witness the scene no longer. I turned and walked away, and William A. Hughes was crying, and remarked, "O, law me; this war is a terrible thing." We left them and began again hunting for our wounded. All through that long September night we continued to carry off our wounded, and when the morning sun arose over the eastern hills, the order came to march to Missionary Ridge.

Chapter 10

Missionary Ridge

AFTER retreating from Chickamauga, the Yankees attempted to re-form their broken lines on Missionary Ridge. We advanced to attack them, but they soon fell back to Chattanooga. We knew they were in an impregnable position. We had built those breastworks and forts, and knew whereof we spoke. We stopped on Missionary Ridge, and gnashed our teeth at Chattanooga. I do not know what our generals thought; I do not know what the authorities at Richmond thought, but I can tell you what the privates thought. But here we were on Missionary Ridge and Lookout Mountain, looking right down into Chattanooga. We had but to watch and wait. We would starve them out.

The Federal army had accomplished their purpose. They wanted Chattanooga. They laughed at our triumph, and mocked at our victory. They got Chattanooga. "Now, where are you, Johnny Reb? What are you going to do about it? You've got the dry grins, arn't you? We've got the key; when the proper time comes we'll unlock your doors and go in. You are going to starve us out, eh? We are not very hungry at present, and we don't want any more pie. When we starve out we'll call on you for rations, but at present we are not starving, by a jug full; but if you want any whisky or tobacco, send over and we'll give you some. We've got all we wanted, and assure you we are satisfied."

The above remarks are the supposed colloquy that took place between the two armies. Bragg, in trying to starve the Yankees out, was starved out himself. Ask any old Rebel as to our bill of fare at Missionary Ridge.

In all the history of the war, I cannot remember of more privations and hardships than we went through at Missionary Ridge. And when in the very acme of our privations and hunger, when the army was most dissatisfied and unhappy, we were ordered into line of battle to be reviewed by Honorable Jefferson Davis. When he passed by us, with his great retinue of staff officers and play-outs at full gallop, cheers greeted them, with the words, "Send us something to eat, Massa Jeff. Give us something to eat, Massa Jeff. I'm hungry! I'm hungry!"

Sergeant Tucker and General Wilder

At this place the Yankee outpost was on one side of the Tennessee river, and ours on the other. I was on the detail one Sunday commanded by Sergeant John T. Tucker. When we were approaching we heard the old guard and the Yankee picket talking back and forth across the river. The new guard immediately resumed the conversation. We had to halloo at the top of our voices, the river being about three hundred yards wide at this point. But there was a little island about the middle of the river. A Yankee hallooed out, "O, Johnny, Johnny, meet me half way in the river on the island." "All right," said Sergeant Tucker, who immediately undressed all but his hat, in which he carried the Chattanooga Rebel and some other Southern newspapers, and swam across to the island. When he got there the Yankee was there, but the Yankee had waded. I do not know what he and John talked about, but they got very friendly, and John invited him to come clear across to our side, which invitation he accepted. I noticed at the time that while John swam, the Yankee waded, remarking that he couldn't swim. The river was but little over waist deep. Well, they came across and we swapped a few lies, canteens and tobacco, and then the Yankee went back, wading all the way across the stream. That man was General Wilder, commanding the Federal cavalry, and at the battle of Missionary Ridge he threw his whole division of cavalry across the Tennessee river at that point, thus flanking Bragg's army, and opening the battle. He was examining the ford, and the swapping business was but a mere by-play. He played it sharp, and Bragg had to get further.

Moccasin Point

Maney's brigade fortified on top of Lookout Mountain. From this position we could see five states. The Yankees had built a fort across the river, on Moccasin Point, and were throwing shells at us continually. I have never seen such accurate shooting in my life. It was upon the principle of shooting a squirrel out of a tree, and they had become so perfect in their aim, that I believe they could have killed a squirrel a mile off. We could have killed a great many artillery men if we had been allowed to shoot, but no private soldier was ever allowed to shoot a gun on his own hook. If he shot at all, it must be by the order of an officer, for if just one cartridge was shot away or lost, the private was charged twenty-five cents for it, and had to do extra duty, and I don't think our artillery was ever allowed to fire a single shot under any circumstances. Our rations were cooked up by a special detail ten miles in the rear, and were sent to us every three days, and then those three days' rations were generally eaten up at one meal, and the private soldier had to starve the other two days and a half. Never in all my whole life do I remember of ever experiencing so much oppression and humiliation. The soldiers were starved and almost naked, and covered all over with lice and camp itch and filth and dirt. The men looked sick, hollow-eyed, and heart-broken, living principally upon parched corn, which had been picked out of the mud and dirt under the feet of officers' horses. We thought of nothing but starvation.

The battle of Missionary Ridge was opened from Moccasin

Point, while we were on Lookout Mountain, but I knew nothing of the movements or maneuvers of either army, and only tell what part I took in the battle.

Battle of Missionary Ridge

One morning Theodore Sloan, Hog Johnson and I were standing picket at the little stream that runs along at the foot of Lookout Mountain. In fact, I would be pleased to name our captain, Fulcher, and Lieutenant Lansdown, of the guard on this occasion, because we acted as picket for the whole three days' engagement without being relieved, and haven't been relieved yet. But that battle has gone into history. We heard a Yankee call, "O, Johnny, Johnny Reb!" I started out to meet him as formerly, when he hallooed out, "Go back, Johnny, go back; we are ordered to fire on you." "What is the matter? Is your army going to advance on us?" "I don't know; we are ordered to fire." I jumped back into the picket post, and a minnie ball ruined the only hat I had; another and another followed in quick succession, and the dirt flew up in our faces off our little breastworks. Before night the picket line was engaged from one end to the other. If you had only heard it, dear reader. It went like ten thousand wood-choppers, and an occasional boom of a cannon would remind you of a tree falling. We could hear colonels giving commands to their regiments, and could see very plainly the commotion and hubbub, but what was up, we were unable to tell. The picket line kept moving to our right. The second night found us near the tunnel, and right where two railroads cross each other, or rather one runs over the other high enough for the cars to pass under. We could see all over Chattanooga, and it looked like myriads of blue coats swarming.

Day's and Mannigault's brigades got into a night attack at the foot of Lookout Mountain. I could see the whole of it. It looked like lightning bugs on a dark night. But about midnight everything quieted down. Theodore Sloan, Hog Johnson and myself occupied an old log cabin as vidette. We had not slept any for two nights, and were very drowsy, I assure you, but we knew there was something up, and we had to keep awake. The next morning, nearly day, I think I had dropped off into a pleasant doze, and was dreaming of more pretty things than you ever saw in your life, when Johnson touched me and whispered, "Look, look, there are three Yankees; must I shoot?" I whispered back "Yes." A bang; "a waugh" went a shriek. He had got one, sure. Everything got quiet again, and we heard nothing more for an hour. Johnson touched me again and whispered, "Yonder they come again; look, look!" I could not see them; was too sleepy for that. Sloan could not see them, either. Johnson pulled down, and another unearthly squall rended the night air. The streaks of day had begun to glimmer over Missionary Ridge, and I could see in the dim twilight the Yankee guard not fifty yards off. Said I, "Boys, let's fire into them and run." We took deliberate aim and fired. At that they raised, I thought, a mighty sickly sort of yell and charged the house. We ran out, but waited on the outside. We took a second position where the railroads cross each other, but they began shelling us from the river, when we got on the opposite side of the railroad and they ceased.

I know nothing about the battle; how Grant, with one wing, went up the river, and Hooker's corps went down Wills valley, etc. I heard fighting and commanding and musketry all day long, but I was still on picket. Balls were passing over our heads, both coming and going. I could not tell whether I was standing picket for Yankees or Rebels. I knew that the Yankee line was between me and the Rebel line, for I could see the battle right over the tunnel. We had been placed on picket at the foot of Lookout Mountain, but we were five miles from that place now. If I had tried to run in I couldn't. I had got separated from Sloan and Johnson somehow; in fact, was waiting either for an advance of the Yankees, or to be called in by the captain of the picket. I could see the blue coats fairly lining Missionary Ridge in my head. The Yankees were swarming everywhere. They were passing me all day with their dead and wounded, going back to Chattanooga. No one seemed to notice me; they were passing to and fro, cannon, artillery, and everything. I was willing to be taken prisoner, but no one seemed disposed to do it. I was afraid to look at them, and I was afraid to hide, for fear some one's attention would be attracted toward me. I wished I could make myself invisible. I think I was invisible. I felt that way anyhow. I felt like the boy who wanted to go to the wedding, but had no shoes. Cassabianca never had such feelings as I had that livelong day.

> Say, captain, say, if yet my task be done?
> And yet the sweeping waves rolled on,
> And answered neither yea nor nay.

About two or three o'clock, a column of Yankees advancing to the attack swept right over where I was standing. I was trying to stand aside to get out of their way, but the more I tried to get out of their way, the more in their way I got. I was carried forward, I knew not whither. We soon arrived at the foot of the ridge, at our old breastworks. I recognized Robert Brank's old corn stalk house, and Alf Horsley's fort, an old log house called Fort Horsley. I was in front of the enemy's line, and was afraid to run up the ridge, and afraid to surrender. They were ordered to charge up the hill. There was no firing from the Rebel lines in our immediate front. They kept climbing and pulling and scratching until I was in touching distance of the old Rebel breastworks, right on the very apex of Missionary Ridge. I made one jump, and I heard Captain Turner, who had the very four Napoleon guns we had captured at Perryville, halloo out, "Number four, solid!" and then a roar. The next order was "Limber to the rear." The Yankees were cutting and slashing, and the cannoneers were running in every direction. I saw Day's brigade throw down their guns and break like quarter horses. Bragg was trying to rally them. I heard him say, "Here is your commander," and the soldiers hallooed back, "here is your mule."

The whole army was routed. I ran on down the ridge, and there was our regiment, the First Tennessee, with their guns stacked, and drawing rations as if nothing was going on. Says I,

"Colonel Field, what's the matter? The whole army is routed and running; hadn't you better be getting away from here? The Yankees are not a hundred yards from here. Turner's battery has surrendered, Day's brigade has thrown down their arms; and look yonder, that is the Stars and Stripes." He remarked very coolly, "You seem to be demoralized. We've whipped them here. We've captured two thousand prisoners and five stands of colors."

Just at this time General Bragg and staff rode up. Bragg had joined the church at Shelbyville, but he had back-slid at Missionary Ridge. He was cursing like a sailor. Says he, "What's this? Ah, ha, have you stacked your arms for a surrender?" "No, sir," says Field. "Take arms, shoulder arms, by the right flank, file right, march," just as cool and deliberate as if on dress parade. Bragg looked scared. He had put spurs to his horse, and was running like a scared dog before Colonel Field had a chance to answer him. Every word of this is a fact. We at once became the rear guard of the whole army.[1]

I felt sorry for General Bragg. The army was routed, and Bragg looked so scared. Poor fellow, he looked so hacked and whipped and mortified and chagrined at defeat, and all along the line, when Bragg would pass, the soldiers would raise the yell, "Here is your mule;" "Bully for Bragg, he's h—l on retreat."

Bragg was a god disciplinarian, and if he had cultivated the love and respect of his troops by feeding and clothing them better than they were, the result would have been different. More depends on a good general than the lives of many privates. The private loses his life, the general his country.

Good-Bye, Tom Webb

As soon as the order was given to march, we saw poor Tom Webb lying on the battlefield shot through the head, his blood and brains smearing his face and clothes, and he still alive. He

[1]Author's Note: I remember of General Maney meeting Gary. I do not know who Gary was, but Maney and Gary seemed to be very glad to see each other. Every time I think of that retreat I think of Gary.

was as brave and noble a man as our Heavenly Father, in His infinite wisdom, ever made. Everybody loved him. He was a universal favorite of the company and regiment; was brave and generous, and ever anxious to take some other man's place when there was any skirmishing or fighting to be done. We did not wish to leave the poor fellow in that condition, and A. S. Horsley, John T. Tucker, Tennessee Thompson and myself got a litter and carried him on our shoulders through that livelong night back to Chickamauga Station. The next morning Dr. J. E. Dixon, of Deshler's brigade, passed by and told us that it would be useless for us to carry him any further, and that it was utterly impossible for him ever to recover. The Yankees were then advancing and firing upon us. What could we do? We could not carry him any further, and we could not bury him, for he was still alive. To leave him where he was we thought best. We took hold of his hand, bent over him and pressed our lips to his—all four of us. We kissed him good-bye and left him to the tender mercies of the advancing foe, in whose hands he would be in a few moments. No doubt they laughed and jeered at the dying Rebel. It mattered not what they did, for poor Tom Webb's spirit, before the sun went down, was with God and the holy angels. He had given his all to his country. O, how we missed him. It seemed that the very spirit and life of Company H had died with the death of good, noble and brave Tom Webb.

I thank God that I am no infidel, and I feel and believe that I will again see Tom Webb. Just as sure and certain, reader, as you are now reading these lines, I will meet him up yonder—I know I will.

The Rear Guard

When we had marched about a mile back in the rear of the battlefield, we were ordered to halt so that all stragglers might pass us, as we were detailed as the rear guard. While resting on the road side we saw Day's brigade pass us. They were gunless, cartridge-boxless, knapsackless, canteenless, and all other military accoutermentsless, and swordless, and officerless, and they all seemed to have the 'possum grins, like Bragg looked, and as they passed our regiment, you never heard such fun made of a parcel of soldiers in your life. Every fellow was yelling at the top of his voice, "Yaller-hammer, Alabama, flicker, flicker, flicker, yaller-hammer, Alabama, flicker, flicker, flicker." I felt sorry for the yellow-hammer Alabamians, they looked so hacked, and answered back never a word. When they had passed, two pieces of artillery passed us. They were the only two pieces not captured at Missionary Ridge, and they were ordered to immediately precede us in bringing up the rear. The whole rear guard was placed under the command of the noble, generous, handsome and brave General Gist, of South Carolina. I loved General Gist, and when I mention his name tears gather in my eyes. I think he was the handsomest man I ever knew.

Our army was a long time crossing the railroad bridge across Chickamauga river. Maney's brigade, of Cheatham's division, and General L. E. Polk's brigade, of Cleburne's division, formed a sort of line of battle, and had to wait until the stragglers had all passed. I remember looking at them, and as they passed I could read the character of every soldier. Some were mad, others cowed, and many were laughing. Some were cursing Bragg, some the Yankees, and some were rejoicing at the defeat. I cannot describe it. It was the first defeat our army had ever suffered, but the prevailing sentiment was anathemas and denunciations hurled against Jeff Davis for ordering Longstreet's corps to Knoxville, and sending off Generals Wheeler's and Forrest's cavalry, while every private soldier in the whole army knew that the enemy was concentrating at Chattanooga.

Chickamauga Station

When we arrived at Chickamauga Station, our brigade and General Lucius E. Polk's brigade, of Cleburne's division, were left to set fire to the town and to burn up and destroy all those immense piles of army stores and provisions which had been accumulated there to starve the Yankees out of Chattanooga. Great piles of corn in sacks, and bacon, and crackers, and molasses, and sugar, and coffee, and rice, and potatoes, and onions, and peas, and flour by the hundreds of barrels, all now to be given to the flames, while for months the Rebel soldiers had been stinted and starved for the want of these same provisions. It was enough to make the bravest and most patriotic soul that ever fired a gun in defense of any cause on earth, think of rebelling against the authorities as they then were. Every private soldier knew these stores were there, and for the want of them we lost our cause.

Reader, I ask you who you think was to blame? Most of our army had already passed through hungry and disheartened, and here were all these stores that had to be destroyed. Before setting fire to the town, every soldier in Maney's and Polk's brigades loaded himself down with rations. It was a laughable looking rear guard of a routed and retreating army. Every one of us had cut open the end of a corn sack, emptied out the corn, and filled it with hard-tack, and, besides, every one of us had a side of bacon hung to our bayonets on our guns. Our canteens, and clothes, and faces, and hair were all gummed up with molasses. Such is the picture of our rear guard. Now, reader, if you were ever on the rear guard of a routed and retreating army, you know how tedious it is. You don't move more than ten feet at furthest before you have to halt, and then ten feet again a few minutes afterwards, and so on all day long. You haven't time to sit down a moment before you are ordered to move on again. And the Yankees dash up every now and then, and fire a volley into your rear. Now that is the way we were marched that livelong day, until nearly dark, and then the Yankees began to crowd us. We can see their line forming, and know we have to fight.

The Battle of Cat Creek

About dark a small body of cavalry dashed in ahead of us and captured and carried off one piece of artillery and Colonel

John F. House, General Maney's assistant adjutant-general. We will have to form line of battle and drive them back. Well, we quickly form line of battle, and the Yankees are seen to emerge from the woods about two hundred yards from us. We promptly shell off those sides of bacon and sacks of hard-tack that we had worried and tugged with all day long. Bang, bang, siz, siz. We are ordered to load and fire promptly and to hold our position. Yonder they come, a whole division. Our regiment is the only regiment in the action. They are crowding us; our poor little handful of men are being killed and wounded by scores. There is General George Maney badly wounded and being carried to the rear, and there is Moon, of Fulcher's battalion, killed dead in his tracks. We can't much longer hold our position. A minnie ball passes through my Bible in my side pocket. All at once we are ordered to open ranks. Here comes one piece of artillery from a Mississippi battery, bouncing ten feet high, over brush and logs and bending down little trees and saplings, under whip and spur, the horses are champing the bits, and are muddied from head to foot. Now, quick, quick; look, the Yankees have discovered the battery and are preparing to charge it. Unlimber, horses and caisson to the rear. No. 1 shrapnel, load, fire—boom, boom; load, ablouyat—boom, boom. I saw Sam Seay fall badly wounded and carried to the rear. I stopped firing to look at Sergeant Doyle how he handled his gun. At every discharge it would bounce, and turn its muzzle completely to the rear, when those old artillery soldiers would return it to its place—and it seemed they fired a shot almost every ten seconds. Fire, men. Our muskets roll and rattle, making music like the kettle and bass drum combined. They are checked; we see them fall back to the woods, and night throws her mantle over the scene. We fell back now, and had to strip and wade Chickamauga river. It was up to our armpits, and was as cold as charity. We had to carry our clothes across on the points of our bayonets. Fires had been kindled every few yards on the other side, and we soon got warmed up again.

Ringgold Gap

I had got as far as Ringgold Gap, when I had unconsciously fallen alseep by a fire, it being the fourth night that I had not slept a wink. Before I got to this fire, however, a gentleman whom I never saw in my life—because it was totally dark at the time—handed me a letter from the old folks at home, and a good suit of clothes. He belonged to Colonel Breckinridge's cavalry, and if he ever sees these lines, I wish to say to him, "God bless you, old boy." I had lost every blanket and vestige of clothing, except those I had on, at Missionary Ridge. I laid down by the fire and went to sleep, but how long I had slept I knew not, when I felt a rough hand grab me and give me a shake, and the fellow said, "Are you going to sleep here, and let the Yankees cut your throat?" I opened my eyes, and asked, "Who are you?" He politely and pleasantly, yet profanely, told me that he was General Walker (the poor fellow was killed the 22nd of July, at Atlanta), and that I had better get further. He passed on and waked others. Just then, General Cleburne and staff rode by me, and I heard one of his staff remark, "General, here is a ditch, or gully, that will make a natural breastwork." All I heard General Cleburne say was, "Er, eh, eh!" I saw General Lucius E. Polk's brigade form on the crest of the hill.

I went a little further and laid down again and went to sleep. How long I had lain there, and what was passing over me, I know nothing about, but when I awoke, here is what I saw: I saw a long line of blue coats marching down the railroad track. The first thought I had was, well, I'm gone up now, sure; but on second sight, I discovered that they were prisoners. Cleburne had had the doggondest fight of the war. The ground was piled with dead Yankees; they were piled in heaps. The scene looked unlike any battlefield I ever saw. From the foot to the top of the hill was covered with their slain, all lying on their faces. It had the appearance of the roof of a house shingled with dead Yankees. They were flushed with victory and success, and had determined to push forward and capture the whole of the Rebel army, and set up their triumphant standard at Atlanta—then exit Southern Confederacy. But their dead were so piled in their path at Ringgold Gap that they could not pass them. The Spartans gained a name at Thermopylæ, in which Leonidas and the whole Spartan army were slain while defending the pass. Cleburne's division gained a name at Ringgold Gap, in which they not only slew the victorious army, but captured five thousand prisoners besides. That brilliant victory of Cleburne's made him not only the best general of the army of Tennessee, and covered his men with glory and honor of heroes, but checked the advance of Grant's whole army.

We did not budge an inch further for many a long day, but we went into winter quarters right here at Ringgold Gap, Tunnel Hill and Dalton.

Chapter 11

Dalton

General Joseph E. Johnston

GENERAL JOSEPH E. JOHNSTON now took command of the army. General Bragg was relieved, and had become Jeff Davis' war adviser at Richmond, Virginia. We had followed General Bragg all through this long war. We had got sorter used to his ways, but he was never popular with his troops. I felt sorry for him. Bragg's troops would have loved him, if he had allowed them to do so, for many a word was spoken in his behalf, after he had been relieved of the command. As a general I have spoken of him in these memoirs, not personally. I try to state facts, so that you may see, reader, why our cause was lost. I have no doubt that Bragg ever did what he thought was best. He was but a man, under the authority of another.

But now, allow me to introduce you to old Joe. Fancy, if you please, a man about fifty years old, rather small of stature, but firmly and compactly built, an open and honest countenance, and a keen but restless black eye, that seemed to read your very inmost thoughts. In his dress he was a perfect dandy. He ever wore the very finest clothes that could be obtained, carrying out in every point the dress and paraphernalia of the soldier, as adopted by the war department at Richmond, never omitting anything, even to the trappings of his horse, bridle and saddle.

His hat was decorated with a star and feather, his coat with every star and embellishment, and he wore a bright new sash, big gauntlets, and silver spurs. He was the very picture of a general.

But he found the army depleted by battles; and worse, yea, much worse, by desertion. The men were deserting by tens and hundreds, and I might say by thousands. The morale of the army was gone. The spirit of the soldiers was crushed, their hope gone. The future was dark and gloomy. They would not answer at roll call. Discipline had gone. A feeling of mistrust pervaded the whole army.

A train load of provisions came into Dalton. The soldiers stopped it before it rolled into the station, burst open every car, and carried off all the bacon, meal and flour that was on board. Wild riot was the order of the day; everything was confusion, worse confounded. When the news came, like pouring oil upon the troubled waters, that General Joe E. Johnston, of Virginia, had taken command of the Army of Tennessee, men returned to their companies, order was restored, and "Richard was himself again." General Johnston issued a universal amnesty to all soldiers absent without leave. Instead of a scrimp pattern of one day's rations, he ordered two days' rations to be issued, being extra for one day. He ordered tobacco and whisky to be issued twice a week. He ordered sugar and coffee and flour to be issued instead of meal. He ordered old bacon and ham to be issued instead of blue beef. He ordered new tents and marquees. He ordered his soldiers new suits of clothes, shoes and hats. In fact, there had been a revolution, sure enough. He allowed us what General Bragg had never allowed mortal man—a furlough. He gave furloughs to one-third of his army at a time, until the whole had been furloughed. A new era had dawned; a new epoch had been dated. He passed through the ranks of the common soldiers, shaking hands with every one he met. He restored the soldier's pride; he brought the manhood back to the private's bosom; he changed the order of roll-call, standing guard, drill, and such nonsense as that. The revolution was complete. He was loved, respected, admired; yea, almost worshipped by his troops. I do not believe there was a soldier in his army but would gladly have died for him. With him everything was his soldiers, and the newspapers, criticising him at the time, said, "He would feed his soldiers if the country starved."

We soon got proud; the blood of the old Cavaliers tingled in our veins. We did not feel that we were serfs and vagabonds. We felt that we had a home and a country worth fighting for, and, if need be, worth dying for. One regiment could whip an army, and did do it, in every instance, before the command was taken from him at Atlanta. But of this another time.

Chaplains were brought back to their regiments. Dr. C. T. Quintard and Rev. C. D. Elliott, and other chaplains, held divine services every Sabbath, prayer was offered every evening at retreat, and the morale of the army was better in every respect. The private soldier once more regarded himself a gentleman and a man of honor. We were willing to do and die and dare anything for our loved South, and the Stars and Bars of the Confederacy. In addition to this, General Johnston ordered his soldiers to be paid up every cent that was due them, and a bounty of fifty dollars besides. He issued an order to his troops offering promotion and a furlough for acts of gallantry and bravery on the field of battle.

The cloven foot of tyranny and oppression was not discernible in the acts of officers, from general down to corporal, as formerly. Notwithstanding all this grand transformation in our affairs, old Joe was a strict disciplinarian. Everything moved like clockwork. Men had to keep their arms and clothing in good order. The artillery was rubbed up and put in good condition. The wagons were greased, and the harness and hamestrings oiled. Extra rations were issued to negroes who were acting as servants, a thing unprecedented before in the history of the war.

Well, old Joe was a yerker. He took all the tricks. He was a commander. He kept everything up and well in hand. His lines of battle were invulnerable. The larger his command, the easier he could handle it. When his army moved, it was a picture of battle, everything in its place, as laid down by scientific military rules. When a man was to be shot, he was shot for the crimes he had done, and not to intimidate and cow the living, and he had ten times as many shot as Bragg had. He had seventeen shot at Tunnel Hill, and a whole company at Rockyface Ridge, and two spies hung at Ringgold Gap, but they were executed for their crimes. No one knew of it except those who had to take part as executioners of the law. Instead of the whipping post, he instituted the pillory and barrel shirt. Get Brutus to whistle the barrel shirt for you. The pillory was a new-fangled concern. If you went to the guard-house of almost any regiment, you would see some poor fellow with his head and hands sticking through a board. It had the appearance of a fellow taking a running start, at an angle of forty-five degrees, with a view of bursting a board over his head, but when the board burst his head and both his hands were clamped in the bursted places. The barrel shirt brigade used to be marched on drill and parade. You could see a fellow's head and feet, and whenever one of the barrels would pass, you would hear the universal cry, "Come out of that barrel, I see your head and feet sticking out." There might have been a mortification and a disgrace in the pillory and barrel shirt business to those that had to use them, but they did not bruise and mutilate the physical man. When one of them had served out his time he was as good as new. Old Joe had greater military insight than any general of the South, not excepting even Lee. He was the born soldier; seemed born to command. When his army moved it moved solid. Cavalry, artillery, wagon train, and infantry stepped the same tread to the music of the march. His men were not allowed to be butchered for glory, and to have his name and a battle fought, with the number of killed and wounded, go back to Richmond for his own glory. When he fought, he fought for victory, not for glory. He could fall back right in the face of the foe as quietly and orderly as if on dress parade; and when his enemies crowded him a little too closely, he would about face and give them a terrible chastisement. He could not be taken by surprise by any flank movement of the enemy. His soldiers were to him his children. He loved them. They were never needlessly sacrificed. He was always ready to meet the attack of the enemy. When his line of battle was formed it was like a wall of granite. His adversaries knew him, and dreaded the certain death that awaited them. His troops were brave; they laughed in the face of battle. He had no rear guard to shoot down any one who ran. They couldn't run; the army was solid. The veriest coward that was ever born became a brave man and a hero under his manipulation. His troops had the utmost confidence in him, and feared no evil. They became an army of veterans, whose lines could not be broken by the armies of the world. Battle became a pastime and a pleasure, and the rattle of musketry and roar of cannon were but the music of victory and success.

Commissaries

Before General Joseph E. Johnston took command of the Army of Tennessee, the soldiers were very poorly fed, it is true, but the blame was not entirely attributable to General Bragg. He issued enough and more than enough to have bountifully fed his army, but there was a lot of men in the army, generally denominated commissaries, and their "gizzards," as well as fingers, had to be greased. There was commissary-general, then corps commissary, then division commissary, then brigade commissary, then regimental commissary, then company commissary. Now, you know were you to start a nice hindquarter of beef, which had to pass through all these hands, and every commissary take a choice steak and roast off it, there would be but little ever reach the company, and the poor man among the Johnnies had to feast like bears in winter—they had to suck their paws—but the rich Johnnies who had money could go to almost any of the gentlemen denominated commissaries (they ought to have been called cormorants) and buy of them much nice fat beef and meal and flour and sugar and coffee and nice canvassed hams, etc. I have done it many times. They were keeping back the rations that had been issued to the army, and lining their own pockets. But when General Johnston took command, this manipulating business played out. Rations would "spile" on their hands. Othello's occupation was gone. They received only one hundred and forty dollars a month then, and the high private got plenty to eat, and Mr. Cormorant quit making as much money as he had heretofore done. Were you to go to them and make complaint, they would say, "I have issued regular army rations to your company, and what is left over is mine," and they were mighty exact about it.

Dalton

We went into winter quarters at Dalton, and remained there during the cold, bad winter of 1863–64, about four months. The usual routine of army life was carried on day by day, with not many incidents to vary the monotony of camp life. But occasionally the soldiers would engage in a snow ball battle, in which generals, colonels, captains and privates all took part. They would usually divide off into two grand divisions, one line naturally becoming the attacking party, and the other the defensive. The snow balls would begin to fly hither and thither, with an occasional knock down, and sometimes an ugly wound, where some mean fellow had enclosed a rock in his snow ball. It was fun while it lasted, but after it was over the soldiers were wet, cold and uncomfortable. I have seen charges and attacks and routes and stampedes, etc., but before the thing was over, one side did not know one from the other. It was a general knock down and drag out affair.

Shooting a Deserter

One morning I went over to Deshler's brigade of Cleburne's division to see my brother-in-law, Dr. J. E. Dixon. The snow was on the ground, and the boys were hard at it, "snow balling."

While I was standing looking on, a file of soldiers marched by me with a poor fellow on his way to be shot. He was blindfolded and set upon a stump, and the detail formed. The command, "Ready, aim, fire!" was given, the volley discharged, and the prisoner fell off the stump. He had not been killed. It was the sergeant's duty to give the *coup d'etat*, should not the prisoner be slain. The sergeant ran up and placed the muzzle of his gun at the head of the poor, pleading, and entreating wretch, his gun was discharged, and the wretched man only powder-burned, the gun being one that had been loaded with powder only. The whole affair had to be gone over again. The soldiers had to reload and form and fire. The culprit was killed stone dead this time. He had no sooner been taken up and carried off to be buried, than the soldiers were throwing snow balls as hard as ever, as if nothing had happened.

Ten Men Killed at The Mourners' Bench

At this place (Dalton) a revival of religion sprang up, and there was divine service every day and night. Soldiers became serious on the subject of their souls' salvation. In sweeping the streets and cleaning up, an old tree had been set on fire, and had been smoking and burning for several days, and nobody seemed to notice it. That night there was service as usual, and the singing and sermon were excellent. The sermon was preached by Rev. J. G. Bolton, chaplain of the Fiftieth Tennessee Regiment, assisted by Rev. C. D. Elliott, the services being held in the Fourth Tennessee Regiment. As it was the custom to "call up mourners," a long bench had been placed in proper position for them to kneel down at. Ten of them were kneeling at this mourners' bench, pouring out their souls in prayer to God, asking Him for the forgiveness of their sins, and for the salvation of their souls, for Jesus Christ their Redeemer's sake, when the burning tree, without any warning, fell with a crash right across the ten mourners, crushing and killing them instantly. God had heard their prayers. Their souls had been carried to heaven.

Hereafter, henceforth, and forevermore, there was no more marching, battling, or camp duty for them. They had joined the army of the hosts of heaven.

By order of the general, they were buried with great pomp and splendor, that is, for those times. Every one of them was buried in a coffin. Brass bands followed, playing the "Dead March," and platoons fired over their graves. It was a soldier's funeral. The beautiful burial service of the Episcopal church was read by Rev. Allen Tribble. A hymn was sung, and prayer offered, and then their graves were filled as we marched sadly back to camp.

Dr. C. T. Quintard

Dr. C. T. Quintard was our chaplain for the First Tennessee Regiment during the whole war, and he stuck to us from the beginning even unto the end. During week days he ministered to us physically, and on Sundays spiritually. He was one of the purest and best men I ever knew. He would march and carry his knapsack every day the same as any soldier. He had one text he preached from which I remember now. It was "the flying scroll." He said there was a flying scroll continually passing over our heads, which was like the reflections in a looking-glass, and all of our deeds, both good and bad, were written upon it. He was a good doctor of medicine, as well as a good doctor of divinity, and above either of these, he was a good man *per se*. Every old soldier of the First Tennessee Regiment will remember Dr. C. T. Quintard with the kindest and most sincere emotions of love and respect. He would go off into the country and get up for our regiment clothing and provisions, and wrote a little prayer and song book, which he had published, and gave it to the soldiers. I learned that little prayer and song book off by heart, and have a copy of it in my possession yet, which I would not part with for any consideration. Dr. Quintard's nature was one of love. He loved the soldiers, and the soldiers loved him, and deep down in his heart of hearts was a deep and lasting love for Jesus Christ, the Redeemer of the world, implanted there by God the Father Himself.

Y's You Got My Hog?

One day, a party of "us privates" concluded we would go across the Conasauga river on a raid. We crossed over in a canoe. After traveling for some time, we saw a neat looking farm house, and sent one of the party forward to reconnoiter. He returned in a few minutes and announced that he had found a fine fat sow in a pen near the house. Now, the plan we formed was for two of us to go into the house and keep the inmates interested and the other was to toll and drive off the hog. I was one of the party which went into the house. There was no one there but an old lady and her sick and widowed daughter. They invited us in very pleasantly and kindly, and soon prepared us a very nice and good dinner. The old lady told us of all her troubles and trials. Her husband had died before the war, and she had three sons in the army, two of whom had been killed, and the youngest, who had been conscripted, was taken with the camp fever and died in the hospital at Atlanta, and she had nothing to subsist upon, after eating up what they then had. I was much interested, and remained a little while after my comrade had left. I soon went out, having made up my mind to have nothing to do with the hog affair. I did not know how to act. I was in a bad fix. I had heard the gun fire and knew its portent. I knew the hog was dead, and went on up the road, and soon overtook my two comrades with the hog, which had been skinned and cut up, and was being carried on a pole between them. I did not know what to do. On looking back I saw the old lady coming and screaming at the top of her voice, "You got my hog! You got my hog!" It was too late to back out now. We had the hog, and had to make the most of it, even if we did ruin a needy and destitute family. We went on until we came to the Conasauga river, when lo and behold! the canoe was on the other side of the river. It was dark then, and getting darker, and what was to be done we did not know. The weather was as cold as blue blazes, and spitting snow from the northwest. That river had to be crossed that night. I undressed and determined to swim it, and went in, but the little thin ice at the bank cut my feet. I waded in a little further, but soon found I would cramp if I tried to swim it. I came out and put my clothes on, and thought of a gate about a mile back. We went back and took the gate off its hinges and carried it to the river and put it in the water, but soon found out that all three of us could not ride on it; so one of the party got on it and started across. He did very well until he came to the other bank, which was a high bluff, and if he got off the center of the gate it would capsize and he would get a ducking. He could not get off the gate. I told him to pole the gate up to the bank, so that one side would rest on the bank, and then make a quick run for the bank. He thought he had got the gate about the right place, and then made a run, and the gate went under and so did he, in water ten feet deep. My comrade, Fount C., who was with me on the bank, laughed, I thought, until he had hurt himself; but with me, I assure you, it was a mightly sickly grin, and with the other one, Barkley J., it was anything but a laughing matter. To me he seemed a hero. Barkley did about to liberate me from a very unpleasant position. He soon returned with the canoe, and we crossed the river with the hog. We worried and tugged with it, and got it to camp just before daylight.

I had a guilty conscience, I assure you. The hog was cooked, but I did not eat a piece of it. I felt that I had rather starve, and I believe that it would have choked me to death if I had attempted it.

A short time afterward an old citizen from Maury county visited me. My father sent me, by him, a silver watch—which I am wearing today—and eight hundred dollars in old issue Confederate money. I took two hundred dollars of the money, and had it funded for new issue, 33 1/3 cents discount. The other six hundred I sent to Vance Thompson, then on duty at Montgomery, with instructions to send it to my brother, Dave Watkins, Uncle Asa Freeman, and J. E. Dixon, all of whom were in Wheeler's cavalry, at some other point—I knew not where. After getting my money, I found that I had $133.33 1/3. I could not rest. I took one hundred dollars, new issue, and going by my lone self back to the old lady's house, I said, "Madam, some soldiers were here a short time ago, and took your hog. I was one of that party, and I wish to pay you for it. What was it worth?" "Well, sir," says she, "money is of no value to me; I cannot get any article that I wish; I would much rather have the hog." Says I, "Madam, that is an impossibility; your hog is dead and eat up, and I have come to pay you for it." The old lady's eyes filled with tears. She said that she was perfectly willing to give the soldiers everything she had, and if she thought it had done us any good, she would not charge anything for it.

"Well," says I, "Madam, here is a hundred dollar, new issue, Confederate bill. Will this pay you for your hog?" "Well, sir," she says, drawing herself up to her full height, her cheeks flushed and her eyes flashing, "I do not want your money. I would feel that it was blood money." I saw that there was no further use to offer it to her. I sat down by the fire and the conversation turned upon other subjects.

I helped the old lady catch a chicken (an old hen—about the last she had) for dinner, went with her in the garden and pulled a bunch of eschalots, brought two buckets of water, and cut and brought enough wood to last several days.

After awhile, she invited me to dinner, and after dinner I sat down by her side, took her old hand in mine, and told her the whole affair of the hog, from beginning to end; how sorry I was, and how I did not eat any of that hog; and asked her as a special act of kindness and favor to me, to take the hundred dollars; that I felt bad about it, and if she would take it, it would ease my conscience. I laid the money on the table and left. I have never in my life made a raid upon anybody else.

Target Shooting

By some hook, or crook, or blockade running, or smuggling, or Mason and Slidell, or Raphael Semmes, or something of the sort, the Confederate States government had come in possession of a small number of Whitworth guns, the finest long range guns in the world, and a monopoly by the English government. They were to be given to the best shots in the army. One day Captain Joe P. Lee and Company H went out to shoot at a target for the gun. We all wanted the gun, because if we got it we would be sharpshooters, and be relieved from camp duty, etc.

All the generals and officers came out to see us shoot. The mark was put up about five hundred yards on a hill, and each of us had three shots. Every shot that was fired hit the board, but there was one man who came a little closer to the spot than any other one, and the Whitworth was awarded him; and as we just turned round to go back to camp, a buck rabbit jumped up, and was streaking it as fast as he could make tracks, all the boys whooping and yelling as hard as they could, when Jimmy Webster raised his gun and pulled down on him, and cut the rabbit's head entirely off with a minnie ball right back of his ears. He was about two hundred and fifty yards off. It might have been an accidental shot, but General Leonidas Polk laughed very heartily at the incident, and I heard him ask one of his staff if the Whitworth gun had been awarded. The staff officer responded that it had, and that a certain man in Colonel Farquharson's regiment—the Fourth Tennessee—was the successful contestant, and I heard General Polk remark, "I wish I had another gun to give, I would give it to the young man that shot the rabbit's head off."

None of our regiment got a Whitworth, but it has been subsequently developed that our regiment had some of the finest shots in it the world ever produced. For instance, George and Mack Campbell, of Maury county; Billy Watkins, of Nashville, and Colonel H. R. Field, and many others, who I cannot now recall to mind in this rapid sketch.

Uncle Zack and Aunt Daphne

While at this place, I went out one day to hunt someone to wash my clothes for me. I never was a good washerwoman. I could cook, bring water and cut wood, but never was much on the wash. In fact, it was an uphill business for me to wash up "the things" after "grub time" in our mess.

I took my clothes and started out, and soon came to a little old negro hut. I went in and says to an old negress, "Aunty, I would like for you to do a little washing for me." The old creature was glad to get it, as I agreed to pay her what it was worth. Her name was Aunt Daphne, and if she had been a politician, she would have been a success. I do not remember of a more fluent "conversationalist" in my life. Her tongue seemed to be on a balance, and both ends were trying to out-talk the other—but she was a good woman. Her husband was named Uncle Zack, and was the exact counterpart of Aunt Daphne. He always sat in the chimney corner, his feet in the ashes, and generally fast asleep. I am certain I never saw an uglier or more baboonish face in my life, but Uncle Zack was a good Christian, and I would sometimes wake him up to hear him talk Christian.

He said that when he "fessed 'ligin, de debil come dare one nite, and say, 'Zack, come go wid me,' and den de debil tek me to hell, and jes stretch a wire across hell, and hang me up jes same like a side of bacon, through the tongue. Well, dar I hang like de bacon, and de grease kept droppin' down, and would blaze up all 'round me. I jes stay dar and burn; and after while de debil come 'round wid his gun, and say, 'Zack, I gwine to shoot you,' and jes as he raise de gun, I jes jerk loose from dat wire, and I jes fly to heben."

"Fly! did you have wings?"

"O, yes, sir, I had wings."

"Well, after you got to heaven, what did you do then?"

"Well, I jes went to eatin' grass like all de balance of de lams."

"What! were they eating grass?"

"O, yes, sir."

"Well, what color were the lambs, Uncle Zack?"

"Well, sir, some of dem was white, and some black, and some spotted."

"Were there no old rams or ewes among them?"

"No, sir; dey was all lams."

"Well, Uncle Zack, what sort of a looking lamb were you?"

"Well, sir, I was sort of specklish and brown like."

Old Zack begins to get sleepy.

"Did you have horns, Uncle Zack?"

"Well, some of dem had little horns dat look like dey was jes sorter sproutin' like."

Zack begins to nod and doze a little.

"Well, how often did they shear the lambs, Uncle Zack?"

"Well, w-e-l-l, w—e—l—l—," and Uncle Zack was fast asleep and snoring, and dreaming no doubt of the beautiful pastures glimmering above the clouds of heaven.

Red Tape

While here I applied for a furlough. Now, reader, here commenced a series of red tapeism that always had characterized the officers under Braggism. It had to go through every officer's hands, from corporal up, before it was forwarded to the next officer of higher grade, and so it passed through every officer's hands. He felt it his sworn and bound duty to find some informality in it, and it was brought back for correction according to his notions, you see. Well, after getting the corporal's consent and approval, it goes up to the sergeant. It ain't right! Some informality, perhaps, in the wording and spelling. Then the lieutenants had to have a say in it, and when it got to the captain, it had to be read and re-read, to see that every "i" was dotted and "t" crossed, but returned because there was one word that he couldn't make out. Then it was forwarded to the colonel. He would snatch it out of your hand, grit his teeth, and say, "D—n it;" feel in his vest pocket and take out a lead pencil, and simply write "app." for approved. This would also be returned, with instructions that the colonel must write "approved" in a plain hand, and with pen and ink. Then it went to the brigadier-general. He would be engaged in a game of poker, and would tell you to call again, as he didn't have time to bother with those small affairs at present. "I'll see your five and raise you ten." "I have a straight flush." "Take the pot." After setting him out, and when it wasn't his deal, I get up and walk around, always keeping the furlough in sight. After reading carefully the furlough, he says, "Well, sir, you have failed to get the adjutant's name to it. You ought to have the colonel and adjutant, and you must go back and get their signatures." After this, you go to the major-general. He is an old aristocratic fellow, who never smiles, and tries to look as sour as vinegar. He looks at the furlough, and looks down at the ground, holding the furlough in his hand in a kind of dreamy way, and then says, "Well, sir, this is all informal." You say, "Well, General, what is the matter with it?" He looks at you as if he hadn't heard you, and repeats very slowly, "Well, sir, this is informal," and hands it back to you. You take it, feeling all the while that you wished you had not applied for a furlough, and by summoning all the fortitude that you possess, you say in a husky and choking voice, "Well, general (you say the "general" in a sort of gulp and dry swallow), what's the matter with the furlough?" You look askance, and he very languidly re-takes the furlough and glances over it, orders his negro boy to go and feed his horse, asks his cook how long it will be before dinner, hallooes at some fellow away down the hill that he would like for him to call at 4 o'clock this evening, and tells his adjutant to sign the furlough. The adjutant tries to be smart and polite, smiles a smile both child-like and bland, rolls up his shirt-sleeves, and winks one eye at you, gets astraddle of a camp-stool, whistles a little stanza of schottische, and with a big flourish of his pen, writes the major-general's name in small letters, and his own—the adjutant's—in very large letters, bringing the pen under it with tremendous flourishes, and writes approved and forwarded. You feel relieved. You feel that the anaconda's coil had been suddenly relaxed. Then you start out to the lieutenant-general; you find him. He is in a very learned and dignified conversation about the war in Chili. Well, you get very anxious for the war in Chili to get to an end. The general pulls his side-whiskers, looks wise, and tells his adjutant to look over it, and, if correct, sign it. The adjutant does not deign to condescend to notice you.

He seems to be full of gumbo or calf-tail soup, and does not wish his equanimity disturbed. He takes hold of the document, and writes the lieutenant-general's name, finishes his own name while looking in another direction—approved and forwarded. Then you take it up to the general; the guard stops you in a very formal way, and asks, "What do you want?" You tell him. He calls for the orderly; the orderly gives it to the adjutant, and you are informed that it will be sent to your colonel tonight, and given to you at roll-call in the morning. Now, reader, the above is a pretty true picture of how I got my furlough.

I Get a Furlough

After going through all the formality of red-tapeism, and being snubbed with tweedle-dum and tweedle-dee, I got my furlough. When it started out, it was on the cleanest piece of paper that could be found in Buck Lanier's sutler's store. After it came back, it was pretty well used up, and looked as if it had gone through a very dark place, and been beat with a soot-bag. But, anyhow, I know that I did not appreciate my furlough half as much as I thought I would. I felt like returning it to the gentlemen with my compliments, declining their kind favors. I felt that it was unwillingly given, and, as like begets like, it was very unwillingly received. Honestly, I felt as if I had made a bad bargain, and was keen to rue the trade. I did not know what to do with it; but, anyhow, I thought I would make the best of a bad bargain. I got on the cars at Dalton—now, here is a thing that I had long since forgotten about—it was the first first-class passenger car that I had been in since I had been a soldier. The conductor passed around, and handed me a ticket with these words on it:

> "If you wish to travel with ease,
> Keep this ticket in sight, if you please;
> And if you wish to take a nap,
> Just stick this in your hat or cap."

This was the poetry, reader, that was upon the ticket. The conductor called around every now and then, especially if you were asleep, to look at your ticket, and every now and then a captain and a detail of three soldiers would want to look at your furlough. I thought before I got to Selma, Alabama, that I wished the ticket and furlough both were in the bottom of the ocean, and myself back in camp. Everywhere I went someone wanted to see my furlough. Before I got my furlough, I thought it sounded big. Furlough was a war word, and I did not comprehend its meaning until I got one. The very word "furlough" made me sick then. I feel fainty now whenever I think of furlough. It has a sickening sound in the ring of it—"furlough!" "Furloch," it ought to have been called. Every man I met had a furlough; in fact, it seemed to have the very double-extract of romance about it—"fur too, eh?" Men who I knew had never been in the army in their lives, all had furloughs. Where so many men ever got furloughs from I never knew; but I know now. They were like the old bachelor who married the widow with ten children—he married a "ready-made" family. They had ready-made furloughs. But I have said enough on the furlough question; it enthralled me—let it pass; don't want any more furloughs. But while on my furlough, I got with Captain G. M. V. Kinzer, a fine-dressed and handsome cavalry captain, whom all the ladies (as they do at the present day), fell in love with. The captain and myself were great friends. The captain gave me his old coat to act captain in, but the old thing wouldn't act. I would keep the collar turned down. One night we went to call on a couple of beautiful and interesting ladies near Selma. We chatted the girls until the "wee sma' hours" of morning, and when the young ladies retired, remarked that they would send a servant to show us to our room. We waited; no servant came. The captain and myself snoozed it out as best we could. About daylight the next morning the captain and myself thought that we would appear as if we had risen very early, and began to move about, and opening the door, there lay a big black negro on his knees and face. Now, reader, what do you suppose that negro was doing?

You could not guess in a week. The black rascal! hideous! terrible to contemplate! vile! outrageous! Well, words cannot express it. What do you suppose he was doing? He was fast asleep. He had come thus far, and could go no further, and fell asleep. There is where the captain and myself found him at daylight the next morning. We left for Selma immediately after breakfast, leaving the family in ignorance of the occurrence. The captain and myself had several other adventures, but the captain always had the advantage of me; he had the good clothes, and the good looks, and got all the good presents from the pretty young ladies—well, you might say, "cut me out" on all occasions. "That's what makes me 'spise a furlough." But then furlough sounds big, you know.

Chapter 12

Hundred Days Battle

Rocky Face Ridge

WHEN I got back to Dalton, I found the Yankee army advancing; they were at Rocky Face Ridge. Now, for old Joe's generalship. We have seen him in camp, now we will see him in action. We are marched to meet the enemy; we occupy Turner's Gap at Tunnel Hill. Now, come on, Mr. Yank—we are keen for an engagement. It is like a picnic; the soldiers are ruddy and fat, and strong; whoop! whoop! hurrah! come on, Mr. Yank. We form line of battle on top of Rocky Face Ridge, and here we are face to face with the enemy. Why don't you unbottle your thunderbolts and dash us to pieces? Ha! here it comes; the boom of cannon and the bursting of a shell in our midst. Ha! ha! give us another blizzard! Boom! boom! That's all right, you ain't hurting nothing.

"Hold on, boys," says a sharpshooter, armed with a Whitworth gun, "I'll stop that racket. Wait until I see her smoke again." Boom, boom! the keen crack of the Whitworth rings upon the frosty morning air; the cannoneers are seen to lie down; something is going on. "Yes, yonder is a fellow being carried off on a litter." Bang! bang! goes the Whitworth, and the battery is seen to limber to the rear. What next? a yell! What does this yell mean? A charge right up the hill, and a little sharp skirmish for a few moments. We can see the Yankee line. They are resting on their arms. The valley below is full of blue coats, but a little too far off to do any execution.

Old Joe walks along the line. He happens to see the blue coats in the valley, in plain view. Company H is ordered to fire on them. We take deliberate aim and fire a solid volley of minnie balls into their midst. We see a terrible consplutterment among them, and know that we have killed and wounded several of Sherman's incendiaries. They seem to get mad at our audacity, and ten pieces of cannon are brought up, and pointed right toward us. We see the smoke boil up, and a moment afterwards the shell is roaring and bursting right among us. Ha! ha! ha! that's funny—we love the noise of battle. Captain Joe P. Lee orders us to load and fire at will upon these batteries. Our Enfields crack, keen and sharp; and ha, ha, ha, look yonder! The Yankees are running away from their cannon, leaving two pieces to take care of themselves. Yonder goes a dash of our cavalry. They are charging right up in the midst of the Yankee line. Three men are far in advance. Look out boys! What does that mean? Our cavalry are falling back, and the three men are cut off. They will be captured, sure. They turn to get back to our lines. We can see the smoke boil up, and hear the discharge of musketry from the Yankee lines. One man's horse is seen to blunder and fall, one man reels in his saddle, and falls a corpse, and the other is seen to surrender. But, look yonder! the man's horse that blundered and fell is up again; he mounts his horse in fifty yards of the whole Yankee line, is seen to lie down on his neck, and is spurring him right on toward the solid line of blue coats. Look how he rides, and the ranks of the blue coats open. Hurrah for the brave rebel boy! He has passed and is seen to regain his regiment. I afterwards learned that that brave Rebel boy was my own brother, Dave, who at that time was not more than sixteen years old. The one who was killed was named Grimes, and the one captured was named Houser, and the regiment was the First Tennessee Cavalry, then commanded by Colonel J. H. Lewis. You could have heard the cheers from both sides, it seemed, for miles.

John Branch raised the tune, in which the whole First and Twenty-seventh Regiment joined in:

> *"Cheer, boys, cheer, we are marching on to battle!*
> *Cheer, boys, cheer, for our sweethearts and our wives!*
> *Cheer, boys, cheer, we'll nobly do our duty,*
> *And give to the South our hearts, our arms, our lives.*
>   *Old Lincoln, with his hireling hosts,*
>   *Will never whip the South,*
>   *Shouting the battle cry of freedom."*

All this is taking place while the Yankees are fully one thousand yards off. We can see every movement that is made, and we know that Sherman's incendiaries are already hacked. Sherman himself is a coward, and dares not try his strength with old Joe. Sherman never fights; all that he is after is marching to the sea, while the world looks on and wonders: "What a flank movement!" Yes, Sherman is afraid of minnie balls, and tries the flank movement. We are ordered to march somewhere.

"Falling Back"

Old Joe knows what he is up to. Every night we change our position. The morrow's sun finds us face to face with the Yankee lines. The troops are in excellent spirits. Yonder are our "big guns," our cavalry—Forrest and Wheeler—our sharpshooters, and here is our wagon and supply train, right in our midst. The private's tread is light—his soul is happy.

Another flank movement. Tomorrow finds us face to face. Well, you have come here to fight us; why don't you come on? We are ready; always ready. Everything is working like clockwork; machinery is all in order. Come, give us a tilt, and let us try our metal. You say old Joe has got the brains and you have got the men; you are going to flank us out of the Southern Confederacy. That's your plan, is it? Well, look out; we are going to pick off and decimate your men every day. You will be a picked chicken before you do that.

What? The Yankees are at Resacca, and have captured the bridge across the Oostanaula river. Well, now, that's business; that has the old ring in it. Tell it to us again; we're fond of hearing such things.

The Yankees are tearing up the railroad track between the tank and Resacca. Let's hear it again. The Yankees have opened the attack; we are going to have a battle; we are ordered to strip for the fight. (That is, to take off our knapsacks and blankets, and to detail Bev. White to guard them.) Keep closed up, men. The skirmish line is firing like popping fire-crackers on a Christmas morning. Every now and then the boom of a cannon and the screaming of a shell. Ha, ha, ha! that has the right ring. We will make Sherman's incendiaries tell another tale in a few moments, when—"Halt! about face." Well, what's the matter now? Simply a flank movement. All right; we march back, retake our knapsacks and blankets, and commence to march toward Resacca. Tom Tucker's rooster crows, and John Branch raises the tune, "Just Twenty Years Ago," and after we sing that out, he winds up with, "There Was an Ancient Individual Whose Cognomen Was Uncle Edward," and

> *"The old woman who kept a peanut stand,*
> *And a big policeman stood by with a big stick in his*
>   *hand,"*

And Arthur Fulghum halloes out, "All right; go ahead! toot, toot, toot! puff, puff, puff! Tickets, gentlemen, tickets!" and the Maury Grays raise the yell, "All aboard for Culleoka," while Walker Coleman commences the song, "I'se gwine to jine the rebel band, fightin' for my home." Thus we go, marching back to Resacca.

Battle of Resacca

Well, you want to hear about shooting and banging, now, gentle reader, don't you? I am sorry I cannot interest you on this subject—see history.

The Yankees had got breeches hold on us. They were ten miles in our rear; had cut off our possibility of a retreat. The wire bridge was in their hands, and they were on the railroad in our rear; but we were moving, there was no mistake in that. Our column was firm and strong. There was no excitement, but we were moving along as if on review. We passed old Joe and his staff. He has on a light or mole colored hat, with a black feather in it. He is listening to the firing going on at the front. One little cheer, and the very ground seems to shake with cheers. Old Joe smiles as blandly as a modest maid, raises his hat in acknowledgement, makes a polite bow, and rides toward the firing. Soon we are thrown into line of battle, in support of Polk's corps. We belong to Hardee's corps. Now Polk's corps advances to the attack, and Hardee's corps fifty or seventy-five yards in the rear. A thug, thug, thug; the balls are decimating our men; we can't fire; Polk's corps is in front of us; should it give way, then it will be our time. The air is full of deadly missiles. We can see the two lines meet, and hear the deadly crash of battle; can see the blaze of smoke and fire. The earth trembles. Our little corps rush in to carry off our men as they are shot down, killed and wounded. Lie down! thug, thug! General Hardee passes along the line. "Steady, boys!" (The old general had on a white cravat; he had been married to a young wife not more than three weeks.) "Go back, general, go back, go back, go back," is cried all along the line. He passes through the missiles of death unscathed; stood all through that storm of bullets indifferent to their proximity (we were lying down, you know). The enemy is checked; yonder they fly, whipped and driven from the field. "Attention! By the right flank, file left, march! Double quick!" and we were double quicking, we knew not whither, but that always meant fight. We pass over the hill, and through the valley, and there is old Joe pointing toward the tank with his sword. (He looked like the pictures you see hung upon the walls.) We cross the railroad. Halloo! here comes a cavalry charge from the Yankee line. Now for it; we will see how Yankee cavalry fight. We are not supported; what is the matter? Are we going to be captured? They thunder down upon us. Their flat-footed dragoons shake and jar the earth. They are all around us—we are surrounded. "Form square! Platoons, right and left wheel! Kneel and fire!" There we were in a hollow square. The Yankees had never seen anything like that before. It was something new. They charged right upon us. Colonel Field, sitting on his gray mare, right in the center of the hollow square, gives the command, "Front rank, kneel and present bayonet against cavalry." The front rank knelt down, placing the butts of their guns against their knees. "Rear rank, fire at will; commence firing." Now, all this happened in less time than it has taken me to write it. They charged right upon us, no doubt expecting to ride right over us, and trample us to death with the hoofs of their horses. They tried to spur and whip their horses over us, but the horses had more sense than that. We were pouring a deadly fire right into their faces, and soon men and horses were writhing in the death agonies; officers were yelling at the top of their voices, "Surrender! surrender!" but we were having too good a thing of it. We were killing them by scores, and they could not fire at us; if they did they either overshot or missed their aim. Their ranks soon began to break and get confused, and finally they were routed, and broke and ran in all directions, as fast as their horses could carry them.

When we re-formed our regiment and marched back, we found that General Johnston's army had all passed over the bridge at Resacca. Now, reader, this was one of our tight places. The First Tennessee Regiment was always ordered to hold tight places, which we always did. We were about the last troops that passed over.

Now, gentle reader, that is all I know of the battle of Resacca. We had repulsed every charge, had crossed the bridge with every wagon, and cannon, and everything, and had nothing lost or captured. It beat anything that has ever been recorded in history. I wondered why old Joe did not attack in their rear. The explanation was that Hood's line was being enfiladed, his men decimated, and he could not hold his position.

We are still fighting; battles innumerable. The Yankees had

thrown pontoons across the river below Resacca, in hopes to intercept us on the other side. We were marching on the road; they seemed to be marching parallel with us. It was fighting, fighting, every day. When we awoke in the morning, the firing of guns was our reveille, and when the sun went down it was our "retreat and our lights out." Fighting, fighting, fighting, all day and all night long. Battles were fought every day, and in one respect we always had the advantage; they were the attacking party, and we always had good breastworks thrown up during the night.

Johnston's army was still intact. The soldiers drew their regular rations of biscuit and bacon, sugar and coffee, whisky and tobacco. When we went to sleep we felt that old Joe, the faithful old watch dog, had his eye on the enemy. No one was disposed to straggle and go back to Company Q. (Company Q was the name for play-outs.) They even felt safer in the regular line than in the rear with Company Q.

Well as stated previously, it was battle, battle, battle, every day, for one hundred days. The boom of cannon, and the rattle of musketry was our reveille and retreat, and Sherman knew that it was no child's play.

Today, April 14, 1882, I say, and honestly say, that I sincerely believe the combined forces of the whole Yankee nation could never have broken General Joseph E. Johnston's line of battle, beginning at Rocky Face Ridge, and ending on the banks of the Chattahoochee.

Adairsville—Octagon House—The First Tennessee Always Occupies Tight Places

We had stacked our arms and gone into camp, and had started to build fires to cook supper. I saw our cavalry falling back, I thought, rather hurriedly. I ran to the road and asked them what was the matter? They answered, "Matter enough; yonder are the Yankees, are you infantry fellows going to make a stand here?" I told Colonel Field what had been told to me, and he hooted at the idea; but balls that had shucks tied to their tails were passing over, and our regiment was in the rear of the whole army. I could hardly draw anyone's attention to the fact that the cavalry had passed us, and that we were on the outpost of the whole army, when an order came for our regiment to go forward as rapidly as possible and occupy an octagon house in our immediate front. The Yankees were about a hundred yards from the house on one side and we about a hundred yards on the other. The race commenced as to which side would get to the house first. We reached it, and had barely gotten in, when they were bursting down the paling of the yard on the opposite side. The house was a fine brick, octagon in shape, and as perfect a fort as could be desired. We ran to the windows, up-stairs, down-stairs and in the cellar. The Yankees cheered and charged, and our boys got happy. Colonel Field told us he had orders to hold it until every man was killed, and never to surrender the house. It was a forlorn hope.

We felt we were "gone fawn skins," sure enough. At every discharge of our guns, we would hear a Yankee squall. The boys raised a tune—

> *"I'se gwine to jine the Rebel band,*
> *A fighting for my home"*—

as they loaded and shot their guns. Then the tune of—

> *"Cheer, boys, cheer, we are marching on to battle!*
> *Cheer, boys, cheer, for our sweethearts and our wives!*
> *Cheer, boys, cheer, we'll nobly do our duty,*
> *And give to the South our hearts, our arms, our lives."*

Our cartridges were almost gone, and Lieutenant Joe Carney, Joe Sewell, and Billy Carr volunteered to go and bring a box of one thousand cartridges. They got out of the back window, and through that hail of iron and lead, made their way back with the box of cartridges. Our ammunition being renewed, the fight raged on. Captain Joe P. Lee touched me on the shoulder and said, "Sam, please let me have your gun for one shot." He raised it to his shoulder and pulled down on a fine-dressed cavalry officer, and I saw that Yankee tumble. He handed it back to me to reload. About twelve o'clock, midnight, the Hundred and Fifty-fourth Tennessee, commanded by Colonel McGevney, came to our relief.

The firing had ceased, and we abandoned the octagon house. Our dead and wounded—there were thirty of them—were in strange contrast with the furniture of the house. Fine chairs, sofas, settees, pianos and Brussels carpeting being made the death-bed of brave and noble boys, all saturated with blood. Fine lace and damask curtains, all blackened by the smoke of battle. Fine bureaus and looking-glasses and furniture being riddled by the rude missiles of war. Beautiful pictures in gilt frames, and a library of valuable books, all shot and torn by musket and cannon balls. Such is war.

Kennesaw Line

The battles of the Kennesaw line were fought for weeks. Cannonading and musketry firing was one continual thing. It seemed that shooting was the order of the day, and pickets on both sides kept up a continual firing, that sounded like ten thousand wood-choppers. Sometimes the wood-choppers would get lazy or tired and there was a lull. But you could always tell when the old guard had been relieved, by the accelerated chops of the wood-choppers.

Am Detailed to Go into the Enemy's Line

One day our orderly sergeant informed me that it was my regular time to go on duty, and to report to Captain Beasley, of the Twenty-seventh. I reported to the proper place, and we were taken to the headquarters of General Leonidas Polk. We had to go over into the enemy's lines, and make such observations as we could, and report back by daylight in the morning. Our instructions were to leave everything in camp except our guns and cartridge-boxes. These were to be carried, but, under no circumstances, to be used, except in case of death itself. We were instructed to fall in in the rear of our relief guard, which would go out about sunset; not to attract their attention, but to drop out one or two at a time; to pass the Yankee picket as best we could, even if we had to crawl on our bellies to do so; to go over in the Yankee lines, and to find out all we could, without attracting attention, if possible. These were our instructions. You may be sure my heart beat like a muffled drum when I heard our orders.

I felt like making my will. But, like the boy who was passing the graveyard, I tried to whistle to keep my spirits up. We followed the relief guard, and one by one stepped off from the rear. I was with two others, Arnold Zellner and T. C. Dornin. We found ourselves between the picket lines of the two armies. Fortune seemed to favor us. It was just getting dusky twilight, and we saw the relief guard of the Yankees just putting on their picket. They seemed to be very mild, inoffensive fellows. They kept a looking over toward the Rebel lines, and would dodge if a twig cracked under their feet. I walked on as if I was just relieved, and had passed their lines, when I turned back, and says I "Captain, what guard is this?" He answered, "Nien bocht, you bet," is what I understood him to say. "What regiment are you from?" "Ben bicht mir ein riefel fab bien." "What regiment is your detail from?" "Iet du mein got Donnermetter stefel switzer." I had to give it up—I had run across the detail of a Dutch regiment. I passed on, and came to the regular line of breastworks, and there was an old Irishman sitting on a stump grinding coffee. "General McCook's brigade, be jabbers," he answered to my inquiry as to what regiment it was. Right in front of me the line was full of Irish soldiers, and they were cooking supper. I finally got over their breastworks, and was fearful I would run into some camp or headquarter guard, and the countersign would be demanded of me. I did not know what to do in that case—but I thought of the way that I had gotten in hundreds of times before in our army, when I wanted to slip the guard, and that was to get a gun, go to some cross street or conspicuous place, halt the officer, and get the countersign. And while standing near General Sherman's headquarters, I saw a courier come out of his tent, get on his horse, and ride toward where I stood. As he approached, says I, "Halt! who goes there?" "A friend with the countersign." He advanced, and whispered in my ear the word "United." He rode on. I had gotten their countersign, and felt I was no longer a prisoner. I went all over their camp, and saw no demonstration of any kind. Night had thrown her mantle over the encampment. I could plainly see the sentinels on their weary vigils along the lines, but there was none in their rear. I met and talked with a great many soldiers, but could get no information from them.

About 2 o'clock at night, I saw a body of men approaching where I was. Something told me that I had better get out of their way, but I did not. The person in command said, "Say, there! you, sir; say, you, sir!" Says I, "Are you speaking to me?" "Yes," very curtly and abruptly. "What regiment do you belong to?" Says I, "One hundred and twenty-seventh Illinois." "Well, sir, fall in here; I am ordered to take up all stragglers. Fall in, fall in promptly!" Says I, "I am instructed by General McCook to remain here and direct a courier to General Williams' headquarters." He says, "It's a strange place for a courier to come to." His command marched on. About an hour afterwards—about 3 o'clock—I heard the assembly sound. I knew then that it was about time for me to be getting out of the way. Soon their companies were forming, and they were calling the roll everywhere. Everything had begun to stir. Artillery men were hitching up their horses. Men were dashing about in every direction. I saw their army form and move off. I got back into our lines, and reported to General Polk.

He was killed that very day on the Kennesaw line. General Stephens was killed the very next day.

Every now and then a dead picket was brought in. Times had begun to look bilious, indeed. Their cannon seemed to be getting the best of ours in every fight. The cannons of both armies were belching and bellowing at each other, and the pickets were going it like wood choppers, in earnest. We were entrenched behind strong fortifications. Our rations were cooked and brought to us regularly, and the spirits of the army were in good condition.

We continued to change position, and build new breastworks every night. One-third of the army had to keep awake in the trenches, while the other two-thirds slept. But everything was so systematized, that we did not feel the fatigue.

Pine Mountain—Death of General Leonidas Polk

General Leonidas Polk, our old leader, whom we had followed all through that long war, had gone forward with some of his staff to the top of Pine Mountain, to reconnoiter, as far as was practicable, the position of the enemy in our front. While looking at them with his field glass, a solid shot from the Federal guns struck him on his left breast, passing through his body and through his heart. I saw him while the infirmary corps were bringing him off the field. He was as white as a piece of marble, and a most remarkable thing about him was, that not a drop of blood was ever seen to come out of the place through which the cannon ball had passed. My pen and ability is inadequate to the task of doing his memory justice. Every private soldier loved him. Second to Stonewall Jackson, his loss was the greatest the South ever sustained. When I saw him there dead, I felt that I had lost a friend whom I had ever loved and respected, and that the South had lost one of her best and greatest generals.

His soldiers always loved and honored him. They called him "Bishop Polk." "Bishop Polk" was ever a favorite with the army, and when any position was to be held, and it was known that "Bishop Polk" was there, we knew and felt that "all was well."

Golgotha Church—General Lucius E. Polk Wounded

On this Kennesaw line, near Golgotha Church, one evening about 4 o'clock, our Confederate line of battle and the Yankee line came in close proximity. If I mistake not, it was a dark, drizzly, rainy evening. The cannon balls were ripping and tearing through the bushes. The two lines were in plain view of each other. General Pat Cleburne was at this time commanding Hardee's corps, and General Lucius E. Polk was in command of Cleburne's division. General John C. Brown's division was supporting Cleburne's division, or, rather, "in echelon." Every few moments, a raking fire from the Yankee lines would be poured into our lines, tearing limbs off the trees, and throwing rocks and dirt in every direction; but I never saw a soldier quail, or even dodge. We had confidence in old Joe, and were ready to march right into the midst of battle at a moment's notice. While in this position, a bomb, loaded with shrapnel and grape-shot, came ripping and tearing through our ranks, wounding General Lucius E. Polk, and killing some of his staff. And, right here, I deem it not inappropriate to make a few remarks as to the character and appearance of so brave and gallant an officer. At this time he was about twenty-five years old, with long black hair, that curled, a gentle and attractive black eye that seemed to sparkle with love rather than chivalry, and were it not for a young moustache and goatee that he usually wore, he would have passed for a beautiful girl. In his manner he was as simple and guileless as a child, and generous almost to a fault. Enlisting in the First Arkansas Regiment as a private soldier, and serving for twelve months as orderly sergeant; at the reorganization he was elected colonel of the regiment, and afterwards, on account of merit and ability, was commissioned brigadier-general; distinguishing himself for conspicuous bravery and gallantry on every battlefield, and being "scalped" by a minnie ball at Richmond, Kentucky—which scar marks its furrow on top of his head today. In every battle he was engaged in, he led his men to victory, or held the enemy at bay, while the surge of battle seemed against us; he always seemed the successful general, who would snatch victory out of the very jaws of defeat. In every battle, Polk's brigade, of Cleburne's division, distinguished itself, almost making the name of Cleburne as the Stonewall of the West. Polk was to Cleburne what Murat or the old guard was to Napoleon. And, at the battle of Chickamauga, when it seemed that the Southern army had nearly lost the battle, General Lucius E. Polk's brigade made the most gallant charge of the war, turning the tide of affairs, and routing the Yankee army. General Polk himself led the charge in person, and was the first man on top of the Yankee breastworks (*vide* General D. H. Hill's report of the battle of Chickamauga), and in every attack he had the advance guard, and in every retreat, the rear guard of the army. Why? Because General Lucius E. Polk and his brave soldiers *never* faltered, and with him as leader, the general commanding the army knew that "all was well."

Well, this evening of which I now write, the litter corps ran up and placed him on a litter, and were bringing him back through Company H, of our regiment, when one of the men was wounded, and I am not sure but another one was killed, and they let him fall to the ground. At that time, the Yankees seemed to know that they had killed or wounded a general, and tore loose their batteries upon this point. The dirt and rocks were flying in every direction, when Captain Joe P. Lee, Jim Brandon and myself, ran forward, grabbed up the litter, brought General Polk off the crest of the hill, and assisted in carrying him to the headquarters of General Cleburne. When we got to General Cleburne, he came forward and asked General Polk if he was badly wounded, and General Polk remarked, laughingly: "Well, I think I will be able to get a furlough now." This is a fact. General Polk's leg had been shot almost entirely off. I remember the foot part being twisted clear around, and lying by his side, while the blood was running through the litter in a perfect stream. I remember, also that General Cleburne dashed a tear from his eye with his hand, and saying, "Poor fellow," at once galloped to the front, and ordered an immediate advance of our lines. Cleburne's division was soon engaged. Night coming on, prevented a general engagement, but we drove the Yankee line two miles.

"Dead Angle"

The First and Twenty-seventh Tennessee Regiments will ever remember the battle of "Dead Angle," which was fought June 27th, on the Kennesaw line, near Marietta, Georgia. It was one of the hottest and longest days of the year, and one of the most desperate and determinedly resisted battles fought during the whole war. Our regiment was stationed on an angle, a little spur of the mountain, or rather promontory of a range of hills, extending far out beyond the main line of battle, and was subject to the enfilading fire of forty pieces of artillery of the Federal batteries. It seemed fun for the guns of the whole Yankee army to play upon this point. We would work hard every night to strengthen our breastworks, and the very next day they would be torn down smooth with the ground by solid shots and shells from the guns of the enemy. Even the little trees and bushes which had been left for shade, were cut down as so much stubble. For more than a week this constant firing had been kept up against this salient point. In the meantime, the skirmishing in the valley below resembled the sounds made by ten thousand wood-choppers.

Well, on the fatal morning of June 27th, the sun rose clear and cloudless, the heavens seemed made of brass, and the earth of iron, and as the sun began to mount toward the zenith, everything became quiet, and no sound was heard save a peckerwood on a neighboring tree, tapping on its old trunk, trying to find a worm for his dinner. We all knew it was but the dead calm that precedes the storm. On the distant hills we could plainly see officers dashing about hither and thither, and the Stars and Stripes moving to and fro, and we knew the Federals were making preparations for the mighty contest. We could hear but the rumbling sound of heavy guns, and the distant tread of a marching army, as a faint roar of the coming storm, which was soon to break the ominous silence with the sound of conflict, such as was scarcely ever before heard on this earth. It seemed that the arch-angel of Death stood and looked on with outstretched wings, while all the earth was silent, when all at once a hundred guns from the Federal line opened upon us, and for more than an hour they poured their solid and chain shot, grape and shrapnel right upon this salient point, defended by our regiment alone, when, all of a sudden, our pickets jumped into our works and reported the Yankees advancing, and almost at the same time a solid line of blue coats came up the hill. I discharged my gun, and happening to look up, there was the beautiful flag of the Stars and Stripes flaunting right in my face, and I heard John Branch, of the Rock City Guards, commanded by Captain W. D. Kelley, who were next Company H, say, "Look at that Yankee flag; shoot that fellow; snatch that flag out of his hand!" My pen is unable to describe the scene of carnage and death that ensued in the next two hours. Column after column of Federal soldiers were crowded upon that line, and by referring to the history of the war you will find they were massed in column forty columns deep; in fact, the whole force of the Yankee army was hurled against this point, but no sooner would a regiment mount our works than they were shot down or surrendered, and soon we had every "gopher hole" full of Yankee prisoners. Yet still the Yankees came. It seemed impossible to check the onslaught, but every man was true to his trust, and seemed to think that at that moment the whole responsibility of the Confederate government was rested upon his shoulders. Talk about other battles, victories, shouts, cheers, and triumphs, but in comparison with this day's fight, all others dwarf into insignificance. The sun beaming down on our uncovered heads, the thermometer being one hundred and ten degrees in the shade, and a solid line of blazing fire right from the muzzles of the Yankee guns being poured right into our very faces, singeing our hair and clothes, the hot blood of our dead and wounded spurting on us, the blinding smoke and stifling atmosphere filling our eyes and mouths, and the awful concussion causing the blood to gush out of our noses and

ears, and above all, the roar of battle, made it a perfect pandemonium. Afterward I heard a soldier express himself by saying
that he thought "Hell had broke loose in Georgia, sure enough."

I have heard men say that if they ever killed a Yankee during
the war they were not aware of it. I am satisfied that on this
memorable day, every man in our regiment killed from one
score to four score, yea, five score men. I mean from twenty to
one hundred each. All that was necessary was to load and shoot.
In fact, I will ever think that the reason they did not capture our
works was the impossibility of their living men passing over the
bodies of their dead. The ground was piled up with one solid
mass of dead and wounded Yankees. I learned afterwards from
the burying squad that in some places they were piled up like
cord wood, twelve deep.

After they were time and time again beaten back, they at last
were enabled to fortify a line under the crest of the hill, only
thirty yards from us, and they immediately commenced to ex-
cavate the earth with the purpose of blowing up our line.

We remained here three days after the battle. In the meantime the woods had taken fire, and during the nights and days
of all that time continued to burn, and at all times, every hour
of day and night, you could hear the shrieks and screams of the
poor fellows who were left on the field, and a stench, so sickening as to nauseate the whole of both armies, arose from the de-
caying bodies of the dead left lying on the field.

On the third morning the Yankees raised a white flag, asked
an armistice to bury their dead, not for any respect either army
had for the dead, but to get rid of the sickening stench. I get sick
now when I happen to think about it. Long and deep trenches
were dug, and hooks made from bayonets crooked for the purpose, and all the dead were dragged and thrown pell mell into
these trenches. Nothing was allowed to be taken off the dead,
and finely dressed officers, with gold watch chains dangling over
their vests, were thrown into the ditches. During the whole day
both armies were hard at work, burying the Federal dead.

Every member of the First and Twenty-seventh Tennessee

Regiments deserves a wreath of imperishable fame, and a warm place in the hearts of their countrymen, for their gallant and heroic valor at the battle of Dead Angle. No man distinguished himself above another. All did their duty, and the glory of one is but the glory and just tribute of the others.

After we had abandoned the line, and on coming to a little stream of water, I undressed for the purpose of bathing, and after undressing found my arm all battered and bruised and bloodshot from my wrist to my shoulder, and as sore as a blister. I had shot one hundred and twenty times that day. My gun became so hot that frequently the powder would flash before I could ram home the ball, and I had frequently to exchange my gun for that of a dead comrade.

Colonel H. R. Field was loading and shooting the same as any private in the ranks when he fell off the skid from which he was shooting right over my shoulder, shot through the head. I laid him down in the trench, and he said, "Well, they have got me at last, but I have killed fifteen of them; time about is fair play, I reckon." But Colonel Field was not killed—only wounded, and one side paralyzed. Captain Joe P. Lee, Captain Mack Campbell, Lieutenant T. H. Maney, and other officers of the regiment, threw rocks and beat them in their faces with sticks. The Yankees did the same. The rocks came in upon us like a perfect hail storm, and the Yankees seemed very obstinate, and in no hurry to get away from our front, and we had to keep up the firing and shooting them down in self-defense. They seemed to walk up and take death as coolly as if they were automatic or wooden men, and our boys did not shoot for the fun of the thing. It was, verily, a life and death grapple, and the least flicker on our part, would have been sure death to all. We could not be reinforced on account of our position, and we had to stand up to the rack, fodder or no fodder. When the Yankees fell back, and the firing ceased, I never saw so many broken down and exhausted men in my life. I was as sick as a horse, and as wet with blood and sweat as I could be, and many of our men were vomiting with excessive fatigue, over-exhaustion, and sunstroke; our tongues were parched and cracked for water, and our faces blackened with powder and smoke, and our dead and wounded were piled indiscriminately in the trenches. There was not a single man in the company who was not wounded, or had holes shot through his hat and clothing. Captain Beasley was killed, and nearly all his company killed and wounded. The Rock City Guards were almost piled in heaps and so was our company. Captain Joe P. Lee was badly wounded. Poor Walter Hood and Jim Brandon were lying there among us, while their spirits were in heaven; also, William A. Hughes, my old mess-mate and friend, who had clerked with me for S. F. & J. M. Mayes, and who had slept with me for lo! these many years, and a boy who loved me more than any other person on earth has ever done. I had just discharged the contents of my gun into the bosoms of two men, one right behind the other, killing them both, and was re-loading, when a Yankee rushed upon me, having me at a disadvantage, and said, "You have killed my two brothers, and now I've got you." Everything I had ever done rushed through my mind. I heard the roar, and felt the flash of fire, and saw my more than friend, William A. Hughes, grab the muzzle of the gun, receiving the whole contents in his hand and arm, and mortally wounding him. Reader, he died for me. In saving my life, he lost his own. When the infirmary corps carried him off, all mutilated and bleeding he told them to give me "Florence Fleming" (that was the name of his gun, which he had put on it in silver letters), and to give me his blanket and clothing. He gave his life for me, and everything that he had. It was the last time that I ever saw him, but I know that away up yonder, beyond the clouds, blackness, tempest and night, and away above the blue vault of heaven, where the stars keep their ceaseless vigils, away up yonder in the golden city of the New Jerusalem, where God and Jesus Christ, our Savior, ever reign, we will sometime meet at the marriage supper of the Son of God, who gave His life for the redemption of the whole world.

For several nights they made attacks upon our lines, but in

every attempt, they were driven back with great slaughter. They would ignite the tape of bomb shells, and throw them over in our lines, but, if the shell did not immediately explode, they were thrown back. They had a little shell called *hand grenade*, but they would either stop short of us, or go over our heads, and were harmless. General Joseph E. Johnston sent us a couple of *chevaux-de-frise*. When they came, a detail of three men had to roll them over the works. Those three men were heroes. Their names were Edmund Brandon, T. C. Dornin, and Arnold Zellner. Although it was a solemn occasion, every one of us was convulsed with laughter at the ridiculous appearance and actions of the detail. Every one of them made their wills and said their prayers truthfully and honestly, before they undertook the task. I laugh now every time I think of the ridiculous appearance of the detail, but to them it was no laughing matter. I will say that they were men who feared not, nor faltered in their duty. They were men, and today deserve the thanks of the people of the South. That night about midnight, an alarm was given that the Yankees were advancing. They would only have to run about twenty yards before they would be in our works. We were ordered to "shoot." Every man was hallooing at the top of his voice, "Shoot, shoot, tee, shoot, shootee." On the alarm, both the Confederate and Federal lines opened, with both small arms and artillery, and it seemed that the very heavens and earth were in a grand conflagration, as they will be at the final judgment, after the resurrection. I have since learned that this was a false alarm, and that no attack had been meditated.

Previous to the day of attack, the soldiers had cut down all the trees in our immediate front, throwing the tops down hill and sharpening the limbs of the same, thus making, as we thought, an impenetrable *abattis* of vines and limbs locked together; but nothing stopped or could stop the advance of the Yankee line, but the hot shot and cold steel that we poured into their faces from under our head-logs.

One of the most shameful and cowardly acts of Yankee

treachery was committed there that I ever remember to have seen. A wounded Yankee was lying right outside of our works, and begging most piteously for water, when a member of the railroad company (his name was Hog Johnson, and the very man who stood videt with Theodore Sloan and I at the battle of Missionary Ridge, and who killed the three Yankees, one night, from Fort Horsley), got a canteen of water, and gave the dying Yankee a drink, and as he started back, he was killed dead in his tracks by a treacherous Yankee hid behind a tree. It matters not, for somewhere in God's Holy Word, which cannot lie, He says that "He that giveth a cup of cold water in my name, shall not lose his reward." And I have no doubt, reader, in my own mind, that the poor fellow is reaping his reward in Emanuel's land with the good and just. In every instance where we tried to assist their wounded, our men were killed or wounded. A poor wounded and dying boy, not more than sixteen years of age, asked permission to crawl over our works, and when he had crawled to the top, and just as Blair Webster and I reached up to help the poor fellow, he, the Yankee, was killed by his own men. In fact, I have ever thought that is why the slaughter was so great in our front, that nearly, if not as many, Yankees were killed by their own men as by us. The brave ones, who tried to storm and carry our works, were simply between two fires. It is a singular fanaticism, and curious fact, that enters the mind of a soldier, that it is a grand and glorious death to die on a victorious battlefield. One morning the Sixth and Ninth Regiments came to our assistance—not to relieve us—but only to assist us, and every member of our regiment—First and Twenty-seventh— got as mad as a "wet hen." They felt almost insulted, and I believe we would soon have been in a free fight, had they not been ordered back. As soon as they came up every one of us began to say, "Go back! go back! we can hold this place, and by the eternal God we are not going to leave it." General Johnston came there to look at the position, and told us that a transverse line was about one hundred yards in our rear, and should they come on us too heavy to fall back to that line, when almost every one of us said, "You go back and look at other lines, this place is safe, and can never be taken." And then when they had dug a tunnel under us to blow us up, we laughed, yea, even rejoiced, at the fact of soon being blown sky high. Yet, not a single man was willing to leave his post. When old Joe sent us the two *chevaux-de-frise*, and kept on sending us water, and rations, and whisky, and tobacco, and word to hold our line, we would invariably send word back to rest easy, and that all is well at Dead Angle. I have ever thought that is one reason why General Johnston fell back from this Kennesaw line, and I will say today, in 1882, that while we appreciated his sympathies and kindness toward us, yet we did not think hard of old Joe for having so little confidence in us at that time. A perfect hail of minnie balls was being continually poured into our head-logs the whole time we remained here. The Yankees would hold up small looking-glasses, so that our strength and breastworks could be seen in the reflection in the glass; and they also had small mirrors on the butts of their guns, so arranged that they could hight up the barrels of their guns by looking through these glasses, while they themselves would not be exposed to our fire, and they kept up this continual firing day and night, whether they could see us or not. Sometimes a glancing shot from our head-logs would wound some one.

But I cannot describe it as I would wish. I would be pleased to mention the name of every soldier, not only of Company H alone, but every man in the First and Twenty-seventh Tennessee Consolidated Regiments on this occasion, but I cannot now remember their names, and will not mention any one in particular, fearing to do injustice to some whom I might inadvertently omit. Every man and every company did their duty. Company G, commanded by Captain Mack Campbell, stood side by side with us on this occasion, as they ever had during the whole war. But soldiers of the First and Twenty-seventh Regiments, it is with a feeling of pride and satisfaction to me, today, that I was associated with so many noble and brave men, and who were subsequently complimented by Jeff Davis, then President of the Confederate States of America, in person, who said, "That every member of our regiment was fit to be a captain"—his very words. I mention Captain W. C. Flournoy, of Company K, the Martin Guards; Captain Ledbetter, of the Rutherford Rifles; Captains Kelley and Steele, of the Rock City Guards, and Captain Adkisson, of the Williamson Grays, and Captain Fulcher, and other names of brave and heroic men, some of whom live today, but many have crossed the dark river and are "resting under the shade of the trees" on the other shore, waiting and watching for us, who are left to do justice to their memory and our cause, and when we old Rebels have accomplished God's purpose on earth, we, too, will be called to give an account of our battles, struggles, and triumphs.

Reader mine, I fear that I have wearied you with too long a description of the battle of "Dead Angle," if so, please pardon me, as this is but a sample of the others which will now follow each other in rapid succession. And, furthermore, in stating the above facts, the half has not been told, but it will give you a faint idea of the hard battles and privations and hardships of the soldiers in that stormy epoch—who died, grandly, gloriously, nobly; dyeing the soil of old mother earth, and enriching the same with their crimson life's blood, while doing what? Only trying to protect their homes and families, their property, their constitution and their laws, that had been guaranteed to them as a heritage forever by their forefathers. They died for the faith that each state was a separate sovereign government, as laid down by the Declaration of Independence and the Constitution of our fathers.

Battle of New Hope Church

We were on a forced march along a dusty road. I never in my whole life saw more dust. The dust fairly popped under our feet, like tramping in a snow-drift, and our eyes, and noses, and mouths, were filled with the dust that arose from our footsteps, and to make matters worse, the boys all tried to kick up a "bigger dust." Cavalry and artillery could not be seen at ten paces, being perfectly enveloped in dust. It was a perfect fog of dust.

We were marching along, it then being nearly dark, when we heard the hoarse boom of a cannon in our rear. It sounded as if it had a bad attack of croup. It went, "Croup, croup, croup." The order was given to "about face, double quick, march." We double quicked back to the old church on the road side, when the First Tennessee Cavalry, commanded by Colonel Lewis, and the Ninth Battalion, commanded by Major James H. Akin, passed us, and charged the advance of the Federal forces. We were supporting the cavalry. We heard them open. Deadly missiles were flying in every direction. The peculiar thud of spent balls and balls with shucks tied to their tails were passing over our heads. We were expecting that the cavalry would soon break, and that we would be ordered into action. But the news came from the front, that the cavalry were not only holding their position, but were driving the enemy. The earth jarred and trembled; the fire fiend seemed unchained; wounded men were coming from the front. I asked the litter corps, "Who have you there?" And one answered, "Captain Asa G. Freeman." I asked if he was dangerously wounded, and he simply said, "Shot through both thighs," and passed on. About this time we heard the whoops and cheers of the cavalry, and knew that the Yankees were whipped and falling back. We marched forward and occupied the place held by the cavalry. The trees looked as if they had been cut down for new ground, being mutilated and shivered by musket and cannon balls. Horses were writhing in their death agony, and the sickening odor of battle filled the air. Well, well, those who go to battle may expect to die. An halo ever surrounds the soldier's life, because he is ever willing to die for his country.

Battle of Dallas—Breckinridge Charges the Heights

We are ordered to march to Dallas.

Reader, somehow the name and character of General John C. Breckinridge charms me. That morning he looked grand and glorious. His infantry, artillery, and cavalry were drawn up in line of battle in our immediate front. He passed along the line, and stopping about the center of the column, said, "Soldiers, we have been selected to go forward and capture yon heights. Do you think we can take them? I will lead the attack." The men whooped, and the cry, "We can, we can," was heard from one end of the line to the other. Then, "Forward, guide center, march!" were words re-repeated by colonels and captains. They debouched through the woods, and passed out of sight in a little ravine, when we saw them emerge in an open field and advance right upon the Federal breastworks. It was the grandest spectacle I ever witnessed. We could see the smoke and dust of battle, and hear the shout of the charge, and the roar and rattle of cannon and musketry. But Breckinridge's division continued to press forward, without wavering or hesitating. We can see the line of dead and wounded along the track over which he passed, and finally we see our battle flag planted upon the Federal breastworks. I cannot describe the scene. If you, reader, are an old soldier, you can appreciate my failure to give a pen picture of battle. But Breckinridge could not long hold his position. Why we were not ordered forward to follow up his success, I do not know; but remember, reader, I am not writing history. I try only to describe events as I witnessed them.

We marched back to the old church on the roadside, called New Hope church, and fortified, occupying the battlefield of the day before. The stench and sickening odor of dead men and horses were terrible. We had to breathe the putrid atmosphere.

The next day, Colonel W. M. Voorhies' Forty-eighth Tennessee Regiment took position on our right. Now, here were all the Maury county boys got together at New Hope church. I ate dinner with Captain Joe Love, and Frank Frierson filled my haversack with hardtack and bacon.

Battle of Zion Church, July 4th, 1864

The 4th day of July, twelve months before, Pemberton had surrendered twenty-five thousand soldiers, two hundred pieces of artillery, and other munitions of war in proportion, at Vicksburg.

The Yankees wanted to celebrate the day. They thought it was their lucky day; but old Joe thought he had as much right to celebrate the Sabbath day of American Independence as the Yankees had, and we celebrated it. About dawn, continued boom of cannon reverberated over the hills as if firing a Fourth of July salute. I was standing on top of our works, leveling them off with a spade. A sharpshooter fired at me, but the ball missed me and shot William A. Graham through the heart. He was as noble and brave a soldier as ever drew the breath of life, and lacked but a few votes of being elected captain of Company H, at the reorganization. He was smoking his pipe when he was shot. We started to carry him to the rear, but he remarked, "Boys, it is useless; please lay me down and let me die." I have never in my life seen any one meet death more philosophically. He was dead in a moment. General A. J. Vaughan, commanding General Preston Smith's brigade, had his foot shot off by a cannon ball a few minutes afterwards.

It seemed that both Confederate and Federal armies were celebrating the Fourth of July. I cannot now remember a more severe artillery duel. Two hundred cannon were roaring and belching like blue blazes. It was but a battle of cannonade all day long. It seemed as though the Confederate and Federal cannons were talking to each other. Sometimes a ball passing over would seem to be mad, then again some would seem to be laughing, some would be mild, some sad, some gay, some sorrowful, some rollicking and jolly; and then again some would scream like the ghosts of the dead. In fact, they gave forth every kind of sound that you could imagine. It reminded one of when two storms meet in mid-ocean—the mountain billows of waters coming from two directions, lash against the vessel's side, while the elements are filled with roaring, thundering and lightning. You could almost feel the earth roll and rock like a drunken man, or a ship, when she rides the billows in an awful storm. It seemed that the earth was frequently moved from its foundations, and you could hear it grate as it moved. But all through that storm of battle, every soldier stood firm, for we knew that old Joe was at the helm.

Kingston

Here General Johnston issued his first battle order, that thus far he had gone and intended to go no further. His line of battle was formed; his skirmish line was engaged; the artillery was booming from the Rebel lines. Both sides were now face to face. There were no earthworks on either side. It was to be an open field and a fair fight, when—"Fall back!" What's the matter? I do not know how we got the news, but here is what is told us—and so it was, every position we ever took. When we fell back the news would be, "Hood's line is being enfiladed, and they are decimating his men, and he can't hold his position." But we fell back and took a position at

Cassville

Our line of battle was formed at Cassville. I never saw our troops happier or more certain of success. A sort of grand halo illumined every soldier's face. You could see self-confidence in the features of every private soldier. We were confident of victory and success. It was like going to a frolic or a wedding. Joy was welling up in every heart. We were going to whip and rout the Yankees. It seemed to be anything else than a fight. The soldiers were jubilant. Gladness was depicted on every countenance. I honestly believe that had a battle been fought at this place, every soldier would have distinguished himself. I believe a sort of fanaticism had entered their souls, that whoever was killed would at once be carried to the seventh heaven. I am sure of one thing, that every soldier had faith enough in old Joe to have charged Sherman's whole army. When "Halt!" "Retreat!" What is the matter? General Hood says they are enfilading his line, and are decimating his men, and he can't hold his position.

The same old story repeats itself. Old Joe's army is ever face to face with Sherman's incendiaries. We have faith in old Joe's ability to meet Sherman whenever he dares to attack. The soldiers draw their regular rations. Every time a blue coat comes in sight, there is a dead Yankee to bury. Sherman is getting cautious, his army hacked. Thus we continue to fall back for four months, day by day, for one hundred and ten days, fighting every day and night.

On the Banks of the Chattahoochee

Our army had crossed the Chattahoochee. The Federal army was on the other side; our pickets on the south side, the Yankees on the north side. By a tacit agreement, as had ever been the custom, there was no firing across the stream. That was considered the boundary. It mattered not how large or small the stream, pickets rarely fired at each other. We would stand on each bank, and laugh and talk and brag across the stream.

One day, while standing on the banks of the Chattahoochee, a Yankee called out:

"Johnny, O, Johnny, O, Johnny Reb."

Johnny answered, "What do you want?"

"You are whipped, aren't you?"

"No. The man who says that is a liar, a scoundrel, and a coward."

"Well, anyhow, Joe Johnston is relieved of the command."

"What?"

"General Joseph E. Johnston is relieved."

"What is that you say?"

"General Joseph E. Johnston is relieved, and Hood appointed in his place."

"You are a liar, and if you will come out and show yourself I will shoot you down in your tracks, you lying Yankee galloot."

"That's more than I will stand. If the others will hands off, I will fight a duel with you. Now, show your manhood."

Well, reader, every word of this is true, as is everything in this book. Both men loaded their guns and stepped out to their places. They were both to load and fire at will, until one or both were killed. They took their positions without either trying to get the advantage of the other. Then some one gave the command to "Fire at will; commence firing." They fired seven shots each; at the seventh shot, poor Johnny Reb fell a corpse, pierced through the heart.

Removal of General Joseph E. Johnston

Such was the fact. General Joseph E. Johnston had been removed and General J. B. Hood appointed to take command. Generals Hardee and Kirby Smith, two old veterans, who had been identified with the Army of Tennessee from the beginning, resigned. We had received the intelligence from the Yankees.

The relief guard confirmed the report.

All the way from Rocky Face Ridge to Atlanta was a battle of a hundred days, yet Hood's line was all the time enfiladed and his men decimated, and he could not hold his position. Old Joe Johnston had taken command of the Army of Tennessee when it was crushed and broken, at a time when no other man on earth could have united it. He found it in rags and tatters, hungry and heart-broken, the morale of the men gone, their manhood vanished to the winds, their pride a thing of the past. Through his instrumentality and skillful manipulation, all these had been restored. We had been under his command nearly twelve months. He was more popular with his troops day by day. We had made a long and arduous campaign, lasting four months; there was not a single day in that four months that did not find us engaged in battle with the enemy. History does not record a single instance of where one of his lines was ever broken—not a single rout. He had not lost a single piece of artillery; he had dealt the enemy heavy blows; he was whipping them day by day, yet keeping his own men intact; his men were in as good spirits and as sure of victory at the end of four months as they were at the beginning; instead of the army being depleted, it had grown in strength. 'Tis true, he had fallen back, but it was to give his enemy the heavier blows. He brought all the powers of his army into play; ever on the defensive, 'tis true, yet ever striking his enemy in his most vulnerable part. His face was always to the foe. They could make no movement in which they were not anticipated. Such a man was Joseph E. Johnston, and such his record. Farewell, old fellow! We privates loved you because you made us love ourselves. Hardee, our old corps commander, whom we had followed for nearly four years, and whom we had loved and respected from the beginning, has left us. Kirby Smith has resigned and gone home. The spirit of our good and honored Leonidas Polk is in heaven, and his body lies yonder on the Kennesaw line. General Breckinridge and other generals resigned.[1] I lay down my pen; I can write no more; my heart is too full. Reader, this is the saddest chapter I ever wrote.

But now, after twenty years, I can see where General Joseph E. Johnston made many blunders in not attacking Sherman's line at some point. He was better on the defensive than the aggressive, and hence, *bis peccare in bello non licet.*

General Hood Takes Command

It came like a flash of lightning, staggering and blinding every one. It was like applying a lighted match to an immense magazine. It was like the successful gambler, flushed with continual winnings, who staked his all and lost. It was like the end of the Southern Confederacy. Things that were, were not. It was the end. The soldier of the relief guard who brought us the news while picketing on the banks of the Chattahoochee, remarked, by way of imparting gently the information—

"Boys, we've fought all the war for nothing. There is nothing for us in store now."

"What's the matter now?"

"General Joe Johnston is relieved, Generals Hardee and Kirby Smith has resigned, and General Hood is appointed to take command of the Army of Tennessee."

"My God! is that so?"

"It is certainly a fact."

---

[1] The statements about resignations are erroneous. Hardee was greatly displeased by Hood's appointment and asked to be relieved or transferred. But Davis persuaded him to serve under the new commander.

"Then I'll never fire another gun. Any news or letters that you wish carried home? I've quit, and am going home. Please tender my resignation to Jeff Davis as a private soldier in the C. S. Army."

Five men of that picket—there were just five—as rapidly as they could, took off their cartridge-boxes, after throwing down their guns, and then their canteens and haversacks, taking out of their pockets their gun-wipers, wrench and gun-stoppers, and saying they would have no more use for "them things." They marched off, and it was the last we ever saw of them. In ten minutes they were across the river, and no doubt had taken the oath of allegiance to the United States government. Such was the sentiment of the Army of Tennessee at that time.

Chapter 13

Atlanta

Hood Strikes

G ENERAL JOHN B. HOOD had the reputation of being a fighting man, and wishing to show Jeff Davis what a "bully" fighter he was, lights in on the Yankees on Peachtree creek. But that was "I give a dare" affair. General William B. Bate's division gained their works, but did not long hold them.

Our division, now commanded by General John C. Brown, was supporting Bate's division; our regiment supporting the Hundred and Fifty-fourth Tennessee, which was pretty badly cut to pieces, and I remember how mad they seemed to be, because they had to fall back.

Hood thought he would strike while the iron was hot, and while it could be hammered into shape, and make the Yankees believe that it was the powerful arm of old Joe that was wielding the sledge.

But he was like the fellow who took a piece of iron to the shop, intending to make him an ax. After working for some time and failing, he concluded he would make him a wedge, and, failing in this, said, "I'll make a skeow." So he heats the iron red-hot and drops it into the slacktub, and it went s-k-e-o-w, bubble, bubble, s-k-e-o-w, bust.

Killing a Yankee Scout

On the night of the 20th, the Yankees were on Peachtree creek, advancing toward Atlanta. I was a videt that night, on the outpost of the army. I could plainly hear the moving of their army, even the talking and laughing of the Federal soldiers. I was standing in an old sedge field. About midnight everything quieted down. I was alone in the darkness, left to watch while the army slept. The pale moon was on the wane, a little yellow arc, emitting but a dim light, and the clouds were lazily passing over it, while the stars seemed trying to wink and sparkle and make night beautiful. I thought of God, of heaven, of home, and I thought of Jennie—her whom I had ever loved, and who had given me her troth in all of her maiden purity, to be my darling bride so soon as the war was over. I thought of the scenes of my childhood, my school-boy days. I thought of the time when I left peace and home, for war and privations. I had Jennie's picture in my pocket Bible, alongside of a braid of her beautiful hair. And I thought of how good, how pure, and how beautiful was the woman, who, if I lived, would share my hopes and struggles, my happiness as well as troubles, and who would be my darling bride, and happiness would ever be mine. An owl had lit on an old tree near me and began to "hoo, hoo, hoo are you," and his mate would answer back from the lugubrious depths of the Chattahoochee swamps. A shivering owl also sat on the limb of a tree and kept up its dismal wailings. And ever now and then I could hear the tingle, tingle, tingle of a cow bell in the distance, and the shrill cry of the whip-poor-will. The shivering owl and whip-poor-will seemed to be in a sort of talk, and the jack-o'-lanterns seemed to be playing spirits—when, hush! what is that? listen! It might have been two o'clock, and I saw, or thought I saw, the dim outlines of a Yankee soldier, lying on the ground not more than ten steps from where I stood. I tried to imagine it was a stump or hallucination of the imagination. I looked at it again. The more I looked the more it assumed the outlines of a man. Something glistens in his eyes. Am I mistaken? Tut, tut, it's nothing but a stump; you are getting demoralized. What! it seems to be getting closer. There are two tiny specks that shine like the eyes of a cat in the dark. Look here, thought I, you are getting nervous. Well, I can stand this doubt and agony no longer; I am going to fire at that object anyhow, let come what will. I raised my gun, placed it to my shoulder, took deliberate aim, and fired, and waugh-weouw, the most unearthly scream I ever heard, greeted my ears. I broke and run to a tree nearby, and had just squatted behind it, when zip, zip, two balls from our picket post struck the tree in two inches of my head. I hallooed to our picket not to fire that it was "me," the videt. I went back, and says I, "Who fired those two shots?" Two fellows spoke up and said that they did it. No sooner was it spoken, than I was on them like a duck on a june-bug, *pugnis et calcibus*. We "fout and fit, and gouged and bit," right there in that picket post. I have the marks on my face and forehead where one of them struck me with a Yankee zinc canteen, filled with water. I do not know which whipped. My friends told me that I whipped both of them, and I suppose their friends told them that they had whipped me. All I know is, they both run, and I was bloody from head to foot, from where I had been cut in the forehead and face by the canteens. This all happened one dark night in the month of July, 1864, in the rifle pit in front of Atlanta. When day broke the next morning, I went forward to where I had shot at the "boogaboo" of the night before, and right there I found a dead Yankee soldier, fully accoutered for any emergency, his eyes wide open. I looked at him, and I said, "Old fellow, I am sorry for you; didn't know it was you, or I would have been worse scared than I was. You are dressed mighty fine, old fellow, but I don't want anything you have got, but your haversack." It was a nice haversack, made of chamois skin. I kept it until the end of the war, and when we surrendered at Greensboro, N. C., I had it on. But the other soldiers who were with me, went through him and found twelve dollars in greenback, a piece of tobacco, a gun-wiper and gun-stopper and wrench, a looking-glass and pocket-comb, and various and sundry other articles. I came across that dead Yankee two days afterwards, and he was as naked as the day he came into the world, and was as black as a negro, and was as big as a skinned horse. He had mortified. I recollect of saying, "Ugh, ugh," and of my hat being lifted off my head, by my hair, which stood up like the quills of the fretful porcupine. He scared me worse when dead than when living.

An Old Citizen

But after the little unpleasant episode in the rifle pit, I went back and took my stand. When nearly day, I saw the bright and beautiful star in the east rise above the tree tops, and the gray fog from off the river begun to rise, and every now and then could hear a far off chicken crow.

While I was looking toward the Yankee line, I saw a man riding leisurely along on horseback, and singing a sort of humdrum tune. I took him to be some old citizen. He rode on down the road toward me, and when he had approached, "Who goes there?" He immediately answered, "A friend." I thought that I recognized the voice in the darkness—and said I, "Who are you?" He spoke up, and gave me his name. Then, said I, "Advance, friend, but you are my prisoner." He rode on toward me, and I soon saw that it was Mr. Mumford Smith, the old sheriff of Maury county. I was very glad to see him, and as soon as the relief guard came, I went back to camp with him. I do not remember of ever in my life being more glad to see any person. He had brought a letter from home, from my father, and some Confederate old issue bonds, which I was mighty glad to get, and also a letter from "the gal I left behind me," enclosing a rosebud and two apple blossoms, resting on an arbor vitæ leaf, and this on a little piece of white paper, and on this was written a motto (which I will have to tell for the young folks), "Receive me, such as I am; would that I were of more use for your sake. Jennie." Now, that was the bouquet part. I would not like to tell you what was in that letter, but I read that letter over five hundred times, and remember it today. I think I can repeat the poetry *verbatim et literatim*, and will do so, gentle reader, if you don't laugh at me. I'm married now, and only write from memory, and never in my life have I read it in book or paper, and only in that letter—

"I love you, O, how dearly,
  Words too faintly but express;
This heart beats too sincerely,
  E'er in life to love you less;
No, my fancy never ranges,
  Hopes like mine, can never soar;
If the love I cherish, changes,
  'Twill only be to love you more."

Now, fair and gentle reader, this was the poetry, and you see for yourself that there was no "shenanigan" in that letter; and if a fellow "went back" on that sort of a letter, he would strike his "mammy." And then the letter wound up with "May God shield and protect you, and prepare you for whatever is in store for you, is the sincere prayer of Jennie." You may be sure that I felt good and happy, indeed.

My Friends

Reader mine, in writing these rapid and imperfect recollections, I find that should I attempt to write up all the details that I would not only weary you, but that these memoirs would soon become monotonous and uninteresting. I have written only of what I saw. Many little acts of kindness shown me by ladies and old citizens, I have omitted. I remember going to an old citizen's house, and he and the old lady were making clay pipes. I recollect how they would mold the pipes and put them in a red-hot stove to burn hard. Their kindness to me will never be forgotten. The first time that I went there they seemed very glad to see me, and told me that I looked exactly like their son who was in the army. I asked them what regiment he belonged to. After a moment's silence the old lady, her voice trembling as she spoke, said the Fourteenth Georgia, and then she began to cry. Then the old man said, "Yes, we have a son in the army. He went to Virginia the first year of the war, and we have never heard of him since. These wars are terrible, sir. The last time that we heard of him, he went with Stonewall Jackson away up in the mountains of West Virginia, toward Romney, and I did hear that while standing picket at a little place called Hampshire Crossing, on a little stream called St. John's Run, he and eleven others froze to death. We have never heard of him since." He got up and began walking up and down the room, his hands crossed behind his back. I buckled on my knapsack to go back to camp, and I shook hands with the two good old people, and they told me good-bye, and both said, "God bless you, God bless you." I said the same to them, and said, "I pray God to reward you, and bring your son safe home again." When I got back to camp I found cannon and caissons moving, and I knew and felt that General Hood was going to strike the enemy again. Preparations were going on, but everything seemed to be out of order and system. Men were cursing, and seemed to be dissatisfied and unhappy, but the army was moving.

A Body Without Limbs—An Army Without Cavalry

Forrest's cavalry had been sent to Mississippi; Wheeler's cavalry had been sent to North Carolina and East Tennessee. Hood had sent off both of his "arms"—for cavalry was always called the most powerful "arm" of the service. The infantry were the feet, and the artillery the body. Now, Hood himself had no legs, and but one arm, and that one in a sling. The most terrible and disastrous blow that the South ever received was when Hon. Jefferson Davis placed General Hood in command of the Army of Tennessee. I saw, I will say, thousands of men cry like babies—regular, old-fashioned boohoo, boohoo, boohoo.

Now, Hood sent off all his cavalry right in the face of a powerful army, by order and at the suggestion of Jeff Davis, and was using his cannon as "feelers." O, God! Ye gods! I get sick at heart even at this late day when I think of it.

I remember the morning that General Wheeler's cavalry filed by our brigade, and of their telling us, "Good-bye, boys, good-bye, boys." The First Tennessee Cavalry and Ninth Battalion were both made up in Maury county. I saw John J. Stephenson, my friend and step-brother, and David F. Watkins my own dear brother, and Arch Lipscomb, Joe Fussell, Captain Kinzer, Jack Gordon, George Martin, Major Dobbins, Colonel Lewis, Captain Galloway, Aaron and Sims Latta, Major J. H. Akin, S. H. Armstrong, Albert Dobbins, Alex Dobbins, Jim Cochran, Rafe Grisham, Captain Jim Polk, and many others with whom I was acquainted. They all said, "Good-bye, Sam, good-bye, Sam." I cried. I remember stopping the whole command and begging them to please not leave us; that if they did, Atlanta, and perhaps Hood's whole army, would surrender in a few days; but they told me, as near as I can now remember, "We regret to leave you, but we have to obey orders." The most ignorant private in the whole army saw everything that we had been fighting for for four years just scattered like chaff to the winds. All the Generals resigned, and those who did not resign were promoted; colonels were made brigadier-generals, captains were made colonels, and the private soldier, well, he deserted, don't you see? The private soldiers of the Army of Tennessee looked upon Hood as an over-rated general, but Jeff Davis did not.

Battle of July 22nd, 1864

Cannon balls, at long range, were falling into the city of Atlanta. Details of citizens put out the fires as they would occur from the burning shells. We could see the smoke rise and hear the shells pass away over our heads as they went on toward the doomed city.

One morning Cheatham's corps marched out and through the city, we knew not whither, but we soon learned that we were going to make a flank movement. After marching four or five miles, we "about faced" and marched back again to within two hundred yards of the place from whence we started. It was a "flank movement," you see, and had to be counted that way any-how. Well, now as we had made the flank movement, we had to storm and take the Federal lines, because we had made a flank movement, you see. When one army makes a flank movement it is courtesy on the part of the other army to recognize the flank movement, and to change his base. Why, sir, if you don't recognize a flank movement, you ain't a graduate of West Point. Hood was a graduate of West Point, and so was Sherman. But unfortunately there was Mynheer Dutchman commanding (McPherson had gone to dinner) the corps that had been flanked, and he couldn't speak English worth a cent. He, no doubt, had on board mein lager beer, so goot as vat never vas. I sweitzer, mein Got, you bet. Bang, bang, bang, goes our skirmish line advancing to the attack. Hans, vat fer ish dot shooting mit mein left wing? Ish dot der Repels, Hans?

The Attack

The plan of battle, as conceived and put into action by General Cleburne, was one of the boldest conceptions, and, at the same time, one of the most hazardous that ever occurred in our army during the war, but it only required nerve and pluck to carry it out, and General Cleburne was equal to the occasion. The Yankees had fortified on two ranges of hills, leaving a gap in their breastworks in the valley entirely unfortified and unprotected. They felt that they could enfilade the valley between the two lines so that no troop would or could attack at this weak point. This valley was covered with a dense undergrowth of trees and bushes. General Walker, of Georgia, was ordered to attack on the extreme right, which he did nobly and gallantly, giving his life for his country while leading his men, charging their breastworks. He was killed on the very top of their works. In the meantime General Cleburne's division was marching by the right flank in solid column, the same as if they were marching along the road, right up this valley, and thus passing between the Yankee lines and cutting them in two, when the command

by the left flank was given, which would throw them into line of
battle. By this maneuver, Cleburne's men were right upon their
flank, and enfilading their lines, while they were expecting an attack in their front. It was the finest piece of generalship and the
most successful of the war.

Shineral Mynheer Dutchman says, "Hans, mein Got! mein
Got! vare ish Shineral Mackferson, eh? Mein Got, mein Got! I
shust pelieve dot der Repel ish cooming. Hans, go cotch der filly
colt. Now, Hans, I vants to see vedder der filly colt mid stand fire.
You get on der filly colt, und I vill get pehind der house, und ven
you shust coome galloping py, I vill say 'B-o-o-h,' und if der filly
colt don't shump, den I vill know dot der filly colt mid stand fire."
Hans says, "Pap, being as you have to ride her in the battle, you
get on her, and let me say booh." Well, Shineral Mynheer gets on
the colt, and Hans gets behind the house, and as the general
comes galloping by, Hans had got an umbrella, and on seeing his
father approach, suddenly opens the umbrella, and hallowing at
the top of his voice b-o-o-h! *b-o-o-h!* B-O-O-H! The filly makes a
sudden jump and ker-flop comes down Mynheer. He jumps up
and says, "Hans, I alvays knowed dot you vas a vool. You make
too pig a booh; vy, you said booh loud enuff to scare der ole
horse. Hans, go pring out der ole horse. Der tam Repel vill be
here pefore Mackferson gits pack from der dinner time. I shust
peleve dot der Repel ish flanking, und dem tam fool curnells of
mein ish not got sense enuff to know ven Sheneral Hood is flanking. Hans, bring out der old horse, I vant to find out vedder
Mackferson ish got pack from der dinner time or not."

We were supporting General Cleburne's division. Our division (Cheatham's) was commanded by General John C. Brown.
Cleburne's division advanced to the attack. I was marching by
the side of a soldier by the name of James Galbreath, and a conscript from the Mt. Pleasant country. I never heard a man pray
and "go on" so before in my life. It actually made me feel sorry
for the poor fellow. Every time that our line would stop for a few
minutes, he would get down on his knees and clasp his hands
and commence praying. He kept saying, "O, my poor wife and

children! God have mercy on my poor wife and children! God pity me and have mercy on my soul!" Says I, "Galbreath, what are you making a fool of yourself that way for? If you are going to be killed, why you are as ready now as you ever will be, and you are making everybody feel bad; quit that nonsense." He quit, but kept mumbling to himself, "God have mercy! God have mercy!" Cleburne had reached the Yankee breastworks; the firing had been and was then terrific. The earth jarred, and shook, and trembled, at the shock of battle as the two armies met. Charge men! And I saw the Confederate flag side by side with the Federal flag. A courier dashed up and said, "General Cleburne has captured their works—advance and attack upon his immediate left. Attention, forward!" A discharge of cannon, and a ball tore through our ranks. I heard Galbreath yell out, "O, God, have mercy on my poor soul." The ball had cut his body nearly in two. Poor fellow, he had gone to his reward.

We advanced to the attack on Cleburne's immediate left. Cleburne himself was leading us in person, so that we would not fire upon his men, who were then inside the Yankee line. His sword was drawn. I heard him say, "Follow me, boys." He ran forward, and amid the blazing fires of the Yankee guns was soon on top of the enemy's works. He had on a bob-tail Confederate coat, which looked as if it had been cut out of a scrimp pattern. (You see I remember the little things.) We were but a few paces behind, following close upon him, and soon had captured their line of works. We were firing at the flying foe—astraddle of their lines of battle. This would naturally throw us in front, and Cleburne's corps supporting us. The Yankee lines seemed routed. We followed in hot pursuit; but from their main line of entrenchment—which was diagonal to those that we had just captured, and also on which they had built forts and erected batteries—was their artillery, raking us fore and aft. We passed over a hill and down into a valley being under the muzzles of this rampart of death. We had been charging and running, and had stopped to catch our breath right under their reserve and main line of battle. When General George Maney said, "Soldiers, you

are ordered to go forward and charge that battery. When you
start upon the charge I want you to go, as it were, upon the
wings of the wind. Shoot down and bayonet the cannoneers, and
take their guns at all hazards." Old Pat Cleburne thought he had
better put in a word to his soldiers. He says, "You hear what
General Maney says, boys. If they don't take it, by the eternal
God, you have got to take it!" I heard an Irishman of the "bloody
Tinth," and a "darn good regiment, be jabbers," speak up, and
say, "Faith, gineral, we'll take up a collection and buy you a
batthery, be Jasus." About this time our regiment had re-formed,
and had got their breath, and the order was given to charge, and
take their guns even at the point of the bayonet. We rushed forward up the steep hill sides, the seething fires from ten thousand
muskets and small arms, and forty pieces of cannon hurled right
into our very faces, scorching and burning our clothes, and
hands, and faces from their rapid discharges, and piling the
ground with our dead and wounded almost in heaps. It seemed
that the hot flames of hell were turned loose in all their fury,
while the demons of damnation were laughing in the flames, like
seething serpents hissing out their rage. We gave one long, loud
cheer, and commenced the charge. As we approached their lines,
like a mighty inundation of the river Acheron in the infernal regions, Confederate and Federal meet. Officers with drawn
swords meet officers with drawn swords, and man to man meets
man to man with bayonets and loaded guns. The continued roar
of battle sounded like unbottled thunder. Blood covered the
ground, and the dense smoke filled our eyes, and ears, and faces.
The groans of the wounded and dying rose above the thunder of
battle. But being heavily supported by Cleburne's division, and
by General L. E. Polk's brigade, headed and led by General Cleburne in person, and followed by the First and Twenty-seventh
up the blazing crest, the Federal lines waver, and break and fly,
leaving us in possession of their breastworks, and the battlefield,
and I do not know how many pieces of artillery, prisoners and
small arms.

Here is where Major Allen, Lieutenant Joe Carney, Captain

Joe Carthell, and many other good and brave spirits gave their lives for the cause of their country. They lie today, weltering in their own life's blood. It was one of the bloody battles that characterized that stormy epoch, and it was the 22nd of July, and one of the hottest days I ever felt.

General George Maney led us in the heat of battle, and no general of the war acted with more gallantry and bravery during the whole war than did General George Maney on this occasion.

The victory was complete. Large quantities of provisions and army stores were captured. The Federals had abandoned their entire line of breastworks, and had changed their base. They were fortifying upon our left, about five miles off from their original position. The battlefield was covered with their dead and wounded soldiers. I have never seen so many battleflags left indiscriminately upon any battlefield. I ran over twenty in the charge, and could have picked them up everywhere; did pick up one, and was promoted to fourth corporal for gallantry in picking up a flag on the battlefield.

On the final charge that was made, I was shot in the ankle and heel of my foot. I crawled into their abandoned ditch, which then seemed full and running over with our wounded soldiers. I dodged behind the embankment to get out of the raking fire that was ripping through the bushes, and tearing up the ground. Here I felt safe. The firing raged in front; we could hear the shout of the charge and the clash of battle. While I was sitting here, a cannon ball came tearing down the works, cutting a soldier's head off, spattering his brains all over my face and bosom, and mangling and tearing four or five others to shreds. As a wounded horse was being led off, a cannon ball struck him, and he was literally ripped open, falling in the very place I had just moved from.

I saw an ambulance coming from toward the Yankee line, at full gallop, saw them stop at a certain place, hastily put a dead man in the ambulance, and gallop back toward the Yankee lines. I did not know the meaning of this maneuver until after the battle, when I learned that it was General McPherson's dead body.

We had lost many a good and noble soldier. The casualties on our side were frightful. Generals, colonels, captains, lieutenants, sergeants, corporals and privates were piled indiscriminately everywhere. Cannon, caissons, and dead horses were piled pell-mell. It was the picture of a real battlefield. Blood had gathered in pools, and in some instances had made streams of blood. 'Twas a picture of carnage and death.

Am Promoted

"Why, hello, corporal, where did you get those two yellow stripes from on your arm?"

"Why, sir, I have been promoted for gallantry on the battlefield, by picking up an orphan flag, that had been run over by a thousand fellows, and when I picked it up I did so because I thought it was pretty, and I wanted to have me a shirt made out of it."

"I could have picked up forty, had I known that," said Sloan.

"So could I, but I knew that the stragglers would pick them up."

Reader mine, the above dialogue is true in every particular. As long as I was in action, fighting for my country, there was no chance for promotion, but as soon as I fell out of ranks and picked up a forsaken and deserted flag, I was promoted for it. I felt "sorter" cheap when complimented for gallantry, and the high honor of fourth corporal was conferred upon me. I felt that those brave and noble fellows who had kept on in the charge were more entitled to the honor than I was, for when the ball struck me on the ankle and heel, I did not go any further. And had I only known that picking up flags entitled me to promotion and that every flag picked up would raise me one notch higher, I would have quit fighting and gone to picking up flags, and by that means I would have soon been President of the Confederate States of America. But honors now begin to cluster around my brow. This is the laurel and ivy that is entwined around the noble brows of victorious and renowned generals. I honestly earned the exalted honor of fourth corporal by picking up a Yankee battle-flag on the 22nd day of July, at Atlanta.

28th of July at Atlanta

Another battle was fought by Generals Stephen D. Lee and Stewart's corps, on the 28th day of July. I was not in it, neither was our corps, but from what I afterwards learned, the Yankees got the best of the engagement. But our troops continued fortifying Atlanta. No other battles were ever fought at this place.

I Visit Montgomery

Our wounded were being sent back to Montgomery. My name was put on the wounded list. We were placed in a box-car, and whirling down to West Point, where we changed cars for Montgomery. The cars drew up at the depot at Montgomery, and we were directed to go to the hospital. When we got off the cars, little huckster stands were everywhere—apples, oranges, peaches, watermelons, everything. I know that I never saw a greater display of eatables in my whole life. I was particularly attracted toward an old lady's stand; she had bread, fish, and hard boiled eggs. The eggs were what I was hungry for. Says I:

"Madam, how do you sell your eggs?"

"Two for a dollar," she said.

"How much is your fish worth?"

"A piece of bread and a piece of fish for a dollar."

"Well, madam, put out your fish and eggs." The fish were hot and done to a crisp—actually frying in my mouth, crackling and singing as I bit off a bite. It was good, I tell you. The eggs were a little over half done. I soon demolished both, and it was only an appetizer. I invested a couple of dollars more, and thought that maybe I could make out till supper time. As I turned around, a smiling, one-legged man asked me if I wouldn't like to have a drink. Now, if there was anything that I wanted at that time, it was a drink.

"How do you sell it?" says I.

"A dollar a drink," said he.

"Pour me out a drink."

It was a tin cap-box. I thought that I knew the old fellow, and he kept looking at me as if he knew me. Finally, he said to me:

"It seems that I ought to know you."

I told him that I reckon he did, as I had been there.

"Ain't your name Sam?" said he.

"That is what my mother called me."

Well, after shaking hands, it suddenly flashed upon me who the old fellow was. I knew him well. He told me that he belonged to Captain Ed. O'Neil's company, Second Tennessee Regiment, General William B. Bate's corps, and that his leg had been shot off at the first battle of Manassas, and at that time he was selling cheap whisky and tobacco for a living at Montgomery, Alabama. I tossed off a cap-box full and paid him a dollar. It staggered me, and I said:

"That is raw whisky."

"Yes," said he, "all my cooked whisky is out."

"If this is not quite cooked, it is as hot as fire anyhow, and burns like red-hot lava, and the whole dose seems to have got lodged in my windpipe."

I might have tasted it, but don't think that I did. All I can remember now, is a dim recollection of a nasty, greasy, burning something going down my throat and chest, and smelling, as I remember at this day, like a decoction of red-pepper tea, flavored with coal oil, turpentine and tobacco juice.

The Hospital

I went to the hospital that evening, saw it, and was satisfied with hospital life. I did not wish to be called a hospital rat. I had no idea of taking stock and making my headquarters at this place. Everything seemed clean and nice enough, but the smell! Ye gods! I stayed there for supper. The bill of fare was a thin slice of light bread and a plate of soup, already dished out and placed at every plate. I ate it, but it only made me hungry. At nine o'clock I had to go to bed, and all the lights were put out. Every man had a little bunk to himself. I do not know whether I slept or not, but I have a dim recollection of "sawing gourds," and jumping up several times to keep some poor wretch from strangling. He was only snoring. I heard rats filing away at night, and thought that burglars were trying to get in; my dreams were not pleasant, if I went to sleep at all. I had not slept off of the ground or in a house in three years. It was something new to me, and I could not sleep, for the room was so dark that had I got up I could not have found my way out. I laid there, I do not know how long, but I heard a rooster crow, and a dim twilight began to glimmer in the room, and even footsteps were audible in the rooms below. I got sleepy then, and went off in a doze. I had a beautiful dream—dreamed that I was in heaven, or rather, that a pair of stairs with richly carved balusters and wings, and golden steps overlaid with silk and golden-colored carpeting came down from heaven to my room; and two beautiful damsels kept peeping, and laughing, and making faces at me from the first platform of these steps; and every now and then they would bring out their golden harps, and sing me a sweet and happy song. Others were constantly passing, but always going the same way. They looked like so many schoolgirls, all dressed in shining garments. Two or three times the two beautiful girls would go up the stairs and return, bringing fruits and vegetables that shined like pure gold. I knew that I never had seen two more beautiful beings on earth. The steps began to lengthen out, and seemed to be all around me; they seemed to shine a halo of glory all about. The two ladies came closer, and closer, passing around, having a beautiful wreath of flowers in each hand, and gracefully throwing them backward and forward as they laughed and danced around me. Finally one stopped and knelt down over me and whispered something in my ear. I threw up my arms to clasp the beautiful vision to my bosom, when I felt my arm grabbed, and "D—n ye, I wish you would keep your d—n arm off my wound, ye hurt me," came from the soldier in the next bunk. The sun was shining full in my face. I got up and went down to breakfast. The bill of fare was much better for breakfast than it had been for supper; in fact it was what is called a "jarvis" breakfast. After breakfast, I took a ramble around the city. It was a nice place, and merchandise and other business was being carried on as if there was no war. Hotels were doing a thriving business; steamboats were at the wharf, whistling and playing their calliopes. I remember the one I heard was playing "Away Down on the Sewanee River." To me it seemed that everybody was smiling, and happy, and prosperous.

The Capitol

I went to the capitol, and it is a fine building overlooking the city. When I got there, I acted just like everybody that ever visited a fine building—they wanted to go on top and look at the landscape. That is what they all say. Now, I always wanted to go on top, but I never yet thought of landscape. What I always wanted to see, was how far I could look, and that is about all that any of them wants. It's mighty nice to go up on a high place with your sweetheart, and hear her say, "La! ain't it b-e-a-u-t-i-f-u-l," "Now, now, please don't go there," and how you walk up pretty close to the edge and spit over, to show what a brave man you are. It's "bully," I tell you. Well, I wanted to go to the top of the capitol—I went; wanted to go up in the cupola. Now, there was an iron ladder running up across an empty space, and you could see two hundred feet below from this cupola or dome on top. The ladder was about ten feet long, spanning the dome. It was very easy to go up, because I was looking up all the time, and I was soon on top of the building. I saw how far I could see, and saw the Alabama river, winding and turning until it seemed no larger than a silver thread. Well, I am very poor at describing and going into ecstacies over fancies. I want some abler pen to describe the scene. I was not thinking about the scene or the landscape—I was thinking how I was going to get down that ladder again. I would come to that iron ladder and peep over, and think if I fell, how far would I have to fall. The more I thought about going down that ladder, the more I didn't feel like going down. Well, I felt that I had rather die than go down that ladder.

I'm honest in this. I felt like jumping off and committing suicide rather than go down that ladder. I crossed right over the frightful chasm, but when forbearance ceased to be a virtue, I tremblingly put my foot on the first rung, then grabbed the top of the two projections. There I remained, I don't know how long, but after awhile I reached down with one foot and touched the next rung. After getting that foot firmly placed, I ventured to risk the other foot. It was thus for several backward steps, until I come to see down—away down, down, down below me—and my head got giddy. The world seemed to be turning round and round. A fellow at the bottom hallooed, "Look up! look up, mister! look up!" I was not a foot from the upper floor. As soon as I looked at the floor, everything got steady. I kept my eyes fixed on the top of the building, and soon made the landing on *terra firma*.

I have never liked high places since. I never could bear to go upstairs in a house. I went to the capitol at Nashville, last winter, and McAndrews wanted me to go up in the cupola with him. He went, and paid a quarter for the privilege. I stayed, and—well, if I could estimate its value by dollars—I would say two hundred and fifty million dollars is what I made by staying down.

Am Arrested

The next day, while the ferryboat was crossing the river, I asked the ferryman to let me ride over. I was halted by a soldier who "knowed" his business.

"Your pass, sir!"

"Well, I have no pass!"

"Well, sir, I will have to arrest you, and take you before the provost marshal."

"Very well, sir; I will go with you to the provost or anywhere else."

I appear before the provost marshal.

"What command do you belong to, sir?"

"Well, sir, I belong to Company H, First Tennessee Regiment. I am a wounded man sent to the hospital."

"Well, sir, that's too thin; why did you not get a pass?"

"I did not think one was required."

"Give me your name, sir."

I gave my name.

"Sergeant, take this name to the hospital and ask if such name is registered on their books."

I told him that I knew it was not. The sergeant returns and reports no such name, when he remarks:

"You have to go to the guard-house."

Says I, "Colonel (I knew his rank was that of captain), if you send me to the guard-house, you will do me a great wrong. Here is where I was wounded." I pulled off my shoe and began to unbandage.

"Well, sir, I don't want to look at your foot, and I have no patience with you. Take him to the guard-house."

Turning back I said, "Sir, aye, aye, you are clothed with a little brief authority, and appear to be presuming pretty heavy on that authority; but, sir"—well I have forgotten what I did say. The sergeant took me by the arm, and said, "Come, come, sir, I have my orders."

As I was going up the street, I met Captain Dave Buckner, and told him all the circumstances of my arrest as briefly as I could. He said, "Sergeant, bring him back with me to the provost marshal's office." They were as mad as wet hens. Their faces were burning, and I could see their jugular veins go thump, thump, thump. I do not know what Captain Buckner said to them, all I heard were the words "otherwise insulted me." But I was liberated, and was glad of it.

Those Girls

I then went back to the river, and gave a fellow two dollars to "row me over the ferry." I was in no particular hurry, and limped along at my leisure until about nightfall, when I came to a nice, cosy-looking farm house, and asked to stay all night. I was made very welcome, indeed. There were two very pretty girls here, and

I could have "loved either were 'tother dear charmer away." But I fell in love with both of them, and thereby overdid the thing. This was by a dim fire-light. The next day was Sunday, and we all went to church in the country. We went in an old rockaway carriage. I remember that the preacher used the words, "O, God," nineteen times in his prayer. I had made up my mind which one of the girls I would marry. Now, don't get mad, fair reader mine. I was all gallantry and smiles, and when we arrived at home, I jumped out and took hold the hand of my fair charmer to help her out. She put her foot out, and—well, I came very near telling—she tramped on a cat. The cat squalled.

The Talisman

But then, you know, reader, that I was engaged to Jennie and I had a talisman in my pocket Bible, in the way of a love letter, against the charms of other beautiful and interesting young ladies. Uncle Jimmie Rieves had been to Maury county, and, on returning to Atlanta, found out that I was wounded and in the hospital at Montgomery, and brought the letter to me; and, as I am married now, I don't mind telling you what was in the letter, if you won't laugh at me. You see, Jennie was my sweetheart, and here is my sweetheart's letter:

My Dear Sam.:—I write to tell you that I love you yet, and you alone; and day by day I love you more, and pray, every night and morning for your safe return home again. My greatest grief is that we heard you were wounded and in the hospital, and I cannot be with you to nurse you.

We heard of the death of many noble and brave men at Atlanta; and the death of Captain Carthell, Cousin Mary's husband. It was sent by Captain January; he belonged to the Twelfth Tennessee, of which Colonel Watkins was lieutenant-colonel.

The weather is very beautiful here, and the flowers in the garden are in full bloom, and the apples are getting ripe. I have gathered a small bouquet, which I will put in the letter; I also send by Uncle Jimmie a tobacco bag, and a watch-guard, made out of horse hair, and a woolen hood, knit with my own hands, with love and best respects.

We heard that you had captured a flag at Atlanta, and was promoted for it to corporal. Is that some high office? I know you will be a general yet, because I always hear of your being in every battle, and always the foremost man in the attack. Sam, please take care of yourself for my sake, and don't let the Yankees kill you. Well, good-bye, darling, I will ever pray for God's richest and choicest blessings upon you. Be sure and write a long, long letter— I don't care how long, to your loving and sincere

JENNIE.

The Brave Captain

When I got back to the Alabama river, opposite Montgomery, the ferryboat was on the other shore. A steamboat had just pulled out of its moorings and crossed over to where I was, and began to take on wood. I went on board, and told the captain, who was a clever and good man, that I would like to take a trip with him to Mobile and back, and that I was a wounded soldier from the hospital. He told me, "All right, come along, and I will foot expenses."

It was about sunset, but along the line of the distant horizon we could see the dark and heavy clouds begin to boil up in thick and ominous columns. The lightning was darting to and fro like lurid sheets of fire, and the storm seemed to be gathering; we could hear the storm king in his chariot in the clouds, rumbling as he came, but a dead lull was seen and felt in the air and in nature; everything was in a holy hush, except the hoarse belchings of the engines, the sizzing and frying of the boilers, and the work of the machinery on the lower deck. At last the storm burst upon us in all its fury; it was a tornado and the women and children began to scream and pray—the mate to curse and swear. I was standing by the captain on the main upper deck, as he was trying to direct the pilot how to steer the boat through that awful storm, when we heard the alarm bell ring out, and the hoarse cry of "Fire! fire! fire!" Men were running toward the fire with buckets, and the hose began throwing water on the flames. Men, women, and children were jumping in the water, and the captain used every effort to quiet the panic, and to land his boat with its passengers, but the storm and fire were too much, and down the vessel sank to rise no more. Many had been saved in the lifeboat, and many were drowned. I jumped overboard, and the last thing I saw was the noble and brave captain still ringing the bell, as the vessel went down. He went down amid the flames to fill a watery grave. The water was full of struggling and dying people for miles. I did not go to Mobile.

How I Get Back to Atlanta

When I got to Montgomery, the cars said toot, toot, and I raised the hue and cry and followed in pursuit. Kind friends, I fear that I have wearied you with my visit to Montgomery, but I am going back to camp now, and will not leave it again until our banner is furled never to be again unfurled.

I, you remember, was without a pass, and did not wish to be carried a second time before that good, brave, and just provost marshal; and something told me not to go to the hospital. I found out when the cars would leave, and thought that I would get on them and go back without any trouble. I got on the cars, but was hustled off mighty quick, because I had no pass. A train of box-cars was about leaving for West Point, and I took a seat on top of one of them, and was again hustled off; but I had determined to go, and as the engine began to puff, and tug, and pull, I slipped in between two box-cars, sitting on one part of one and putting my feet on the other, and rode this way until I got to West Point. The conductor discovered me, and had put me off several times before I got to West Point, but I would jump on again as soon as the cars started. When I got to West Point, a train of cars started off, and I ran, trying to get on, when Captain Peebles reached out his hand and pulled me in, and I arrived safe and sound at Atlanta.

On my way back to Atlanta, I got with Dow Akin and Billy March. Billy March had been shot through the under jaw by a minnie ball at the octagon house, but by proper attention and nursing, he had recovered. Conner Akin was killed at the octagon house, and Dow wounded. When we got back to the regiment, then stationed near a fine concrete house (where Shepard and I would sleep every night), nearly right on our works, we found two thirty-two-pound parrot guns stationed in our immediate front, and throwing shells away over our heads into the city of Atlanta. We had just begun to tell all the boys howdy, when I saw Dow Akin fall. A fragment of shell had struck him on his backbone, and he was carried back wounded and bleeding. We could see the smoke boil up, and it would be nearly a minute before we would hear the report of the cannon, and then a few moments after we would hear the scream of the shell as it went on to Atlanta. We used to count from the time we would see the smoke boil up until we would hear the noise, and some fellow would call out, "Look out boys, the United States is sending iron over into the Southern Confederacy; let's send a little lead back to the United States." And we would blaze away with our Enfield and Whitworth guns, and every time we would fire, we would silence those parrot guns. This kind of fun was carried on for forty-six days.

Death of Tom Tuck's Rooster

Atlanta was a great place to fight chickens. I had heard much said about cock pits and cock fights, but had never seen such a thing. Away over the hill, outside of the range of Thomas' thirty-pound parrot guns, with which he was trying to burn up Atlanta, the boys had fixed up a cock pit. It was fixed exactly like a circus ring, and seats and benches were arranged for the spectators. Well, I went to the cock fight one day. A great many roosters were to be pitted that day, and each one was trimmed and gaffed. A gaff is a long keen piece of steel, as sharp as a needle, that is fitted over the spurs. Well, I looked on at the fun. Tom Tuck's rooster was named Southern Confederacy; but this was abbreviated to Confed., and as a pet name, they called him Fed. Well, Fed was a trained rooster, and would "clean up" a big-foot rooster as soon as he was put in the pit. But Tom always gave Fed every advantage. One day a green-looking country hunk came in with a rooster that he wanted to pit against Fed. He looked like a common rail-splitter. The money was soon made up, and the stakes placed in proper hands. The gaffs were fitted, the roosters were placed in the pit and held until both were sufficiently mad to fight, when they were turned loose, and each struck at the same time. I looked and poor Fed was dead. The other rooster had popped both gaffs through his head. He was a dead rooster; yea, a dead cock in the pit. Tom went and picked up his rooster, and said, "Poor Fed, I loved you; you used to crow every morning at day-light to wake me up. I have carried you a long time, but, alas! alas! poor Fed, your days are numbered, and those who fight will sometimes be slain. Now, friends, conscripts, countrymen, if you have any tears to shed, prepare to shed them now. I will not bury Fed. The evil that roosters do live after them, but the good is oft interred with their bones. So let it not be with Confed. Confed left no will, but I will pick him, and fry him, and dip my biscuit in his gravy. Poor Fed, Confed, Confederacy, I place one hand on my heart and one on my head, regretting that I have not another to place on my stomach, and whisper, softly whisper, in the most doleful accents, Good-bye, farewell, a long farewell."

> "Not a laugh was heard—not even a joke—
>   As the dead rooster in the camp-kettle they hurried;
> For Tom had lost ten dollars, and was broke,
>   In the cock-pit where Confed was buried.

"They cooked him slowly in the middle of the day,
  As the frying-pan they were solemnly turning;
The hungry fellows looking at him as he lay,
  With one side raw, the other burning.

"Some surplus feathers covered his breast,
  Not in a shroud, but in a tiara they soused him;
He lay like a 'picked chicken' taking his rest,
  While the Rebel boys danced and cursed around
    him.

"Not a few or short were the cuss words they said,
  Yet, they spoke many words of sorrow;
As they steadfastly gazed on the face of the dead,
  And thought 'what'll we do for chicken tomorrow?'

"Lightly they'll talk of the Southern Confed. that's gone,
  And o'er his empty carcass upbraid him;
But nothing he'll reck, if they let him sleep on,
  In the place where they have laid him.

"Sadly and slowly they laid him down,
  From the field of fame fresh and gory;
They ate off his flesh, and threw away his bones,
  And then left them alone in their glory."

When, cut, slash, bang, debang, and here comes a dash of Yankee cavalry, right in the midst of the camp, under whip and spur, yelling like a band of wild Comanches, and bearing right down on the few mourners around the dead body of Confed. After making this bold dash, they about faced, and were soon out of sight. There was no harm done, but, alas! that cooked chicken was gone. Poor Confed! To what a sad end you have come. Just to think, that but a few short hours ago, you was a proud rooster—was "cock of the walk," and was considered invincible. But, alas! you have sunk so low as to become food for Federals! *Requiescat in pace* you can crow no more.

Old Joe Brown's Pets

By way of grim jest, and a fitting burlesque to tragic scenes, or, rather, to the thing called "glorious war," old Joe Brown, then Governor of Georgia, sent in his militia. It was the richest picture of an army I ever saw. It beat Forepaugh's double-ringed circus. Every one was dressed in citizen's clothes, and the very best they had at that time. A few had double-barreled shot-guns, but the majority had umbrellas and walking-sticks, and nearly every one had on a duster, a flat-bosomed "biled" shirt, and a plug hat; and, to make the thing more ridiculous, the dwarf and the giant were marching side by side; the knock-kneed by the side of the bow-legged; the driven-in by the side of the drawn-out; the pale and sallow dyspeptic, who looked like Alex. Stephens, and who seemed to have just been taken out of a chimney that smoked very badly, and whose diet was goobers and sweet potatoes, was placed beside the three hundred-pounder, who was dressed up to kill, and whose looks seemed to say, "I've got a substitute in the army, and twenty negroes at home besides—h-a-a-m, h-a-a-m." Now, that is the sort of army that old Joe Brown had when he seceded from the Southern Confederacy, declaring that each state was a separate sovereign government of itself; and, as old Joe Brown was an original secessionist, he wanted to exemplify the grand principles of secession, that had been advocated by Patrick Henry, John Randolph, of Roanoke, and John C. Calhoun, in all of whom he was a firm believer. I will say, however, in all due deference to the Georgia militia and old Joe Brown's pets, that there was many a gallant and noble fellow among them. I remember on one occasion that I was detailed to report to a captain of the Fourth Tennessee Regiment (Colonel Farquharson, called "Guidepost"); I have forgotten that captain's name. He was a small-sized man, with a large, long set of black whiskers. He was the captain, and I the corporal of the detail. We were ordered to take a company of the Georgia militia on a scout. We went away around to our extreme right wing, passing through Terry's mill pond, and over the old battlefield of the

22nd, and past the place where General Walker fell, when we came across two ladies. One of them kept going from one tree to another, and saying: "This pine tree, that pine tree; this pine tree, that pine tree." In answer to our inquiry, they informed us that the young woman's husband was killed on the 22nd, and had been buried under a pine tree, and she was nearly crazy because she could not find his dead body. We passed on, and as soon as we came in sight of the old line of Yankee breastworks, an unexpected volley of minnie balls was fired into our ranks, killing this captain of the Fourth Tennessee Regiment and killing and wounding seven or eight of the Georgia militia. I hallooed to lay down, as soon as possible, and a perfect whizz of minnie balls passed over, when I immediately gave the command of attention, forward, charge and capture that squad. That Georgia militia, every man of them, charged forward, and in a few moments we ran into a small squad of Yankees, and captured the whole "lay out." We then carried back to camp the dead captain and the killed and wounded militia. I had seen a great many men killed and wounded, but some how or other these dead and wounded men, of that day, made a more serious impression on my mind than in any previous or subsequent battles. They were buried with all the honors of war and I never will forget the incidents and scenes of this day as long as I live.

We Go After Stoneman

One morning our regiment was ordered to march, double-quick, to the depot to take the cars for somewhere. The engine was under steam, and ready to start for that mysterious somewhere. The whistle blew long and loud, and away we went at break-neck speed for an hour, and drew up at a little place by the name of Jonesboro. The Yankees had captured the town, and were tearing up the railroad track. A regiment of Rebel infantry and a brigade of cavalry were already in line of battle in their rear. We jumped out of the cars and advanced to attack them in front. Our line had just begun to open a pretty brisk fire on the Yankee cavalry, when they broke, running right through and over the lines of the regiment of infantry and brigade of cavalry in their rear, the men opening ranks to get out of the way of the hoofs of their horses. It was Stoneman's cavalry, upon its celebrated raid toward Macon and Andersonville to liberate the Federal prisoners. We went to work like beavers, and in a few hours the railroad track had been repaired so that we could pass. Every few miles we would find the track torn up, but we would get out of the cars, fix up the track, and light out again. We were charging a brigade of cavalry with a train of cars, as it were. They would try to stop our progress by tearing up the track, but we were crowding them a little too strong. At last they thought it was time to quit that foolishness, and then commenced a race between cavalry and cars for Macon, Georgia. The cars had to run exceedingly slow and careful, fearing a tear up or ambuscade, but at last Macon came in sight. Twenty-five or thirty thousand Federal prisoners were confined at this place, and it was poorly guarded and protected. We feared that Stoneman would only march in, overpower the guards, and liberate the prisoners, and we would have some tall fighting to do, but on arriving at Macon, we found that Stoneman and all of his command had just surrendered to a brigade of cavalry and the Georgia militia, and we helped march the gentlemen inside the prison walls at Macon. They had furnished their own transportation, paying their own way and bearing their own expenses, and instead of liberating any prisoners, were themselves imprisoned. An extra detail was made as guard from our regiment to take them on to Andersonville, but I was not on this detail, so I remained until the detail returned.

Macon is a beautiful place. Business was flourishing like a green bay tree. The people were good, kind, and clever to us. Everywhere the hospitality of their homes was proffered us. We were regarded as their liberators. They gave us all the good things they had—eating, drinking, etc. We felt our consequence, I assure you, reader. We felt we were heroes, indeed; but the benzine and other fluids became a little promiscuous and the libations of the boys a little too heavy. They began to get boisterous—I might say, riotous. Some of the boys got to behaving badly, and would go into stores and places, and did many things they ought not to have done. In fact, the whole caboodle of them ought to have been carried to the guard-house. They were whooping, and yelling, and firing off their guns, just for the fun of the thing. I remember of going into a very nice family's house, and the old lady told the dog to go out, go out, sir! and remarked rather to herself, "Go out, go out! I wish you were killed, anyhow." John says, "Madam, do you want that dog killed, sure enough?" She says, "Yes, I do. I do wish that he was dead." Before I could even think or catch my breath, bang went John's gun, and the dog was weltering in his blood right on the good lady's floor, the top of his head entirely torn off. I confess, reader, that I came very near jumping out of my skin, as it were, at the unexpected discharge of the gun. And other such scenes, I reckon, were being enacted elsewhere, but at last a detail was sent around to arrest all stragglers, and we were soon rolling back to Atlanta.

"Bellum Lethale"

Well, after "jugging" Stoneman, we go back to Atlanta and occupy our same old place near the concrete house. We found everything exactly as we had left it, with the exception of the increased number of graybacks, which seemed to have propagated a thousand-fold since we left, and they were crawling about like ants, making little paths and tracks in the dirt as they wiggled and waddled about, hunting for ye old Rebel soldier. Sherman's two thirty-pound parrot guns were in the same position, and every now and then a lazy-looking shell would pass over, speeding its way on to Atlanta.

The old citizens had dug little cellars, which the soldiers called "gopher holes," and the women and children were crowded together in these cellars, while Sherman was trying to burn the city over their heads. But, as I am not writing history, I refer you to any history of the war for Sherman's war record in and around Atlanta.

As John and I started to go back, we thought we would visit the hospital. Great God! I get sick today when I think of the agony, and suffering, and sickening stench and odor of dead and dying; of wounds and sloughing sores, caused by the deadly gangrene; of the groaning and wailing. I cannot describe it. I remember, I went in the rear of the building, and there I saw a pile of arms and legs, rotting and decomposing; and, although I saw thousands of horrifying scenes during the war, yet today I have no recollection in my whole life, of ever seeing anything that I remember with more horror than that pile of legs and arms that had been cut off our soldiers. As John and I went through the hospital, and were looking at the poor suffering fellows, I heard a weak voice calling, "Sam, O, Sam." I went to the poor fellow, but did not recognize him at first, but soon found out that it was James Galbreath, the poor fellow who had been shot nearly in two on the 22nd of July. I tried to be cheerful, and said, "Hello, Galbreath, old fellow, I thought you were in heaven long before this." He laughed a sort of dry, cracking laugh, and asked me to hand him a drink of water. I handed it to him. He then began to mumble and tell me something in a rambling and incoherent way, but all I could catch was for me to write to his family, who were living near Mt. Pleasant. I asked him if he was badly wounded. He only pulled down the blanket, that was all. I get sick when I think of it. The lower part of his body was hanging to the upper part by a shred, and all of his entrails were lying on the cot with him, the bile and other excrements exuding from them, and they full of maggots. I replaced the blanket as tenderly as I could, and then said, "Galbreath, good-bye." I then kissed him on his lips and forehead, and left. As I passed on, he kept trying to tell me something, but I could not make out what he said, and fearing I would cause him to exert himself too much, I left.

It was the only field hospital that I saw during the whole war, and I have no desire to see another. Those hollow-eyed and sunken-cheeked sufferers, shot in every conceivable part of the body; some shrieking, and calling upon their mothers; some laughing the hard, cackling laugh of the sufferer without hope, and some cursing like troopers, and some writhing and groaning as their wounds were being bandaged and dressed. I saw a man of the Twenty-seventh, who had lost his right hand, another his leg, then another whose head was laid open, and I could see his brain thump, and another with his under jaw shot off; in fact, wounded in every manner possible.

Ah! reader, there is no glory for the private soldier, much less a conscript. James Galbreath was a conscript, as was also Fain King. Mr. King was killed at Chickamauga. He and Galbreath were conscripted and joined Company H at the same time. Both were old men, and very poor, with large families at home; and they were forced to go to war against their wishes, while their wives and little children were at home without the necessaries of life. The officers have all the glory. Glory is not for the private soldier, such as die in the hospitals, being eat up with the deadly gangrene, and being imperfectly waited on. Glory is for generals, colonels, majors, captains, and lieutenants. They have all the glory, and when the poor private wins battles by dint of sweat, hard marches, camp and picket duty, fasting and broken bones, the officers get the glory. The private's pay was eleven dollars per month, if he got it; the general's pay was three hundred dollars per month, and he always got his. I am not complaining. These things happened sixteen to twenty years ago. Men who never fired a gun, nor killed a Yankee during the whole war, are today the heroes of the war. Now, I tell you what I think about it: I think that those of us who fought as private soldiers, fought as much for glory as the general did, and those of us who stuck it out to the last, deserve more praise than the general who resigned because some other general was placed in command over him. A general could resign. That was honorable. A private could not resign, nor choose his branch of service, and if he deserted, it was death.

The Scout and Death of a Yankee Lieutenant

General Hood had sent off all his cavalry, and a detail was made each day of so many men for a scout, to find out all we could about the movements of the Yankees. Colonel George Porter, of the Sixth Tennessee, was in command of the detail. We passed through Atlanta, and went down the railroad for several miles, and then made a flank movement toward where we expected to come in contact with the Yankees. When we came to a skirt of woods, we were deployed as skirmishers. Colonel Porter ordered us to re-prime our guns and to advance at twenty-five paces apart, being deployed as skirmishers, and to keep under cover as much as possible. He need not have told us this, because we had not learned war for nothing. We would run from one tree to another, and then make a careful reconnoiter before proceeding to another. We had begun to get a little careless, when bang! bang! bang! It seemed that we had got into a Yankee ambush. The firing seemed to be from all sides, and was rattling among the leaves and bushes. It appeared as if some supernatural, infernal battle was going on and the air was full of smoke. We had not seen the Yankees. I ran to a tree to my right, and just as I got to it, I saw my comrade sink to the ground clutching at the air as he fell dead. I kept trying to see the Yankees, so that I might shoot. I had been looking a hundred years ahead, when happening to look not more than ten paces from me, I saw a big six-foot Yankee with a black feather in his hat, aiming deliberately at me. I dropped to the ground, and at the same moment heard the report, and my hat was knocked off in the bushes. I remained perfectly still, and in a few minutes I saw a young Yankee lieutenant peering through the bushes. I would rather not have killed him, but I was afraid to fire and afraid to run, and yet I did not wish to kill him. He was as pretty as a woman, and somehow I thought I had met him before. Our eyes met. He stood like a statue. He gazed at me with a kind of scared expression. I still did not want to kill him, and am sorry today that I did, for I believe I could have captured him, but I fired, and saw the blood spurt all over his face. He was the prettiest youth I ever saw. When I fired, the Yankees broke and run, and I went up to the boy I had killed, and the blood was gushing out of his mouth. I was sorry.

Atlanta Forsaken

One morning about the break of day our artillery opened along our breastworks, scaring us almost to death, for it was the first guns that had been fired for more than a month. We sprang to our feet and grabbed our muskets, and ran out and asked some one what did that mean. We were informed that they were "feeling" for the Yankees. The comment that was made by the private soldier was simply two words, and those two words were "O, shucks." The Yankees had gone—no one knew whither—and our batteries were shelling the woods, feeling for them. "O, shucks."

"Hello," says Hood. "Whar in the Dickens and Tom Walker are them Yanks, hey? Feel for them with long-range 'feelers.'" A boom, boom. "Can anybody tell me whar them Yanks are? Send out a few more 'feelers.' The feelers in the shape of cannon balls will bring them to taw." Boom, boom, boom.

> *"For the want of a nail, the shoe was lost,*
> *For the want of a shoe the horse was lost,*
> *For the want of a horse the general was lost,*
> *For the want of a general the battle was lost."*

Forrest's cavalry had been sent off somewhere. Wheeler's cavalry had been sent away yonder in the rear of the enemy to tear up the railroad and cut off their supplies, etc., and we had to find out the movements of the enemy by "feeling for them" by shelling the vacant woods. The Yankees were at that time twenty-five miles in our rear, "a hundred thousand strong," at a place called Jonesboro. I do not know how it was found out that they were at Jonesboro, but anyhow, the news had come and Cheatham's corps had to go and see about it.

Stewart's corps must hold Atlanta, and Stephen D. Lee's corps must be stretched at proper distance, so that the word could be passed backward and forward as to how they were getting along. As yet it is impossible to tell of the movements of the enemy, because our cannon balls had not come back and re-ported any movements to us. We had always heard that cannon balls were blind, and we did not suppose they could see to find their way back. Well, our corps made a forced march for a day and a night, and passed the word back that we had seen some signs of the Yankees being in that vicinity, and thought perhaps, a small portion—about a hundred thousand—were nigh about there somewhere. Says he, "It's a strange thing you don't know; send out your feelers." We sent out a few feelers and they report back very promptly that the Yankees are here sure enough, or that is what our feelers say. Pass the word up the line. The word is passed from mouth to mouth of Lee's skirmish line twenty-five miles back to Atlanta. Well, if that be the case, we will set fire to all of our army stores, spike all our cannon, and play "smash" generally, and forsake Atlanta.

In the meantime, just hold on where you are till Stewart gets through his job of blowing up arsenals, burning up the army stores, and spiking the cannon, and we will send our negro boy Cæsar down to the horse lot to see if he can't catch old Nance, but she is such a fool with that young suckling colt of hers, that it takes him almost all day to catch her, and if the draw-bars hap-pen to be down, she'll get in the clover patch, and I don't think he will catch her today. But if he don't catch her, I'll ride Balaam anyhow. He's got a mighty sore back, and needs a shoe put on his left hind foot, and he cut his ankle with a broken shoe on his fore foot, and has not been fed today. However, I will be along by-and-by. Stewart, do you think you will be able to get through with your job of blowing up by day after tomorrow, or by Saturday at twelve o'clock? Lee, pass the word down to Cheatham, and ask him what he thinks the Yankees are doing. Now, Kinlock, get my duster and umbrella, and bring out Balaam.

Now, reader, that was the impression made on the private's mind at that time.

Chapter 14

Jonesboro

The Battle of Jonesboro

STEWART'S CORPS was at Atlanta, Lee's corps was between Atlanta and Jonesboro, and Cheatham's corps, then numbering not more than five thousand men—because the woods and roads were full of straggling soldiers, who were not in the fight—was face to face with the whole Yankee army, and he was compelled to flee, fight, or surrender. This was the position and condition of the grand Army of Tennessee on this memorable occasion.

If I am not mistaken, General Cleburne was commanding Cheatham's corps at that time. We expected to be ordered into action every moment, and kept see-sawing backward and forward, until I did not know which way the Yankees were, or which way the Rebels. We would form line of battle, charge bayonets, and would raise a whoop and yell, expecting to be dashed right against the Yankee lines, and then the order would be given to retreat. Then we would immediately re-form and be ordered to charge again a mile off at another place. Then we would march and counter-march backward and forward over the same ground, passing through Jonesboro away over the hill, and then back through the town, first four forward and back; your right hand to your left hand lady, swing half round and balance all. This sort of a movement is called a "feint." A feint is what is called in poker a "bluff," or what is called in a bully a "brag." A feint means anything but a fight. If a lady faints she is either scared or in love, and wants to fall in her lover's arms. If an army makes a feint movement, it is trying to hide some other movement.

"Hello, Lee, what does Cleburne say the Yankees are doing at Jonesboro?"

"They are fanning themselves."

"Well keep up that feint movement until all the boys faint from sheer exhaustion."

"Hello, Stewart, do you think you will be able to burn up those ten locomotives, and destroy those hundred car loads of provisions by day after tomorrow?"

"Lee, ask Cleburne if he feels feinty? Ask him how a fellow feels when he feints?"

Cleburne says: "I have feinted, feinted, and feinted, until I can't feint any longer."

"Well," says Hood, "if you can't feint any longer, you had better flee, fight, or faint; Balaam gets along mighty slow, but I'll be thar after awhile."

At one o'clock we were ordered to the attack. We had to pass through an osage orange hedge that was worse than the enemy's fire. Their breastworks were before us. We yelled, and charged, and hurrahed, and said booh! booh! we're coming, coming, look out, don't you see us coming? Why don't you let us hear the cannon's opening roar? Why don't you rattle a few old muskets over there at us? Booh! booh! we are coming. Tag. We have done got to your breastworks. Now, we tagged first, why don't you tag back? A Yankee seems to be lying on the other side of the breastworks sunning himself, and raising himself on his elbow, says, "Fool who with your fatty bread? W-e are too o-l-d a-birds to be caught with that kind of chaff. We don't want any of that kind of pie. What you got there wouldn't make a mouthful. Bring on your pudding and pound-cake, and then we will talk to ye."

General Granberry, who, poor fellow, was killed in the butchery at Franklin afterwards, goes up to the breastworks, and says, "Look here, Yank, we're fighting, sure enough."

Meynheer Dutchman comes out, and says, "Ish dot so? Vel I ish peen von leetle pit hungry dish morning, und I yust gobble you up for mein lunch pefore tinner dime. Dot ish der kind of mans vot I bees!"

Now, reader, that is a fine description of this memorable battle. That's it—no more, no less. I was in it all, and saw General Granberry captured. We did our level best to get up a fight, but it was no go, any way we could fix it up. I mean no disrespect to General Hood. He was a noble, brave, and good man, and we loved him for his many virtues and goodness of heart. I do not propose to criticize his generalship or ability as a commander. I only write of the impression and sentiment that were made upon the private's mind at the time, and as I remember them now. But Atlanta had fallen into the hands of the Yankees, and they were satisfied for the time.

Death of Lieutenant John Whittaker

At this place we built small breastworks, but for what purpose I never knew. The Yankees seemed determined not to fight, no way we could fix it. Every now and then they would send over a "feeler," to see how we were getting along. Sometimes these "feelers" would do some damage. I remember one morning we were away over a hill, and every now and then here would come one of those lazy-looking "feelers," just bouncing along as if he were in no hurry, called in military "ricochet." They were very easy to dodge, if you could see them in time. Well, one morning as before remarked, Lieutenant John Whittaker, then in command of Company H, and myself were sitting down eating breakfast out of the same tin plate. We were sopping gravy out with some cold corn bread, when Captain W. C. Flournoy, of the Martin Guards, hallooed out, "Look out, Sam; look! look!" I just turned my head, and in turning, the cannon ball knocked my hat off, and striking Lieutenant Whittaker full in the side of the head, carried away the whole of the skull part, leaving only the face. His brains fell in the plate from which we were sopping, and his head fell in my lap, deluging my face and clothes with his blood. Poor fellow, he never knew what hurt him. His spirit went to its God that morning. Green Rieves carried the poor boy off on his shoulder, and, after wrapping him up in a blanket, buried him. His bones are at Jonesboro today. The cannon ball did not go twenty yards after accomplishing its work of death. Captain Flournoy laughed at me, and said, "Sam, that came very near getting you. One-tenth of an inch more would have cooked your goose." I saw another man try to stop one of those balls that was just rolling along on the ground. He put his foot out to stop the ball but the ball did not stop, but, instead, carried the man's leg off with it. He no doubt today walks on a cork-leg, and is tax collector of the county in which he lives. I saw a thoughtless boy trying to catch one in his hands as it bounced along. He caught it, but the next moment his spirit had gone to meet its God. But, poor John, we all loved him. He died for his country. His soul is with his God. He gave his all for the country he loved, and may he rest in peace under the shade of the tree where he is buried, and may the birds sing their sweetest songs, the flowers put forth their most beautiful blooms, while the gentle breezes play about the brave boy's grave. Green Rieves was the only person at the funeral; no tears of a loving mother or gentle sister were there. Green interred his body, and there it will remain till the resurrection. John Whittaker deserves more than a passing notice. He was noble and brave, and when he was killed, Company H was without an officer then commanding. Every single officer had been killed, wounded, or captured. John served as a private soldier the first year of the war, and at the reorganization at Corinth, Mississippi, he, W. J. Whitthorne and myself all ran for orderly sergeant of Company H, and John was elected, and the first vacancy occurring after the death of Captain Webster, he was commissioned brevet second lieutenant. When the war broke out, John was clerking for John L. & T. S. Brandon, in Columbia. He had been in every march, skirmish, and battle that had been fought during the war. Along the dusty road, on the march, in the bivouac and on the battlefield, he was the same noble, generous boy; always, kind, ever gentle, a smile ever lighting up his countenance. He was one of the most even tempered men I ever knew. I never knew him to speak an unkind word to anyone, or use a profane or vulgar word in my life.

One of those ricochet cannon balls struck my old friend, N. B. Shepard. Shep was one of the bravest and best soldiers who ever shouldered a musket. It is true, he was but a private soldier, but he was the best friend I had during the whole war. In intellect he was far ahead of most of the generals, and would have honored and adorned the name of general in the C. S. A. He was ever brave and true. He followed our cause to the end, yet all the time an invalid. Today he is languishing on a bed of pain and sickness, caused by that ball at Jonesboro. The ball struck him on his knapsack, knocking him twenty feet, and breaking one or two ribs and dislocating his shoulder. He was one of God's noblemen, indeed—none braver, none more generous. God alone controls our destinies, and surely He who watched over us and took care of us in those dark and bloody days, will not forsake us now. God alone fits and prepares for us the things that are in store for us. There is none so wise as to foresee the future or foretell the end. God sometimes seems afar off, but He will never leave or forsake anyone who puts his trust in Him. The day will come when the good as well as evil will all meet on one broad platform, to be rewarded for the deeds done in the body, when time shall end, with the gates of eternity closed, and the key fastened to the girdle of God forever. Pardon me, reader, I have wandered. But when my mind reverts to those scenes and times, I seem to live in another age and time and I sometime think that "after us comes the end of the universe."

I am not trying to moralize, I am only trying to write a few scenes and incidents that came under the observation of a poor old Rebel webfoot private soldier in those stormy days and times. Histories tell the great facts, while I only tell of the minor incidents.

But on this day of which I now write, we can see in plain view more than a thousand Yankee battle-flags waving on top the red earthworks, not more than four hundred yards off. Every private soldier there knew that General Hood's army was scattered all the way from Jonesboro to Atlanta, a distance of twenty-five miles, without any order, discipline, or spirit to do anything. We could hear General Stewart, away back yonder in Atlanta, still blowing up arsenals, and smashing things generally, while Stephen D. Lee was somewhere between Lovejoy Station and Macon, scattering. And here was but a demoralized remnant of Cheatham's corps facing the whole Yankee army. I have ever thought that Sherman was a poor general, not to have captured Hood and his whole army at that time. But it matters not what I thought, as I am not trying to tell the ifs and ands, but only of what I saw. In a word, we had everything against us. The soldiers distrusted everything. They were broken down with their long days' hard marching—were almost dead with hunger and fatigue. Every one was taking his own course, and wishing and praying to be captured. Hard and senseless marching, with little sleep, half rations, and lice, had made their lives a misery. Each one prayed that all this foolishness might end one way or the other. It was too much for human endurance. Every private soldier knew that such things as this could not last. They were willing to ring down the curtain, put out the foot-lights and go home. There was no hope in the future for them.

Then Comes the Farce

From this time forward until the close of the war, everything was a farce as to generalship. The tragedy had been played, the glory of war had departed. We all loved Hood; he was such a clever fellow, and a good man.

Well, Yank, why don't you come on and take us? We are ready to play quits now. We have not anything to let you have, you know; but you can parole us, you know; and we'll go home and be good boys, you know—good Union boys, you know; and we'll

be sorry for the war, you know; and we wouldn't have the negroes in any way, shape, form, or fashion, you know; and the
American continent has no north, no south, no east, no west—
boohoo, boohoo, boohoo.

Tut, tut, Johnny; all that sounds tolerable nice, but then you
might want some favor from Uncle Sam, and the teat is too full
of milk at the present time for us to turn loose. It's a sugar teat,
Johnny, and just begins to taste sweet; and, besides, Johnny,
once or twice you have put us to a little trouble; we haven't for-
got that; and we've got you down now—our foot is on your neck,
and you must feel our boot heel. We want to stamp you a little—
"that's what's the matter with Hannah." And, Johnny, you've
fought us hard. You are a brave boy; you are proud and aristocratic, Johnny, and we are going to crush your cursed pride and
spirit. And now, Johnny, come here; I've something to whisper
in your ear. Hold your ear close down here, so that no one can
hear: "We want big fat offices when the war is over. Some of us
want to be presidents, some governors, some go to congress,
and be big ministers to 'Urup,' and all those kind of things,
Johnny, you know. Just go back to your camp, Johnny, chase
round, put on a bold front, flourish your trumpets, blow your
horns. And, Johnny, we don't want to be hard on you, and we'll
tell you what we'll do for you. Away back in your territory, between Columbia and Nashville, is the most beautiful country,
and the most fertile, and we have lots of rations up there, too.
Now, you just go up there, Johnny, and stay until we want you.
We ain't done with you yet, my buy—O, no, Johnny. And, another thing, Johnny; you will find there between Mt. Pleasant
and Columbia, the most beautiful country that the sun of
heaven ever shone upon; and half way between the two places is
St. John's Church. Its tower is all covered over with a beautiful
vine of ivy; and, Johnny, you know that in olden times it was the
custom to entwine a wreath of ivy around the brows of victorious generals. We have no doubt that many of your brave generals will express a wish, when they pass by, to be buried beneath
the ivy vine that shades so gracefully and beautifully the wall of

this grand old church. And, Johnny, you will find a land of beauty and plenty, and when you get there, just put on as much style as you like; just pretend, for our sake, you know, that you are a bully boy with a glass eye, and that you are the victorious army that has returned to free an oppressed people. We will allow you this, Johnny, so that we will be the greater when we want you, Johnny. And now, Johnny, we did not want to tell you what we are going to say to you now, but will, so that you'll feel bad. Sherman wants to 'march to the sea, while the world looks on and wonders.' He wants to desolate the land and burn up your towns, to show what a coward he is, and how dastardly, and one of our boys wants to write a piece of poetry about it. But that ain't all, Johnny. You know that you fellows have got a great deal of cotton at Augusta, Savannah, Charleston, Mobile, and other places, and cotton is worth two dollars a pound in gold, and as Christmas is coming, we want to go down there for some of that cotton to make a Christmas gift to old Abe and old Clo, don't you see? O, no, Johnny, we don't want to end the war just yet awhile. The sugar is mighty sweet in the teat, and we want to suck a while longer. Why, sir, we want to rob and then burn every house in Georgia and South Carolina. We will get millions of dollars by robbery alone, don't you see?"

Palmetto

"Hark from the tomb that doleful sound,
My ears attend the cry."

General J. B. Hood established his headquarters at Palmetto, Georgia, and here is where we were visited by his honor, the Honorable Jefferson Davis, President of the Confederate States of America, and the Right Honorable Robert Toombs, secretary of state under the said Davis. Now, kind reader, don't ask me to write history. I know nothing of history. See the histories for grand movements and military maneuvers. I can only tell of what I saw and how I felt. I can remember now General Robert Toombs' and Hon. Jeff Davis' speeches. I remember how funny

Toombs' speech was. He kept us all laughing, by telling us how quick we were going to whip the Yankees, and how they would skedaddle back across the Ohio river like a dog with a tin oyster can tied to his tail. Captain Joe P. Lee and I laughed until our sides hurt us. I can remember today how I felt. I felt that Davis and Toombs had come there to bring us glad tidings of great joy, and to proclaim to us that the ratification of a treaty of peace had been declared between the Confederate States of America and the United States. I remember how good and happy I felt when these two leading statesmen told of when grim visaged war would smooth her wrinkled front, and when the dark clouds that had so long lowered o'er our own loved South would be in the deep bosom of the ocean buried. I do not know how others felt, but I can say never before or since did I feel so grand. (I came very near saying gloomy and peculiar.) I felt that I and every other soldier who had stood the storms of battle for nearly four long years, were now about to be discharged from hard marches, and scant rations, and ragged clothes, and standing guard, etc. In fact, the black cloud of war had indeed drifted away, and the beautiful stars that gemmed the blue ether above, smiling, said, "Peace, peace, peace." I felt bully, I tell you. I remember what I thought—that the emblem of our cause was the Palmetto and the Texas Star, and the town of Palmetto, were symbolical of our ultimate triumph, and that we had unconsciously, nay, I should say, prophetically, fallen upon Palmetto as the most appropriate place to declare peace between the two sections. I was sure Jeff Davis and Bob Toombs had come there for the purpose of receiving the capitulation of and to make terms with our conquered foes. I knew that in every battle we had fought, except Missionary Ridge, we had whipped the Yankees, and I knew that we had no cavalry, and but little artillery, and only two corps of infantry at Missionary Ridge, and from the way Jeff and Bob talked, it was enough to make us old private soldiers feel that swelling of the heart we ne'er should feel again. I remember that other high dignitaries and big bugs, then the controlling spirits of the government at Richmond, visited us, and most all of these high dignitaries shook hands with the boys. It was all hands round, swing the corner, and balance your partner. I shook hands with Hon. Jeff Davis, and he said howdy, captain; I shook hands with Toombs, and he said howdy, major; and every big bug that I shook hands with put another star on my collar and chicken guts on my sleeve. My pen is inadequate to describe the ecstasy and patriotic feeling that permeated every vein and fiber of my animated being. It was Paradise regained. All the long struggles we had followed the Palmetto flag through victory and defeat, through storms and rains, and snows and tempest, along the dusty roads, and on the weary marches, we had been true to our country, our cause, and our people; and there was a conscious pride within us that when we would return to our homes, we would go back as conquerors, and that we would receive the plaudits of our people—well done, good and faithful servants; you have been true and faithful even to the end.

Jeff Davis Makes a Speech

"Sinner come view the ground
Where you shall shortly lie."

I remember that Hon. Jeff Davis visited the army at this place, and our regiment, the First Tennessee, serenaded him. After playing several airs, he came out of General Hood's marquee, and spoke substantially as follows, as near as I can remember:

"SOLDIERS OF THE FIRST TENNESSEE REGIMENT:— I should have said captains, for every man among you is fit to be a captain. I have heard of your acts of bravery on every battlefield during the whole war, and 'captains,' so far as my wishes are concerned, I today make every man of you a captain, and I say honestly today, were I a private soldier, I would have no higher ambition on earth than to belong to the First Tennessee Regiment. You have been loyal and brave; your ranks have never yet, in the whole history of the war, been broken, even though the army was routed; yet, my brave soldiers, Tennesseans all, you have ever remained in your places in the ranks of the regiment, ever subject to the command of your gallant Colonel Field in every battle, march, skirmish, in an advance or a retreat. There are on the books of the war department at Richmond, the names of a quarter of a million deserters, yet, you, my brave soldiers, captains all, have remained true and steadfast. I have heard that some have been dissatisfied with the removal of General Joe E. Johnston and the appointment of General Hood; but, my brave and gallant heroes, I say, I have done what I thought best for your good. Soon we commence our march to Kentucky and Tennessee. Be of good cheer, for within a short while your faces will be turned homeward, and your feet will press Tennessee soil, and you will tread your native heath, amid the blue-grass regions and pastures green of your native homes. We will flank General Sherman out of Atlanta, tear up the railroad and cut off his supplies, and make Atlanta a perfect Moscow of defeat to the Federal army. Situated as he is in an enemy's country, with his communications all cut off, and our army in the rear, he will be powerless, and being fully posted and cognizant of our position, and of the Federal army, this movement will be the *ultima thule*, the grand crowning stroke for our independence, and the conclusion of the war."

Armistice in Name Only

About this time the Yankees sent us a flag of truce, asking an armistice to move every citizen of Atlanta south of their lines. It was granted. They wanted to live in fine houses awhile, and then rob and burn them, and issued orders for all the citizens of Atlanta to immediately abandon the city. They wanted Atlanta for themselves, you see.

For weeks and months the roads were filled with loaded wagons of old and decrepit people, who had been hunted and hounded from their homes with a relentless cruelty worse, yea, much worse, than ever blackened the pages of barbaric or savage history. I remember assisting in unloading our wagons that

General Hood, poor fellow, had kindly sent in to bring out the citizens of Atlanta to a little place called Rough-and-Ready about half way between Palmetto and Atlanta. Every day I would look on at the suffering of delicate ladies, old men, and mothers with little children clinging to them, crying, "O, mamma, mamma," and old women, and tottering old men, whose gray hairs should have protected them from the savage acts of Yankee hate and Puritan barbarity; and I wondered how on earth our generals, including those who had resigned—that is where the shoe pinches—could quietly look on at this dark, black, and damning insult to our people, and not use at least one effort to rescue them from such terrible and unmitigated cruelty, barbarity, and outrage. General Hood remonstrated with Sherman against the insult, stating that it "transcended in studied and ingenious cruelty, all acts ever before brought to my attention in the dark history of war."

In the great crisis of the war, Hardee, Kirby Smith, Breckinridge, and many brigadiers, resigned, thus throwing all the responsibility upon poor Hood.[1]

I desire to state that they left the army on account of rank. O, this thing of rank!

Many other generals resigned, and left us privates in the lurch. But the gallant Cheatham, Cleburne, Granberry, Gist, Strahl, Adams, John C. Brown, William B. Bate, Stewart, Lowery, and others, stuck to us to the last.

The sinews of war were strained to their utmost tension.

A Scout

At this place I was detailed as a regular scout, which position I continued to hold during our stay at Palmetto. It was a good thing. It beat camp guard all hollow. I had answered "hear" at

---

[1] Author's Note: In the Southern army the question was, who ranked? Not who was the best general, or colonel, or captain—but "who ranked?" The article of rank finally got down to corporals; and rank finally bursted the government.

roll-call ten thousand times in these nearly four years. But I had sorter got used to the darn thing.

Now, reader, I will give you a few chapters on the kind of fun I had for awhile. Our instructions were simply to try and find out all we could about the Yankees, and report all movements.

One dark, rainy evening, while out as a scout, and, after traveling all day, I was returning from the Yankee outposts at Atlanta, and had captured a Yankee prisoner, who I then had under my charge, and whom I afterwards carried and delivered to General Hood. He was a considerable muggins, and a great coward, in fact, a Yankee deserter. I soon found out that there was no harm in him, as he was tired of war anyhow, and was anxious to go to prison. We went into an old log cabin near the road until the rain would be over. I was standing in the cabin door looking at the rain drops fall off the house and make little bubbles in the drip, and listening to the pattering on the clapboard roof, when happening to look up, not fifty yards off, I discovered a regiment of Yankee cavalry approaching. I knew it would be utterly impossible for me to get away unseen, and I did not know what to do. The Yankee prisoner was scared almost to death. I said, "Look, look!" I turned in the room, and found the planks of the floor were loose. I raised two of them, and Yank and I slipped through. I replaced the planks, and could peep out beneath the sill of the house, and see the legs of the horses. They passed on and did not come to the old house. They were at least a half hour in passing. At last the main regiment had all passed, and I saw the rear guard about to pass, when I heard the captain say, "Go and look in that old house." Three fellows detached themselves from the command and came dashing up to the old house. I thought, "Gone up, sure," as I was afraid the Yankee prisoner would make his presence known. When the three men came up, they pushed open the door and looked around, and one fellow said "Booh!" They then rode off. But that "Booh!" I was sure I was caught, but I was not.

"What Is This Rebel Doing Here?"

I would go up to the Yankee outpost, and if some popinjay of a tacky officer didn't come along, we would have a good time. One morning I was sitting down to eat a good breakfast with the Yankee outpost. They were cavalry, and they were mighty clever and pleasant fellows. I looked down the road toward Atlanta, and not fifty yards from the outpost, I saw a body of infantry approaching. I don't know why I didn't run. I ought to have done so, but didn't. I stayed there until this body of infantry came up. They had come to relieve the cavalry. It was a detail of negro soldiers, headed by the meanest looking white man as their captain, I ever saw.

In very abrupt words he told the cavalry that he had come to take their place, and they were ordered to report back to their command. Happening to catch sight of me, he asked, "What is this Rebel doing here?" One of the men spoke up and tried to say something in my favor, but the more he said the more the captain of the blacks would get mad. He started toward me two or three times. He was starting, I could see by the flush of his face, to take hold of me, anyhow. The cavalrymen tried to protest, and said a few cuss words. The captain of the blacks looks back very mad at the cavalry. Here was my opportunity, now or never. Uncle negro looked on, not seeming to care for the cavalry, captain, or for me. I took up my gun very gently and cocked it. I had the gentleman. I had made up my mind if he advanced one step further, that he was a dead man. When he turned to look again, it was a look of surprise. His face was as red as a scalded beet, but in a moment was as white as a sheet. He was afraid to turn his head to give a command. The cavalry motioned their hands at me, as much as to say, "Run, Johnny, run." The captain of the blacks fell upon his face, and I broke and ran like a quarter-horse. I never saw or heard any more of the captain of the blacks or his guard afterward.

"Look Out, Boys"

One night, five of us scouts, I thought all strangers to me, put up at an old gentleman's house. I took him for a Catholic priest. His head was shaved and he had on a loose gown like a lady's dress, and a large cord and tassel tied around his waist, from which dangled a large bunch of keys. He treated us very kindly and hospitably, so far as words and politeness went, but we had to eat our own rations and sleep on our own blankets.

At bedtime, he invited us to sleep in a shed in front of his double log cabin. We all went in, lay down, and slept. A little while before day, the old priest came in and woke us up, and said he thought he saw in the moonlight a detachment of cavalry coming down the road from toward the Rebel lines. One of our party jumped up and said there was a company of cavalry coming that way, and then all four broke toward the old priest's room. I jumped up, put on one boot, and holding the other in my hand, I stepped out in the yard, with my hat and coat off—both being left in the room. A Yankee captain stepped up to me and said, "Are you No. 200?" I answered very huskily, "No, sir, I am not." He then went on in the house, and on looking at the fence, I saw there was at least two hundred Yankee cavalry right at me. I did not know what to do. My hat, coat, gun, cartridge-box, and knapsack were all in the room. I was afraid to stay there, and I was afraid to give the alarm. I soon saw almost every one of the Yankees dismount, and then I determined to give the alarm and run. I hallooed out as loud as I could, "Look out, boys," and broke and run. I had to jump over a garden picket fence, and as I lit on the other side, bang! bang! bang! was fired right after me. They stayed there but a short time, and I went back and got my gun and other accouterments.

Am Captured

When I left the old priest's house, it was then good day— nearly sun up—and I had started back toward our lines, and had walked on about half a mile, not thinking of danger, when four Yankees jumped out in the middle of the road and said, "Halt, there! O, yes, we've got you at last." I was in for it. What could I do? Their guns were cocked and leveled at me, and if I started to run, I would be shot, so I surrendered. In a very short time the regiment of Yankee cavalry came up, and the first greeting I had was, "Hello, you ain't No. 200, are you?" I was taken prisoner. They, I thought, seemed to be very gleeful about it, and I had to march right back by the old priest's house, and they carried me to the headquarters of General Stephen Williams. As soon as he saw me, he said, "Who have you there—a prisoner, or a deserter?" They said a prisoner. From what command? No one answered. Finally he asked me what command I belonged to. I told him the Confederate States army. Then, said he, "What is your name?" Said I, "General, if that would be any information, I would have no hesitancy in giving it. But I claim your protection as a prisoner of war. I am a private soldier in the Confederate States army, and I don't feel authorized to answer any question you may ask." He looked at me with a kind of quizzical look, and said, "That is the way with you Rebels. I have never yet seen one of you, but thought what little information he might possess to be of value to the Union forces." Then one of the men spoke up and said, "I think he is a spy or a scout, and does not belong to the regular army." He then gave me a close look, and said, "Ah, ah, a guerrilla," and ordered me to be taken to the provost marshal's office. They carried me to a large, fine house, upstairs, and I was politely requested to take a seat. I sat there some moments, when a dandy-looking clerk of a fellow came up with a book in his hand, and said, "The name." I appeared not to understand, and he said, "The name." I still looked at him, and he said, "The name." I did not know what he meant by "The name." Finally, he closed the book with a slam and started off, and said I, "Did you want to find out my name?" He said, "I asked you three times." I said, "When? If you ever asked me my name, I have never heard it." But he was too mad to listen to anything else. I was carried to another room in the same building, and locked up. I remained there until about dark, when a man brought me a tolerably good supper, and then left me alone to my own meditations. I could hear the sentinels at all times of the night calling out the hours. I did not sleep a wink, nor even lay down. I had made up my mind to escape, if there was any possible chance. About three o'clock everything got perfectly still. I went to the window, and it had a heavy bolt across it, and I could not open it. I thought I would try the door, but I knew that a guard was stationed in the hall, for I could see a dim light glimmer through the key-hole. I took my knife and unscrewed the catch in which the lock was fastened, and soon found out that I could open the door; but then there was the guard, standing at the main entrance down stairs. I peeped down, and he was quietly walking to and fro on his beat, every time looking to the hall. I made up my mind by his measured tread as to how often he would pass the door, and one time, after he had just passed, I came out in the hall, and started to run down the steps. About midway down the steps, one of them cracked very loud, but I ran on down in the lower hall and ran into a room, the door of which was open. The sentinel came back to the entrance of the hall, and listened a few minutes, and then moved on again. I went to the window and raised the sash, but the blind was fastened with a kind of patent catch. I gave one or two hard pushes, and felt it move. After that I made one big lunge, and it flew wide open, but it made a noise that woke up every sentinel. I jumped out in the yard, and gained the street, and, on looking back, I heard the alarm given, and lights began to glimmer everywhere, but, seeing no one directly after me, I made tracks toward Peachtree creek, and went on until I came to the old battlefield of July 22nd, and made my way back to our lines.

Chapter 15

Advance into Tennessee

General Hood Makes a Flank Movement

AFTER remaining a good long time at Jonesboro, the news came that we were going to flank Atlanta. We flanked it. A flank means "a go around."

Yank says, "What you doing, Johnny?"

Johnny says, "We are flanking."

Yank says, "Bully for you!"

We passed around Atlanta, crossed the Chattahoochee, and traveled back over the same route on which we had made the arduous campaign under Joe Johnston. It took us four months in the first instance, and but little longer than as many days in the second, to get back to Dalton, our starting point. On our way up there, the Yankee cavalry followed us to see how we were getting along with the flanking business. We had pontoons made for the purpose of crossing streams. When we would get to a stream, the pontoons would be thrown across, and Hood's army would cross. Yank would halloo over and say, "Well, Johnny, have you got everything across?" "Yes," would be the answer. "Well, we want these old pontoons, as you will not need them again." And they would take them.

We passed all those glorious battlefields, that have been made classic in history, frequently coming across the skull of some poor fellow sitting on top of a stump, grinning a ghastly smile; also the bones of horses along the road, and fences burned and destroyed, and occasionally the charred remains of a once fine dwelling house. Outside of these occasional reminders we could see no evidence of the desolation of the track of an invading army. The country looked like it did at first. Citizens came out, and seemed glad to see us, and would divide their onions, garlic, and leek with us. The soldiers were in good spirits, but it was the spirit of innocence and peace, not war and victory.

Where the railroads would cross a river, a block-house had been erected, and the bridge was guarded by a company of Federals. But we always flanked these little affairs. We wanted bigger and better meat.

We Capture Dalton

When we arrived at Dalton, we had a desire to see how the old place looked; not that we cared anything about it, but we just wanted to take a last farewell look at the old place. We saw the United States flag flying from the ramparts, and thought that Yank would probably be asleep or catching lice, or maybe engaged in a game of seven-up. So we sent forward a physician with some white bandages tied to the end of a long pole. He walked up and says, "Hello, boys!" "What is it, boss?" "Well, boys, we've come for you." "Hyah, ha; hyah, ha; hyah, ha; a hee, he, he, he; if it ain't old master, sho." The place was guarded by negro troops. We marched the black rascals out. They were mighty glad to see us, and we were kindly disposed to them. We said, "Now, boys, we don't want the Yankees to get mad at you, and to blame you; so, just let's get out here on the railroad track, and tear it up, and pile up the crossties, and then pile the iron on top of them, and we'll set the thing a-fire, and when the Yankees come back they will say, 'What a bully fight *them nagers* did make.'" (A Yankee always says "nager.") Reader, you should have seen how that old railroad did flop over, and how the darkies did sweat, and how the perfume did fill the atmosphere.

But there were some Yankee soldiers in a block-house at Ringgold Gap, who thought they would act big. They said that Sherman had told them not to come out of that block-house, any how. But General William B. Bate begun to persuade the gentlemen, by sending a few four-pound parrot "feelers." Ah! those *feelers!*

They persuaded eloquently. They persuaded effectually— those feelers did. The Yanks soon surrendered. The old place looked natural like, only it seemed to have a sort of grave-yard loneliness about it.

A Man in the Well

On leaving Dalton, after a day's march, we had stopped for the night. Our guns were stacked, and I started off with a comrade to get some wood to cook supper with. We were walking along, he a little in the rear, when he suddenly disappeared. I could not imagine what had become of him. I looked everywhere. The earth seemed to have opened and swallowed him. I called, and called, but could get no answer. Presently I heard a groan that seemed to come out of the bowels of the earth; but, as yet, I could not make out where he was. Going back to camp, I procured a light, and after whooping and hallooing for a long time, I heard another groan, this time much louder than before. The voice appeared to be overhead. There was no tree or house to be seen; and then again the voice seemed to answer from under the ground, in a hollow, sepulchral tone, but I could not tell where he was. But I was determined to find him, so I kept on hallooing and he answering. I went to the place where the voice appeared to come out of the earth. I was walking along rather thoughtlessly and carelessly, when one inch more and I would have disappeared also. Right before me I saw the long dry grass all bending toward a common center, and I knew that it was an old well, and that my comrade had fallen in it. But how to get him out was the unsolved problem. I ran back to camp to get assistance, and everybody had a great curiosity to see "the man in the well." They would get chunks of fire and shake over the well, and, peeping down, would say, "Well, he's in there," and go off, and others would come and talk about his "being in there." The poor fellow stayed in that well all night. The next morning we got a long rope from a battery and let it down in the well, and soon had him on *terra firma*. He was worse scared than hurt.

Tuscumbia

We arrived and remained at Tuscumbia several days, awaiting the laying of the pontoons across the Tennessee river at Florence, Alabama, and then we all crossed over. While at Tuscumbia, John Branch and I saw a nice sweet potato patch, that looked very tempting to a hungry Rebel. We looked all around, and thought that the coast was clear. We jumped over the fence, and commenced grabbling for the sweet potatoes. I had got my haversack full, and had started off, when we heard, "Halt, there." I looked around, and there was a soldier guard. We broke and run like quarter-horses, and the guard pulled down on us just as we jumped the fence. I don't think his gun was loaded, though, because we did not hear the ball whistle.

We marched from Decatur to Florence. Here the pontoon bridges were nicely and beautifully stretched across the river. We walked over this floating bridge, and soon found ourselves on the Tennessee side of Tennessee river.

In driving a great herd of cattle across the pontoon, the front one got stubborn, and the others, crowding up all in one bulk, broke the line that held the pontoon, and drowned many of the drove. We had beef for supper that night.

En Route for Columbia

"And nightly we pitch our moving tent
A day's march nearer home."

How every pulse did beat and leap, and how every heart did throb with emotions of joy, which seemed nearly akin to heaven, when we received the glad intelligence of our onward march to-ward the land of promise, and of our loved ones. The cold November winds coming off the mountains of the northwest were blowing right in our faces, and nearly cutting us in two.

We were inured to privations and hardships; had been upon every march, in every battle, in every skirmish, in every advance, in every retreat, in every victory, in every defeat. We had laid under the burning heat of a tropical sun; had made the cold, frozen earth our bed, with no covering save the blue canopy of heaven; had braved dangers, had breasted floods; had seen our comrades slain upon our right and our left hand; had heard guns that carried death in their missiles; had heard the shouts of the charge; had seen the enemy in full retreat and flying in every direction; had heard the shrieks and groans of the wounded and dying; had seen the blood of our countrymen dyeing the earth and enriching the soil; had been hungry when there was nothing to eat; had been in rags and tatters. We had marked the frozen earth with bloody and unshod feet; had been elated with victory and crushed by defeat; had seen and felt the pleasure of the life of a soldier, and had drank the cup to its dregs. Yes, we had seen it all, and had shared in its hopes and its fears; its love and its hate; its good and its bad; its virtue and its vice; its glories and its shame. We had followed the successes and reverses of the flag of the Lost Cause through all these years of blood and strife.

I was simply one of hundreds of thousands in the same fix. The tale is the same that every soldier would tell, except Jim Whitler. Jim had dodged about, and had escaped being conscripted until "Hood's raid," he called it. Hood's army was taking up every able-bodied man and conscripting him into the army. Jim Whitler had got a position as overseer on a large plantation, and had about a hundred negroes under his surveillance. The army had been passing a given point, and Jim was sitting quietly on the fence looking at the soldiers. The conscripting squad nabbed him. Jim tried to beg off, but all entreaty was in vain. He wanted to go by home and tell his wife and children good-bye, and to get his clothes. It was no go. But, after awhile, Jim says,

"Gentlemen, ay, Ganny, the law!" You see, Jim "knowed" the law. He didn't know B from a bull's foot in the spelling-book. But he said, *the law.* Now, when anyone says anything about the "law," every one stops to listen. Jim says, "Ah, Ganny, *the law*" (laying great stress upon the law)—"allows every man who has twenty negroes to stay at home. Ah, Ganny!" Those old soldiers had long, long ago, forgotten about that old "law" of the long gone past; but Jim had treasured it up in his memory, lo! these many years, and he thought it would serve him now, as it had, no doubt, frequently done in the past. The conscript officer said, "Law or no law—you fall into line, take this gun and cartridge-box, and *march!*" Jim's spirits sank; his hopes vanished into air. Jim was soon in line, and was tramping to the music of the march. He stayed with the company two days. The third day it was reported that the Yankees had taken position on the Murfreesboro pike. A regiment was sent to the attack. It was Jim's regiment. He advanced bravely into battle. The minnie balls began to whistle around his ears. The regiment was ordered to fire. He hadn't seen anything to shoot at, but he blazed away. He loaded and fired the second time, when they were ordered to retreat. He didn't see anything to run from, but the other soldiers began to run, and Jim run, too. Jim had not learned the word "halt!" and just kept on running. He run, and he run, and he run, and he kept on running until he got home, when he jumped in his door and shouted, "Whoopee, Rhoda! Aye, Ganny, *I've served four years in the Rebel army.*"

Chapter 16

Battles in Tennessee

Columbia

"This is my own, my native land"

ONCE more the Maury Grays are permitted to put their feet upon their native heath, and to revisit their homes and friends, after having followed their tattered, and torn, and battle-riddled flag, which they had borne aloft for four long years, on every march, and in every battle that had been fought by the Army of Tennessee. We were a mere handful of devoted braves, who had stood by our colors when sometimes it seemed that God himself had forsaken us. But, parents, here are your noble and brave sons; and, ladies, four years ago you gave us this flag, and we promised you "That we would come back with the flag as victors, or we would come not at all." We have been true to our promise and our trust. On every battlefield the flag that you entrusted to our hands has been borne aloft by brave and heroic men, amid shot and shell, bloody battle, and death. We have never forsaken our colors. Are we worthy to be called the sons of old Maury county? Or have we fought in vain? Have our efforts been appreciated, or have four years of our lives been wasted, while we were battling for constitutional government, the supremacy of our laws over centralization, and our rights, as guaranteed to us by the blood of our forefathers on the battlefields of the Revolution? It is for you to make up your verdict. If our lives as soldiers have been a *failure*, we can but bow our heads on our bosoms, and say, "Surely, four years of our lives have been given for naught, and our efforts to please you have been in vain."

Yet, the invader's foot is still on our soil, but there beats in our bosoms the blood of brave and patriotic men, and we will continue to follow our old and war-worn and battle-riddled flag until it goes down forever.

The Maury Grays, commanded by Captain A. M. Looney, left Columbia, four years ago, with 120 men. How many of those 120 original members are with the company today? Just twelve. Company H has twenty members, but some of this number had subsequently enlisted. But we twelve will stick to our colors till she goes down forever, and until five more of this number fall dead and bleeding on the battlefield.

A Fiasco

When we arrived in sight of Columbia, we found the Yankees still in possession of the town, fortified and determined to resist our advance. We send forward a "feeler," and the "feeler" reports back very promptly, "Yes, the Yankees are there." Well, if that be the case, we'll just make a flank movement. We turn off the main turnpike at J. E. R. Carpenter's, and march through the cedars, and cross Duck river at Davis' ferry, on pontoon bridges, near Lowell's mill. We pass on, and cross Rutherford creek, near Burick's mill, about three o'clock in the afternoon. We had marched through fields in the heavy mud, and the men, weary and worn out, were just dragging themselves along, passing by the old Union Seminary, and then by Mr. Fred Thompson's, until we came to the Rally Hill turnpike—it being then nearly dark— we heard some skirmishing, but, exhausted as we were, we went into bivouac. The Yankees, it seems to me, might have captured the whole of us. But that is a matter of history. But I desire to state that no blunder was made by either Generals Cheatham or

Stewart, neither of whom ever failed to come to time. Jeff Davis is alone responsible for the blunder. About two hours after sun up the next morning we received the order to "Fall in, fall in, quick, make haste, hurrah, promptly, men; each rank count two; by the right flank, quick time, march; keep promptly closed up." Everything indicated an immediate attack. When we got to the turnpike near Spring Hill, lo! and behold; wonder of wonders! the whole Yankee army had passed during the night. The bird had flown. We made a quick and rapid march down the turnpike, finding Yankee guns and knapsacks, and now and then a broken down straggler, also two pieces of howitzer cannon, and at least twenty broken wagons along the road. Everything betokened a rout and a stampede of the Yankee army. Double quick! Forrest is in the rear. Now for fun. All that we want to do now is to catch the blue-coated rascals, ha! ha! We all want to see the surrender, ha! ha! Double quick! A rip, rip, rip; wheuf; pant, pant, pant. First one man drops out, and then another. The Yankees are routed and running, and Forrest has crossed Harpeth river in the rear of Franklin. Hurrah, men! keep closed up; we are going to capture Schofield. Forrest is in the rear; never mind the straggler and cannon. Kerflop we come against the breastworks at Franklin.

Franklin

"The death-angel gathers its last harvest."

Kind reader, right here my pen, and courage, and ability fail me. I shrink from butchery. Would to God I could tear the page from these memoirs and from my own memory. It is the blackest page in the history of the war of the Lost Cause. It was the bloodiest battle of modern times in any war. It was the finishing stroke to the independence of the Southern Confederacy. I was there. I saw it. My flesh trembles, and creeps, and crawls when I think of it today. My heart almost ceases to beat at the horrid recollection. Would to God that I had never witnessed such a scene!

I cannot describe it. It beggars description. I will not attempt to describe it. I could not. The death-angel was there to gather its last harvest. It was the grand coronation of death. Would that I could turn the page. But I feel, though I did so, that page would still be there, teeming with its scenes of horror and blood. I can only tell of what I saw.

Our regiment was resting in the gap of a range of hills in plain view of the city of Franklin. We could see the battleflags of the enemy waving in the breeze. Our army had been depleted of its strength by a forced march from Spring Hill, and stragglers lined the road. Our artillery had not yet come up, and could not be brought into action. Our cavalry was across Harpeth river, and our army was but in poor condition to make an assault. While resting on this hill-side, I saw a courier dash up to our commanding general, B. F. Cheatham, and the word, "Attention!" was given. I knew then that we would soon be in action. Forward, march. We passed over the hill and through a little skirt of woods.

The enemy were fortified right across the Franklin pike, in the suburbs of the town. Right here in these woods a detail of skirmishers was called for. Our regiment was detailed. We deployed as skirmishers, firing as we advanced on the left of the turnpike road. If I had not been a skirmisher on that day, I would not have been writing this today, in the year of our Lord 1882.

It was four o'clock on that dark and dismal December day when the line of battle was formed, and those devoted heroes were ordered forward, to

> "Strike for their altars and their fires,
> For the green graves of their sires,
> For God and their native land."

As they marched on down through an open field toward the rampart of blood and death, the Federal batteries began to open and mow down and gather into the garner of death, as brave, and good, and pure spirits as the world ever saw. The twilight of evening had begun to gather as a precursor of the coming black-ness of midnight darkness that was to envelop a scene so sick-ening and horrible that it is impossible for me to describe it. "Forward, men," is repeated all along the line. A sheet of fire was poured into our very faces, and for a moment we halted as if in despair, as the terrible avalanche of shot and shell laid low those brave and gallant heroes, whose bleeding wounds attested that the struggle would be desperate. Forward, men! The air loaded with death-dealing missiles. Never on this earth did men fight against such terrible odds. It seemed that the very elements of heaven and earth were in one mighty uproar. Forward, men! And the blood spurts in a perfect jet from the dead and wounded. The earth is red with blood. It runs in streams, mak-ing little rivulets as it flows. Occasionally there was a little lull in the storm of battle, as the men were loading their guns, and for a few moments it seemed as if night tried to cover the scene with her mantle. The death-angel shrieks and laughs and old Fa-ther Time is busy with his sickle, as he gathers in the last har-vest of death, crying, More, more, more! while his rapacious maw is glutted with the slain.

But the skirmish line being deployed out, extending a little wider than the battle did—passing through a thicket of small lo-custs, where Brown, orderly sergeant of Company B, was killed—we advanced on toward the breastworks, on and on. I had made up my mind to die—felt glorious. We pressed forward until I heard the terrific roar of battle open on our right. Cle-burne's division was charging their works. I passed on until I got to their works, and got over on their (the Yankees') side. But in fifty yards of where I was the scene was lit up by fires that seemed like hell itself. It appeared to be but one line of stream-ing fire. Our troops were upon one side of the breastworks, and the Federals on the other. I ran up on the line of works, where our men were engaged. Dead soldiers filled the entrenchments. The firing was kept up until after midnight, and gradually died out. We passed the night where we were. But when the morrow's sun began to light up the eastern sky with its rosy hues, and we

looked over the battlefield, O, my God! what did we see! It was
a grand holocaust of death. Death had held high carnival there
that night. The dead were piled the one on the other all over the
ground. I never was so horrified and appalled in my life. Horses,
like men, had died game on the gory breastworks. General
Adams' horse had his fore feet on one side of the works and his
hind feet on the other, dead. The general seems to have been
caught so that he was held to the horse's back, sitting almost as
if living, riddled, and mangled, and torn with balls. General Cleburne's mare had her fore feet on top of the works, dead in that
position. General Cleburne's body was pierced with forty-nine
bullets, through and through. General Strahl's horse lay by the
roadside and the general by his side, both dead, and all his staff.
General Gist, a noble and brave cavalier from South Carolina,
was lying with his sword reaching across the breastworks still
grasped in his hand. He was lying there dead. All dead! They
sleep in the graveyard yonder at Ashwood, almost in sight of my
home, where I am writing today. They sleep the sleep of the
brave. We love and cherish their memory. They sleep beneath
the ivy-mantled walls of St. John's church, where they expressed
a wish to be buried. The private soldier sleeps where he fell,
piled in one mighty heap. Four thousand five hundred privates!
all lying side by side in death! Thirteen generals were killed and
wounded. Four thousand five hundred men slain, all piled and
heaped together at one place. I cannot tell the number of others
killed and wounded. God alone knows that. We'll all find out on
the morning of the final resurrection.

Kind friends, I have attempted in my poor and feeble way to
tell you of this (I can hardly call it) battle. It should be called by
some other name. But, like all other battles, it, too, has gone
into history. I leave it with you. I do not know who was to blame.
It lives in the memory of the poor old Rebel soldier who went
through that trying and terrible ordeal. We shed a tear for the
dead. They are buried and forgotten. We meet no more on earth.
But up yonder, beyond the sunset and the night, away beyond
the clouds and tempest, away beyond the stars that ever twinkle

and shine in the blue vault above us, away yonder by the great white throne, and by the river of life, where the Almighty and Eternal God sits, surrounded by the angels and archangels and the redeemed of earth, we will meet again and see those noble and brave spirits who gave up their lives for their country's cause that night at Franklin, Tennessee. A life given for one's country is never lost. It blooms again beyond the grave in a land of beauty and of love. Hanging around the throne of sapphire and gold, a rich garland awaits the coming of him who died for his country, and when the horologe of time has struck its last note upon his dying brow, Justice hands the record of life to Mercy, and Mercy pleads with Jesus, and God, for his sake, receives him in his eternal home beyond the skies at last and forever.

Nashville

A few more scenes, my dear friends, and we close these memoirs. We march toward the city of Nashville. We camp the first night at Brentwood. The next day we can see the fine old building of solid granite, looming up on Capitol Hill—the capitol of Tennessee. We can see the Stars and Stripes flying from the dome. Our pulse leaps with pride when we see the grand old architecture. We can hear the bugle call, and the playing of the bands of the different regiments in the Federal lines. Now and then a shell is thrown into our midst from Fort Negley, but no attack or demonstrations on either side. We bivouac on the cold and hard-frozen ground, and when we walk about, the echo of our footsteps sound like the echo of a tombstone. The earth is crusted with snow, and the wind from the northwest is piercing our very bones. We can see our ragged soldiers, with sunken cheeks and famine-glistening eyes. Where were our generals? Alas! there were none. Not one single general out of Cheatham's division was left—not one. General B. F. Cheatham himself was the only surviving general of his old division. Nearly all our captains and colonels were gone. Companies mingled with companies, regiments with regiments, and brigades with brigades. A few raw-boned horses stood shivering under the ice-covered trees, nibbling the short, scanty grass. Being in range of the Federal guns from Fort Negley, we were not allowed to have fires at night, and our thin and ragged blankets were but poor protection against the cold, raw blasts of December weather—the coldest ever known. The cold stars seem to twinkle with unusual brilliancy, and the pale moon seems to be but one vast heap of frozen snow, which glimmers in the cold gray sky, and the air gets colder by its coming; our breath, forming in little rays, seems to make a thousand little coruscations that scintillate in the cold frosty air. I can tell you nothing of what was going on among the generals. But there we were, and that is all that I can tell you. One morning about daylight our army began to move. Our division was then on the extreme right wing, and then we were transferred to the left wing. The battle had begun. We were continually moving to our left. We would build little temporary breastworks, then we would be moved to another place. Our lines kept on widening out, and stretching further and further apart, until it was not more than a skeleton of a skirmish line from one end to the other. We started at a run. We cared for nothing. Not more than a thousand yards off, we could see the Yankee cavalry, artillery, and infantry, marching apparently still further to our left. We could see regiments advancing at double-quick across the fields, while, with our army, everything seemed confused. The private soldier could not see into things. It seemed to be somewhat like a flock of wild geese when they have lost their leader. We were willing to go anywhere, or to follow anyone who would lead us. We were anxious to flee, fight, or fortify. I have never seen an army so confused and demoralized. The whole thing seemed to be tottering and trembling. When, *Halt! Front! Right dress!* and Adjutant McKinney reads us the following order:

"SOLDIERS:—The commanding general takes pleasure in announcing to his troops that victory and success are now within their grasp; and the commanding general feels proud and gratified that in every attack and assault the enemy have been repulsed; and the commanding general will further say to his noble and gallant troops, 'Be of good cheer—all is well.'

> "GENERAL JOHN B. HOOD,
> "General Commanding.
> "KINLOCK FALCONER,
> "Acting Adjutant-General."

I remember how this order was received. Every soldier said, "O, shucks; that is all shenanigan," for we knew that we had never met the enemy or fired a gun outside of a little skirmishing. And I will further state that that battle order, announcing success and victory, was the cause of a greater demoralization than if our troops had been actually engaged in battle. They at once mistrusted General Hood's judgment as a commander. And every private soldier in the whole army knew the situation of affairs. I remember when passing by Hood, how feeble and decrepit he looked, with an arm in a sling, and a crutch in the other hand, and trying to guide and control his horse. And, reader, I was not a Christian then, and am but little better today; but, as God sees my heart tonight, I prayed in my heart that day for General Hood. Poor fellow, I loved him, not as a General, but as a good man. I knew when that army order was read, that General Hood had been deceived, and that the poor fellow was only trying to encourage his men. Every impulse of his nature was but to do good, and to serve his country as best he could. Ah! reader, some day all will be well.

We continued marching toward our left, our battle-line getting thinner and thinner. We could see the Federals advancing, their blue coats and banners flying, and could see their movements and hear them giving their commands. Our regiment was ordered to double quick to the extreme left wing of the army, and we had to pass up a steep hill, and the dead grass was wet and as slick as glass, and it was with the greatest difficulty that we could get up the steep hill side. When we got to the top, we, as skirmishers, were ordered to deploy still further to the left. Billy Carr and J. E. Jones, two as brave soldiers as ever breathed the breath of life—in fact, it was given up that they were the bravest and most daring men in the Army of Tennessee—and myself, were on the very extreme left wing of our army. While we were deployed as skirmishers, I heard, "Surrender, surrender," and on looking around us, I saw that we were right in the midst of a Yankee line of battle. They were lying down in the bushes, and we were not looking for them so close to us. We immediately threw down our guns and surrendered. J. E. Jones was killed at the first discharge of their guns, when another Yankee raised up and took deliberate aim at Billy Carr, and fired, the ball striking him below the eye and passing through his head. As soon as I could, I picked up my gun, and as the Yankee turned I sent a minnie ball crushing through his head, and broke and run. But I am certain that I killed the Yankee who killed Billy Carr, but it was too late to save the poor boy's life. As I started to run, a fallen dogwood tree tripped me up, and I fell over the log. It was all that saved me. The log was riddled with balls, and thousands, it seemed to me, passed over it. As I got up to run again, I was shot through the middle finger of the very hand that is now penning these lines, and the thigh. But I had just killed a Yankee, and was determined to get away from there as soon as I could. How I did get back I hardly know, for I was wounded and surrounded by Yankees. One rushed forward, and placing the muzzle of his gun in two feet of me, discharged it, but it missed its aim, when I ran at him, grabbed him by the collar, and brought him off a prisoner. Captain Joe P. Lee and Colonel H. R. Field remember this, as would Lieutenant-Colonel John House, were he alive; and all the balance of Company H, who were there at the time. I had eight bullet holes in my coat, and two in my hand, beside the one in my thigh and finger. It was a hail storm of bullets. The above is true in every particular, and is but one incident of the war, which happened to hundreds of others. But, alas! all our valor and victories were in vain, when God and the whole world were against us.

Billy Carr was one of the bravest and best men I ever knew. He never knew what fear was, and in consequence of his reckless bravery, had been badly wounded at Perryville, Murfreesboro, Chickamauga, the octagon house, Dead Angle, and the 22nd of July at Atlanta. In every battle he was wounded, and finally, in the very last battle of the war, surrendered up his life for his country's cause. No father and mother of such a brave and gallant boy, should ever sorrow or regret having born to them such a son. He was the flower and chivalry of his company. He was as good as he was brave. His bones rest yonder on the Overton hills today, while I have no doubt in my own mind that his spirit is with the Redeemer of the hosts of heaven. He was my friend. Poor boy, farewell!

When I got back to where I could see our lines, it was one scene of confusion and rout. Finney's Florida brigade had broken before a mere skirmish line, and soon the whole army had caught the infection, had broken, and were running in every direction. Such a scene I never saw. The army was panic-stricken. The woods everywhere were full of running soldiers. Our officers were crying, "Halt! halt!" and trying to rally and re-form their broken ranks. The Federals would dash their cavalry in amongst us, and even their cannon joined in the charge. One piece of Yankee artillery galloped past me, right on the road, un-limbered their gun, fired a few shots, and galloped ahead again.

Hood's whole army was routed and in full retreat. Nearly every man in the entire army had thrown away his gun and ac-couterments. More than ten thousand had stopped and allowed themselves to be captured, while many, dreading the horrors of a Northern prison, kept on, and I saw many, yea, even thousands, broken down from sheer exhaustion, with despair and pity written on their features. Wagon trains, cannon, artillery, cavalry, and infantry were all blended in inextricable confusion. Broken down and jaded horses and mules refused to pull, and the badly-scared drivers looked like their eyes would pop out of their heads from fright. Wagon wheels, interlocking each other, soon clogged the road, and wagons, horses and provisions were left indiscriminately. The officers soon became effected with the demoralization of their troops, and rode on in dogged indifference. General Frank Cheatham and General Loring tried to form a line at Brentwood, but the line they formed was like trying to stop the current of Duck river with a fish net. I believe the army would have rallied, had there been any colors to rally to. And as the straggling army moves on down the road, every now and then we can hear the sullen roar of the Federal artillery booming in the distance. I saw a wagon and team abandoned, and I unhitched one of the horses and rode on horse-back to Franklin, where a surgeon tied up my broken finger, and bandaged up my bleeding thigh. My boot was full of blood, and my clothing saturated with it. I was at General Hood's headquarters. He was much agitated and affected, pulling his hair with his one hand (he had but one), and crying like his heart would break. I pitied him, poor fellow. I asked him for a wounded furlough, and he gave it to me. I never saw him afterward. I always loved and honored him, and will ever revere and cherish his memory. He gave his life in the service of his country, and I know today he wears a garland of glory beyond the grave, where Justice says "well done," and Mercy has erased all his errors and faults.

I only write of the under *strata* of history; in other words, the *privates' history*—as I saw things then, and remember them now.

The winter of 1864–5 was the coldest that had been known for many years. The ground was frozen and rough, and our soldiers were poorly clad, while many, yes, very many, were entirely barefooted. Our wagon trains had either gone on, we knew not whither, or had been left behind. Everything and nature, too, seemed to be working against us. Even the keen, cutting air that whistled through our tattered clothes and over our poorly covered heads, seemed to lash us in its fury. The floods of waters that had overflowed their banks, seemed to laugh at our calamity, and to mock us in our misfortunes.

All along the route were weary and footsore soldiers. The citizens seemed to shrink and hide from us as we approached them. And, to cap the climax, Tennessee river was overflowing its banks, and several Federal gun-boats were anchored just below Mussel Shoals, firing at us while crossing.

The once proud Army of Tennessee had degenerated to a mob. We were pinched by hunger and cold. The rains, and sleet, and snow never ceased falling from the winter sky, while the winds pierced the old, ragged, gray-back Rebel soldier to his very marrow. The clothing of many were hanging around them in shreds of rags and tatters, while an old slouched hat covered their frozen ears. Some were on old, raw-boned horses, without saddles.

Hon. Jefferson Davis perhaps made blunders and mistakes, but I honestly believe that he ever did what he thought best for the good of his country. And there never lived on this earth from the days of Hampden to George Washington, a purer patriot or a nobler man than Jefferson Davis; and, like Marius, grand even in ruins.

Hood was a good man, a kind man, a philanthropic man, but he is both harmless and defenseless now. He was a poor general in the capacity of commander-in-chief. Had he been mentally qualified, his physical condition would have disqualified him. His legs and one of his arms had been shot off in the defense of his country.[1] As a soldier, he was brave, good, noble, and gallant, and fought with the ferociousness of the wounded tiger, and with the everlasting grit of the bull-dog; but as a general he was a failure in every particular.

Our country is gone, our cause is lost. *"Actum est de Republica."*

---

[1] This is an error. Hood was seriously wounded in the left arm at Gettysburg but did not lose it. He lost his right leg at Chickamauga.

Chapter 17

The Surrender

The Last Act of the Drama

ON THE 10th day of May, 1861, our regiment, the First Tennessee, left Nashville for the camp of instruction, with twelve hundred and fifty men, officers and line. Other recruits continually coming in swelled this number to fourteen hundred. In addition to this Major Fulcher's battalion of four companies, with four hundred men (originally), was afterwards attached to the regiment; and the Twenty-seventh Tennessee Regiment was afterwards consolidated with the First. And besides this, there were about two hundred conscripts added to the regiment from time to time. To recapitulate: The First Tennessee, numbering originally, 1,250; recruited from time to time, 150; Fulcher's battalion, 400; the Twenty-seventh Tennessee, 1,200; number of conscripts (at the lowest estimate), 200—making the sum total 3,200 men that belonged to our regiment during the war. The above I think a low estimate. Well, on the 26th day of April, 1865, General Joe E. Johnston surrendered his army at Greensboro, North Carolina. The day that we surrendered our regiment it was a pitiful sight to behold. If I remember correctly, there were just sixty-five men in all, including officers, that were paroled on that day. Now, what became of the original 3,200? A grand army, you may say. Three thousand two hundred men!

Only sixty-five left! Now, reader, you may draw your own con-
clusions. It lacked just four days of four years from the day we
were sworn in to the day of the surrender, and it was just four
years and twenty-four days from the time that we left home for
the army to the time that we got back again. It was indeed a sad
sight to look at, the Old First Tennessee Regiment. A mere squad
of noble and brave men, gathered around the tattered flag that
they had followed in every battle through that long war. It was
so bullet-riddled and torn that it was but a few blue and red
shreds that hung drooping while it, too, was stacked with our
guns forever.

Thermopylæ had one messenger of defeat, but when General
Joe E. Johnston surrendered the Army of the South there were
hundreds of regiments, yea, I might safely say thousands, that
had not a representative on the 26th day of April, 1865.

Our cause was lost from the beginning. Our greatest victories—Chickamauga and Franklin—were our greatest defeats.
Our people were divided upon the question of Union and secession. Our generals were scrambling for "Who ranked." The private soldier fought and starved and died for naught. Our
hospitals were crowded with sick and wounded, but half provided with food and clothing to sustain life. Our money was de-
preciated to naught and our cause lost. We left our homes four
years previous. Amid the waving of flags and handkerchiefs and
the smiles of the ladies, while the fife and drum were playing
Dixie and the Bonnie Blue Flag, we bid farewell to home and
friends. The bones of our brave Southern boys lie scattered over
our loved South. They fought for their "country," and gave their
lives freely for that country's cause; and now they who survive
sit, like Marius amid the wreck of Carthage, sublime even in
ruins. Other pens abler than mine will have to chronicle their
glorious deeds of valor and devotion. In these sketches I have
named but a few persons who fought side by side with me during that long and unholy war. In looking back over these pages,
I ask, Where now are many whose names have appeared in
these sketches? They are up yonder, and are no doubt waiting

and watching for those of us who are left behind. And, my kind reader, the time is coming when we, too, will be called, while the archangel of death is beating the long roll of eternity, and with us it will be the last reveille. God Himself will sound the "assembly" on yonder beautiful and happy shore, where we will again have a grand "reconfederation." We shed a tear over their flower-strewn graves. We live after them. We love their memory yet. But one generation passes away and another generation follows. We know our loved and brave soldiers. We love them yet.

But when we pass away, the impartial historian will render a true verdict, and a history will then be written in justification and vindication of those brave and noble boys who gave their all in fighting the battles of their homes, their country, and their God.

"The United States has no North, no South, no East, no West." *"We are one and undivided."*

Adieu

My kind friends—soldiers, comrades, brothers, all: The curtain is rung down, the foot-lights are put out, the audience has all left and gone home, the seats are vacant, and the cold walls are silent. The gaudy tinsel that appears before the footlights is exchanged for the dress of the citizen. Coming generations and historians will be the critics as to how we have acted our parts. The past is buried in oblivion. The blood-red flag, with its crescent and cross, that we followed for four long, bloody, and disastrous years, has been folded never again to be unfurled. We have no regrets for what we did, but we mourn the loss of so many brave and gallant men who perished on the field of battle and honor. I now bid you an affectionate adieu.

But in closing these memoirs, the scenes of my life pass in rapid review before me. In imagination, I am young again tonight. I feel the flush and vigor of my manhood—am just twenty-one years of age. I hear the fife and drum playing Dixie and Bonnie Blue Flag. I see and hear our fire-eating stump-orators tell of the right of secession and disunion. I see our fair and beautiful women waving their handkerchiefs and encouraging their sweethearts to go to the war. I see the marshaling of the hosts for "glorious war." I see the fine banners waving and hear the cry everywhere, *"To arms! to arms!"* And I also see our country at peace and prosperous, our fine cities look grand and gay, our fields rich in abundant harvests, our people happy and contented. All these pass in imagination before me. Then I look and see glorious war in all its splendor. I hear the shout and charge, the boom of artillery and the rattle of small arms. I see gaily-dressed officers charging backwards and forwards upon their mettled war horses, clothed in the panoply of war. I see victory and conquest upon flying banners. I see our arms triumph in every battle. And, O, my friends, I see another scene. I see broken homes and broken hearts. I see war in all of its desolation. I see a country ruined and impoverished. I see a nation disfranchised and maltreated. I see a commonwealth forced to pay dishonest and fraudulent bonds that were issued to crush that people. I see sycophants licking the boots of the country's oppressor. I see other and many wrongs perpetrated upon a conquered people. But maybe it is but the ghosts and phantoms of a dreamy mind, or the wind as it whistles around our lonely cabin-home. The past is buried in oblivion. The mantle of charity has long ago fallen upon those who think differently from us. We remember no longer wrongs and injustice done us by anyone on earth. We are willing to forget and forgive those who have wronged and falsified us. We look up above and beyond all these petty groveling things and shake hands and forget the past. And while my imagination is like the weaver's shuttle, playing backward and forward through these two decades of time, I ask myself, Are these things real? did they happen? are they being enacted today? or are they the fancies of the imagination in forgetful reverie? Is it true that I have seen all these things? that they are real incidents in my life's history? Did I see those brave and noble countrymen of mine laid low in death and weltering in their blood? Did I see our country laid waste and in ruins? Did I see soldiers marching, the earth trembling and jarring beneath their measured tread? Did I see the ruins of smouldering cities and deserted homes? Did I see my comrades buried and see the violet and wild flowers bloom over their graves? Did I see the flag of my country, that I had followed so long, furled to be no more unfurled forever? Surely they are but the vagaries of mine own imagination. Surely my fancies are running wild tonight. But, hush! I now hear the approach of battle. That low, rumbling sound in the west is the roar of cannon in the distance. That rushing sound is the tread of soldiers. That quick, lurid glare is the flash that precedes the cannon's roar. And listen! that loud report that makes the earth tremble and jar and sway, is but the bursting of a shell, as it screams through the dark, tempestuous night. That black, ebon cloud, where the lurid lightning flickers and flares, that is rolling through the heavens, is the smoke of battle; beneath is being enacted a carnage of blood and death. Listen! the soldiers are charging now. The flashes and roaring now are blended with the shouts of soldiers and confusion of battle.

But, reader, time has brought his changes since I, a young, ardent, and impetuous youth, burning with a lofty patriotism first shouldered my musket to defend the rights of my country.

Lifting the veil of the past, I see many manly forms, bright in youth and hope, standing in view by my side in Company H, First Tennessee Regiment. Again I look and half those forms are gone. Again, and gray locks and wrinkled faces and clouded brows stand before me.

Before me, too, I see, not in imagination, but in reality, my own loved Jennie, the partner of my joys and the sharer of my sorrows, sustaining, comforting, and cheering my pathway by her benignant smile; pouring the sunshine of domestic comfort and happiness upon our humble home; making life more worth the living as we toil on up the hill of time together, with the bright pledges of our early and constant love by our side while the sunlight of hope ever brightens our pathway, dispelling darkness and sorrow as we hand in hand approach the valley of the great shadow.

The tale is told. The world moves on, the sun shines as brightly as before, the flowers bloom as beautifully, the birds sing their carols as sweetly, the trees nod and bow their leafy tops as if slumbering in the breeze, the gentle winds fan our brow and kiss our cheek as they pass by, the pale moon sheds her silvery sheen, the blue dome of the sky sparkles with the trembling stars that twinkle and shine and make night beautiful, and the scene melts and gradually disappears forever.

INDEX